T0215467

TECHNOLOGIES FOR MODERN DIGITAL ENTREPRENEURSHIP

UNDERSTANDING EMERGING TECH AT THE CUTTING-EDGE OF THE WEB 3.0 ECONOMY

Abeba N. Turi

Apress®

Technologies for Modern Digital Entrepreneurship: Understanding Emerging Tech at the Cutting-Edge of the Web 3.0 Economy

Abeba N. Turi
Vancouver, BC, Canada

ISBN-13 (pbk): 978-1-4842-6004-3   ISBN-13 (electronic): 978-1-4842-6005-0
https://doi.org/10.1007/978-1-4842-6005-0

Managing Director, Apress Media LLC: Welmoed Spahr
Acquisitions Editor: Shiva Ramachandran
Development Editor: Rita Fernando
Coordinating Editor: Rita Fernando

Cover designed by eStudioCalamar

Distributed to the book trade worldwide by Springer Science+Business Media New York, 1 New York Plaza, New York, NY 100043. Phone 1-800-SPRINGER, fax (201) 348-4505, e-mail orders-ny@springer-sbm.com, or visit www.springeronline.com. Apress Media, LLC is a California LLC and the sole member (owner) is Springer Science + Business Media Finance Inc (SSBM Finance Inc). SSBM Finance Inc is a **Delaware** corporation.

For information on translations, please e-mail rights@apress.com, or visit http://www.apress.com/rights-permissions.

Apress titles may be purchased in bulk for academic, corporate, or promotional use. eBook versions and licenses are also available for most titles. For more information, reference our Print and eBook Bulk Sales web page at http://www.apress.com/bulk-sales.

Any source code or other supplementary material referenced by the author in this book is available to readers on GitHub via the book's product page, located at www.apress.com/9781484260043. For more detailed information, please visit http://www.apress.com/source-code.

Printed on acid-free paper

To the Turi family.
And to my very own Y and V, with love.

Contents

About the Author

Dr. Abeba N. Turi is a scholar with expertise in Digital Economy. She obtained her Ph.D. specializing in the areas of the Digital Economy at the Rovira i Virgili University in Spain. Dr. Turi has worked as an assistant researcher with the UNESCO Chair in Data Privacy, Spain. She has also served in various international research and teaching positions in Africa, Europe and Canada. Currently, Dr. Turi is an instructor at the University Canada West in Vancouver. She has experience working in the areas of web-based business models, which is at the core of modern digital entrepreneurship. Dr. Turi's works have been presented in several international conferences in China, Canada, Germany, Italy, Spain, and the United Kingdom. Dr. Turi identifies herself as a disruptive tech and decentralization enthusiast.

About the Author

Acknowledgments

God, you never stop working.

Coming from an interdisciplinary background, I owe an enormous debt of gratitude to the individuals and organizations that allowed me to develop my skill set around the digital economy space through projects, trainings, workshops, and conference engagements over the last few years. Next, I'd like to thank Prof. Victoria Lemieux for taking the time to read the book manuscript and provide detailed and constructive comments. I'd also like to acknowledge an encouraging friend, Dr. Anwar Seid, and a supportive colleague, Dave Keighron, for the superb chat we had around this topic, which helped to substantiate some of the content coverage of the book. Additionally, my special thanks to Dr. Yitagesu Zewdu for his fascinating insight into the geopolitics of the information society. Besides, I am grateful to Blockchain@UBC, for I was given the opportunity to learn and explore more about DLTs through the Blockchain Summer Institute. My sincere gratitude also goes to Rita and Shivangi, who polished and gave this book its current shape.

Introduction

The fourth industrial revolution has created big tech winners and monopolistic companies that lead the digital economy space today. The unfolding mount in the digital economy is leaving a significant footprint across industries from production, distribution to consumption of goods and services. This economic system is flooded with a dense carpet of tech megatrends. These technological advancements have significantly contributed to the contemporary global inter-state and intra-state order. To this effect, regional and business competitiveness depends on how states and industries respond to the dynamics of emerging technologies around them.

As technology plays a strategically vital role in perceived power of a state through national security and economic competitiveness, some of the major innovations like the Web, robotics, Internet of Things, cloud computing, artificial intelligence, and mobile technology (fifth generation of wireless communications, 5G) have created a technological rivalry between global powers.[1] Of course, these enabling technologies come with tremendous opportunities. For example, not to mention all, the World Economic Forum report indicates that about 10% of the global economy, by 2027, will be recorded on blockchain.[2] In the mobile technology space, McKinsey predicts that in the coming ten years, the 5G connectivity revolution alone could boost the global GDP by 1.2–2 trillion USD, mainly in healthcare, manufacturing, transportation, and retail sectors.[3] As the Chinese tech company Huawei holds the upper hand in 5G tech, the Western world is racing to conquer the perceived challenge posed by China, mainly on a geopolitical basis.[4] That being the case, the fight over technological leadership thus has both political and economic incentives for nations.

Notably, enabled by emerging technologies, data-driven decision-making has continued to be a growing field of the knowledge economy. For example, real-time data access to patients accelerates research and development in the

---

[1] See Hoffmann et al. (2019), Brown (2019), and Johnson (2019) for details on the technology geopolitics.

[2] www3.weforum.org/docs/WEF_GAC15_Technological_Tipping_Points_report_2015.pdf

[3] www.mckinsey.com/industries/technology-media-and-telecommunications/our-insights/connected-world-an-evolution-in-connectivity-beyond-the-5g-revolution

[4] www.economist.com/business/2020/04/08/america-does-not-want-china-to-dominate-5g-mobile-networks

medical industry. In this regard, tech has a track record of effectively facilitating and providing robust solutions to the medical industry. To mention some, Kinsa's smart thermometer has helped in tracking flu trends of the United States in 2018.[5] Recently, as the pandemic challenges major economies, trends in digital tech for tracking, testing, and treating tools show tremendous growth.

Similarly, in Canada, an app developed by the Self Care Catalysts (SCC) enables tracking of COVID-19 health.[6] By leveraging the technologies in the space and facilitating the access to the aggregated real-time data (big data) on patients, such applications lend promising future to our "new normal" world of the COVID-19 pandemic. Another development toward fighting the coronavirus through tech solutions is the US-initiated supercomputing consortium, COVID-19 High-Performance Computing, in collaboration with tech companies and academia.[7, 8] Beyond the med-tech, social media platforms, and mobile technologies that kept people connected while maintaining physical distances to enabling software of working from home and digitized financial service access, digitization has played a significant role.

However, as centralized mega-platforms work with authorities in combating the COVID-19 pandemic, the issues of user data privacy remain to be a concern. A typical example here is the usage of mobile ad location data in 500 US cities by the Centers for Disease Control and Prevention in tracing stay-at-home compliance and the spread of the coronavirus.[9] On the other end, data liberation is on the verge, which could potentially boost global GDPs through the replication of data. It is interesting to see the giant tech, Microsoft, embracing the previously unthinkable move toward open data.[10] Such developments in data accessibility hold enormous opportunities both for established businesses and startups. This will significantly allow for the minimization of digital waste and enable efficient utilization of previously underutilized aggregated data for broader purposes such as AI algorithms and business intelligence systems.

---

[5]www.mobihealthnews.com/content/kinsas-crowdsourced-smart-thermometer-data-now-rivals-cdc-tracking-flu-trends
[6]www.newswire.ca/news-releases/free-covid-19-health-tracking-app-launched-to-help-canadians-track-and-manage-their-health-and-provide-frontline-researchers-and-public-health-officials-real-time-large-scale-open-source-public-data-816809411.html
[7]https://covid19-hpc-consortium.org/
[8]www.whitehouse.gov/briefings-statements/white-house-announces-new-partnership-unleash-u-s-supercomputing-resources-fight-covid-19/
[9]www.wsj.com/articles/government-tracking-how-people-move-around-in-coronavirus-pandemic-11585393202
[10]www.economist.com/business/2020/04/23/microsoft-embraces-big-data

In addition to a significant socioeconomic and political catalyzation, the digital economic system has paved the way for innovation misconduct that has distorted human interactions. From the social media fake contents, business misconducts of the Theranos' fraud charges[11] and China's med-tech faulty vaccine scandal,[12] Facebook and Cambridge Analytica scandal[13] to the Russian election meddling in the sociopolitical discord of the United States, tech has been in place.[14]

The preceding discussion clearly illustrates how emerging technologies hold root in every aspect of our socioeconomic and political interactions today. Thus, excelling in this is a crucial strategic decision one could make to remain competent in the dynamically changing digital world. More importantly, from a business perspective, irreversible consumer behavior is here to tap through technological solutions. As the baby boomers and millennials continue to migrate to the digital world and the digital native Gen Z immerses itself into the new digitized lifestyle, the digital transformation of businesses and application of robust emerging tech solutions are a crucial thing to consider.

Accordingly, this book is designed to flesh out the main developments in the digital economy space with an emphasis on emerging technologies of the web-based business models and distributed ledger technologies that facilitate modern digital entrepreneurship. More specifically, transformation within the digital economic system will be presented in depth by taking the cases of centralized crowd-based business models of the Web 2.0 economy with a further discussion on the distributed network economic system of the Web 3.0. In an effort to bridge the gap between advances in the digital economy space and reader interest, each chapter presents up-to-date data and illustrative examples.

---

[11]www.businessinsider.com/the-history-of-silicon-valley-unicorn-theranos-and-ceo-elizabeth-holmes-2018-5
[12]www.nytimes.com/2018/10/17/business/china-vaccine-fine.html
[13]www.vox.com/policy-and-politics/2018/3/23/17151916/facebook-cambridge-analytica-trump-diagram
[14]www.cnn.com/2017/10/12/us/2016-presidential-election-investigation-fast-facts/index.html

Digital Economy and the Information Society

About a decade has now passed since the fourth industrial revolution took root in our post-modern society. With the aim of giving a clear picture of the digital economy, this chapter is designed to cover the state of the art and major developments under this economic system. Accordingly, we will look at the information society and the digital economy on which such society is built on. An extensive discussion on the monopolization of digital platforms, free riding of the Web, smart business models, and emerging technologies will be presented. In addition, by having a closer look at the business models of major digital companies, the chapter will give an insight into the digital businesses of this economic system. Here, we will briefly discuss the business models of tech giants such as Google, Amazon, Alibaba, Uber, Airbnb, and Shopify and also discuss the startups with Fintech solutions. On the governance side of

© Abeba N. Turi 2020
A. N. Turi, *Technologies for Modern Digital Entrepreneurship*,
https://doi.org/10.1007/978-1-4842-6005-0_1

networks of the information society, we will have a look at the issue of trust and social capital built through rating and reputation schemes in digital platforms. Further, the chapter will cover the major regulatory frameworks and policies toward this economic system and identify the main influences such policies have on the information society and the digital economy. Major regulatory developments such as the global consumer protection initiative, e-consumer.gov, the General Data Protection Regulation (GDPR), California Consumer Privacy Act, taxation of multinationals, and lobbying by the tech giants are some of the points to be covered under this section. In the section that follows, we will have an overview of this economic system.

An Overview of the Digital Economy

The digital world has become a venue for entertainment, news, shopping, and social interaction, easing the way for the current trends of the collaborative economy. The Internet and digitization are the drivers of the mesh economy. The data-driven collaborative economic system of the millennial era, which relies on information technology as the primary catalyst, is known as the digital economy.

In 2013, Owyang et al. argued that one of the catalysts of this digital economy is social media, which impacts communications, marketing, and customer care business functions. Mesh, peer, and sharing economy are the other terms that are interchangeably used to refer to hybrid models of this economy (Hamari et al., 2015). The main developments of this digital economic system include the Internet of Things, Internet of People, cloud computing, artificial intelligence (AI), big data and business intelligence, financial technologies—including the smart business models of peer-to-peer (P2P) transactions, crowdfunding and crowdsourcing, innovation and educational marketplaces—and blockchain-powered nano-economic settings. The web-based business models are at the core of the modern digital entrepreneurship.

Digital Transformation at a Scale

With the advent of growing digital platforms and marketplaces, there are newly growing economic units known as *prosumers*. These economic units are the producers and consumers of digitally driven value. Thus, in the digital economic system, value is co-created at a near-zero marginal cost (e.g., reputation system which will be discussed in depth later in this chapter). Zero marginal cost[1] and ease of entry and exit help this economic system easily create value in real time. The economic system is powered by various emerging technologies that allow efficient utilization of scarce resources, avoid

---

[1]Rifkin, 2014

hyper-consumption, create a new chain of value, and rewrite economic power grid and legacy order of things. The societal structure in the information society, in general, is categorized into two groups: the *digital natives* (those born in the digital era*)* and the *digital immigrants* (those who adopted the digital world's way of life) (Prensky, 2001).

Table 1-1 shows the possible size of the digital sector in the United States as of 2015.

Table 1-1. Possible size of the digital sector in the United States, 2015[2]

Product Group	Percentage of GDP
Included in GDP (on a value-added basis):	
ICT equipment, semiconductors, and software	2.8
Telecommunication and Internet access services	3.3
Data processing and other information services	0.7
Online platforms, including ecommerce platforms	1.3
Platform-enabled services (e.g., the "sharing economy")	0.2
Total (with incomplete adjustment for double counting of output)	**8.3**
Conceptually not included in GDP, or missed for procedural reasons:	
Wikipedia and open source software	0.2
Free media from online platforms funded by advertising	0.1
"Do-it-yourself" fixed capital formation of online platforms	0.3
The output of MNEs attributed to tax havens	0.4
Total (with incomplete adjustment for double counting of output)	**1.0**

Currently, these new collaborative business models account for a significant segment of the global economy and exhibit a fast pace of growth and adoption across different sectors. In 2014, PricewaterhouseCoopers reported that five sectors of the collaborative economy—P2P financing (P2P lending and crowdfunding), crowdsourcing, P2P homestay networks, ride-sharing, and music/video streaming—are predicted to generate about $335 billion global revenue by the year 2025. UN Digital Economy Report 2019 shows that the digital economy accounts for up to 15.5% of the global GDP. According to the

---

[2]Source: IMF Staff Report, 2018, on Measuring the Digital Economy, www.imf.org/en/ Publications/Policy-Papers/Issues/2018/04/03/022818-measuring-the- digital-economy

EU Commission, multinational companies with the digital business model have average annual revenue growth of 14%, which is significantly higher than the multinationals with a traditional business model with an average annual growth rate of 0.2% to 3%. In 2016, the EU's information and communications technology (ICT) services accounted for about 3.75% of the GDP.[3] By 2023, ecommerce (the way of transacting goods and services over the Internet) is estimated to have a share of about 22% in global retail sales. A forecast by Statista shows a growing migration of people to the digital space with over 2.14 billion online buyers of goods and services in 2021.[4] This is triggered by increasing access to smartphones and the Internet. According to the ITU, as of 2019, there are 4.1 billion global Internet users. Furthermore, R&D, ICT spending, and infrastructural developments contribute to the rapid growth in the digital economy and mass adoption of the underlying economic activities. Gartner predicted that, in 2020, the global ICT spending would increase by 3.7% (see Table 1-2).

Table 1-2. Worldwide IT spending forecast (in billion USD)[5]

IT Sector	2019 Spending	2019 Growth (%)	2020 Spending	2020 Growth (%)	2021 Spending	2021 Growth (%)
Data Center Systems	205	−2.5	210	2.6	212	1.0
Enterprise Software	457	8.8	507	10.9	560	10.5
Devices	675	−5.3	683	1.2	685	0.4
IT Services	1031	3.7	1088	5.5	1147	5.5
Communications Services	1364	−1.1	1384	1.5	1413	2.1
Overall IT	**3732**	**0.4**	**3872**	**3.7**	**4018**	**3.8**

Challenges with the Growing Digital Economy

Despite an increase in the adoption of the Internet, there is a growing digital divide. The main digital divides are the digital gender gap, digital age gap (generation: digital natives vs. immigrants), and digital usage gap (a.k.a. skill gap). In the latter case, the gap arises mainly due to the degree of sophistication (in terms of digital literacy) of users with the advances in Internet applications. See Figure 1-1.

[3] https://ec.europa.eu/eurostat/statistics-explained/index.php/ ICT_sector_-_value_added,_employment_and_R%26D
[4] See ecommerce forecast at statista.com.
[5] Gartner (2019), available at www.gartner.com/en/newsroom/press-releases/2019-10-23-gartner-says-global-it-spending-to-grow-3point7-percent-in-2020

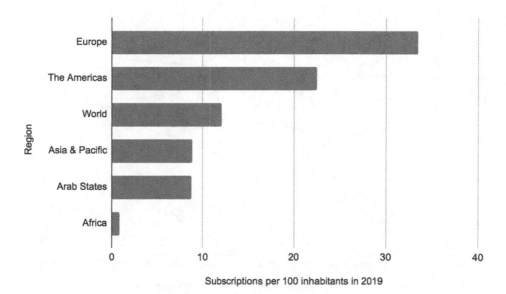

Figure 1-1. Individuals using the Internet per 100 inhabitants by region, 2019[6]

To better harness the value created through this economic system and achieve more inclusive growth, smart business models also have to consider how they can engage less sophisticated users who use only basic features of the Internet, like communication channels. Moreover, in the current era of the digitally shrinking world, more significant work in harnessing the potentials of the information society through higher digital financial inclusion for the previously underserved regions like that of Africa and minimizing the digital gender gap is crucial by the digital financial inclusion; we mean affordable and ease of virtual access to financial services. Such regions are also prone to a significant gender disparities in access to digital services (we will discuss this further later under the "Digital Economy in the Developing Regions" section of this chapter). Figure 1-2 shows international trade in digitally deliverable services as a percentage of total trade in services by region.

---

[6]Source: Author's extraction based on ITU Statistics, available at www.itu.int/ict/ statistics

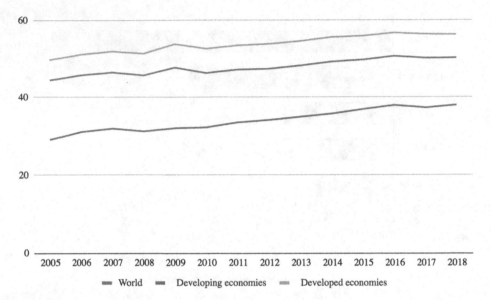

Figure 1-2. International trade in digitally deliverable services as a percentage of total trade in services by region[7]

As this collaborative form of value creation emerges, the economic system gets complicated and becomes prone to many serious problems that hamper its efficiency. Some of the challenges and uncertainties in this economic system include central point of failure, blockade of platforms, privacy risks, security and operational risks (fraud, cybercrime, and operational outages), lack of trust resulting from the information asymmetry, risk of default, usury and systemic financial risks due to liquidity, and credit risks with the business cycle uncertainties. Apart from its externalities to the traditional business models, this economic system also poses a challenge to the government in enacting new rules and regulations. This trend also creates tension in the labor market resulting in the substitution of the manually performed tasks to automation. However, scholars in the field argue that the existing trend can co-exist until the traditional way of operation fades out and the transformation to the new digital economy matures. According to Intuit's Future of Accountancy Report (2013), with the demographic shifts from the digital immigrants to the digital natives, irreversible consumer behavior emerges, and the transformation of the traditional service sector to the modern digitized service naturally smooths by itself as the millennials hold the market through time, and the baby boomers retire. In line with this, in analyzing the pace of disruption from the digital wave to the banking industry, Marco Marinc argued

---

[7]Source: Author's extraction based on UNCTADstat, available at https://unctadstat.unctad.org/

that automated decision-making in transaction lending techniques cannot make human decision-making based on the relational banking soft information obsolete (Marinc, 2015). Soft information is contextual and qualitative, which is difficult to store and transmit impersonally. Such information play important role for relaxing credit constraints in lending relationships. Soft information which a banker gains through a front desk service, for instance, allows individual decision-making on physically observed information. However, a direct interaction and transmission of soft information is not viable in fintech solutions which are digital by nature. Online platform-based and app-enabled lending solutions mainly relay on artificial intelligence and different algorithms for decision-making (we will go through some of the reputation protocols and rating mechanisms underlying P2P lending later in this book). Thus, in addition to hard quantifiable information, frequent and personal contacts with clients can help in identifying the creditworthiness of a client. For example, in relational banking, a direct interaction history, and in-person experience of talking with a potential borrower, provides a signal that helps a decision-maker in the approval process. Marinc's argument is based on the grounds that a game of incomplete information, such as a poker game, is much more difficult for computers to master compared to chess, and hence that human decision-making surpasses that of automated actors when it comes to strategic decision-making. However, algorithms built in some technologies like artificial intelligence surpass human decision-making in object recognition and detection, which can be used for dermatology or lip-reading.

Thus, inclusive policy measures and strategies toward the digital transformation are needed in order to harness the fruits of this economic system fully. Moreover, at a policy level, in the current era of the digitally shrinking world, greater work in harnessing the potentials of the information society and minimizing the digital gap of all forms is crucial. Lastly, most of the underlying business models of this economic system are not stress-tested since they are mostly recent developments.

Monopolistic Digital Platforms: The Billionaires' Pulse

There is a significant concentration of wealth created through the digital economy in the hands of few advanced regions (the United States and China) and monopolistic tech giants (such as Microsoft, Apple, Amazon, Google, Facebook, Uber, Airbnb, Tencent, and Alibaba). In terms of geographic distribution, the United States and China alone account for about 40% of global value-added, 75% of both global distributed ledger technology (DLT) patents and cloud computing market, and about 50% of Internet of Things

(IoT) global spending and generate about 90% of the market cap of the biggest global digital platforms.[8]

The digital economy has been referred to as the sharing economy, implying the collaborative commons under this economic system. For example, today, thanks to Craigslist, Facebook marketplace, and similar platforms, you can get a free access to used and brand new items listed by the Internet community in your neighborhood. This is due to the nearly zero and essentially priceless access to goods and services which the Web 2.0 economy allowed like never before. However, the system is not sharing in its core settings. Under this economic system, few tech giants and digital platforms have proved to generate billions of revenues by redefining the legacy business models, monetizing digital data and aggregating services, and selling them back. Privacy practice and market control are the main issues regarding the tech giants. Increasing monopolization of the Internet in this regard is a typical example to mention (Candeub, 2013). For example, monopolistic digital platforms in the search engine (Google has about 90% of global market dominance[9]), social media, and ads (Facebook has about 66% global dominance[10] and WeChat with a pure monopoly of the Chinese market) are some to mention. The tech giants, according to *Forbes*, are one of the top 100 companies by market value in the world. In 2019, Apple, Microsoft, and Amazon.com made up the top three list in the world with 961.3, 946.5, and 916.1 US billion dollars of market values, respectively. Alphabet (Google), Facebook, Alibaba, and Tencent Holdings followed closely with market values of 863.2, 472.1, 480.8, and 512 billion US dollars, respectively.[11] See Figure 1-3.

---

[8]UNCTAD Digital Economy Report 2019
[9]Statista, available at www.statista.com/statistics/216573/worldwide-market-share-of-search-engines/
[10]Statista, available at www.statista.com/statistics/272014/global-social-networks-ranked-by-number-of-users/
[11]See Forbes Top 100 Digital Companies, available at www.forbes.com/top-digital-companies/list/#tab:rank

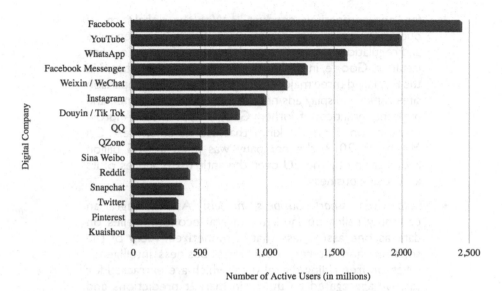

Figure 1-3. Most popular social networks worldwide as of January 2020, ranked by number of active users (in millions)[12]

Some of the main factors that result in digital market concentration are

- *Network effects and economies of scope:* This has a spillover effect and externality on a digital company's business lines and ease of market penetration for their new products.

- *Strategic service bundling and acquisitions:* Digital companies collude or acquire other companies or startups to limit competition and strengthen their market power. For example, Facebook acquired several companies, including Instagram, on April 9, 2012, and WhatsApp on April 19, 2014. Some other technology acquisitions include Fitbit by Google, Tableau and ClickSoftware by Salesforce, Intel's smartphone modem business by Apple, and so on. Antitrust laws against mergers and acquisitions and anti-competitive conducts of digital companies have been in place. *The Guardian* on June 4, 2019, reported Congress' intention to investigate tech giants (Facebook, Google, and Amazon)

---

[12]Source: Author's extraction based on data from Statista, available at www.statista.com/ statistics/272014/global-social-networks-ranked-by-number-of-users/

for "anti-competitive conduct."[13] With the global form of operation of such digital companies, they face uneven rules and regulations depending on the region of operation. For instance, Google, in addition to its US antitrust probes,[14] in the EU, faced three major cases for its shopping comparison sites ranking, display ads network usage requirements, and bundling practice of other Google apps with Android software on phone makings that use its software.[15] On March 20, 2019, the company was fined a €1.5 billion antitrust fine by the EU over the antitrust practices of its advertising business.[16]

- *Data-driven smart business models:* As the agrarian economy relies on land, the digital economy relies on data as one asset class that is monetized. Most of the software and Internet companies' business intelligence relies on free riding digital data, which are extracted for sale or aggregated to utilize in market predictions and understanding customers. In this regard, data control, analytical power, and business intelligence are vital competitive advantages in the knowledge-based economy of today's world. Various companies generate revenues over the Internet by aggregating and providing access to the psychographic and behavioral consumer data of product users, which is fetched from major social platforms.

- *Emerging technologies including artificial intelligence, cloud computing, and machine learning:* The big techs have a massive investment, research, and development toward emerging technologies that enhance their core business lines.

---

[13]The Guardian News available at www.theguardian.com/technology/2019/jun/03/tech-monopoly-congress-increases-antitrust-scrutiny-on-facebook-google-amazon, accessed on May 22, 2020.

[14]Ars Technica "Justice Department launches antitrust probe into big tech," available at https://arstechnica.com/tech-policy/2019/07/justice-department-launches-antitrust-probe-into-big-tech/, accessed on May 22, 2020.

[15]Bloomberg Technology, www.bloomberg.com/news/articles/2019-06-03/google-has-antitrust-playbook-ready-for-doj-after-eu-challenges, accessed on May 22, 2020.

[16]The Verge, www.theverge.com/2019/3/20/18270891/google-eu-antitrust-fine-adsense-advertising, accessed on May 22, 2020.

- *Size of a digital company and financial resources:* The tech giants in the digital economy space have a massive resource, thus enjoying economies of scale that sustain their core business lines and further invest in high tech solutions. These companies also have control of unique technological infrastructure that is not easily duplicated. Besides, they can afford to invest huge money for lobbying, in policy battles, to influence government regulations and curb amendments to their benefit.

Smart Business Models and Emerging Technologies

The digital economic system is shaping the trends in consumption, production, distribution, and, more generally, utilization of scarce resources. Scarce resources are those resources that have limited availability making them mostly excludable and of rivalry in ownership. Because of this, some of such goods and services tend to be overused (hyper-consumption), underutilized, or wasted due to a lack of robust exchange system that can facilitate the exchange of any item of value in an organized way. Thus, technology-oriented channels have now enabled access to such goods and services in real time. For instance, think of a car-share platform that enables the sharing of the ride at a reasonable price. Here, the technology-enabled real-time transaction can allow a potential client to track available rides to share. The transaction is also win-win for the driver heading the same way as you with an open empty seat, while you can save on time, money, and usage of alternative means like public transport. Another example of this can be the human capital, which is made easily accessible through the crowdsourcing marketplaces of the collaborative economy business models. The digital economy is mainly characterized by the disintermediation of the legacy centralized form of economic system. The rise of information networks and the advances in information technology have led to a dramatic shift in the traditional forms of economic systems and organizations.

The peer-to-peer business models underlying this economic system are enabled by the digital platforms that facilitate direct peer-to-peer transactions. Digitized online marketplaces add significant value to users in terms of interactive and accessible transactions through mobile apps, online marketplaces with a large network of global players, and reduced transaction costs. Ecommerce marketplaces are typical examples of features of the digital economic system.

The service sector of this economy is booming with the catalyzing advancements in digital technology. For example, video conferencing and streaming and online collaboration portals without a need for a face-to-face contact have eased the access to education. Also, the traditional healthcare sector is affected by the availability of remote diagnosis, drug, and other treatment mechanism's advertisement and the sharing of patient experience through electronic health records. The same is true in the broadcasting and media sector with vast social media networks and user-generated content.

In addition to self-publishing, free digital content generation (such as video on demand, OTT (over-the-top) delivery, and streaming media), and online blogging, digital companies like Facebook's and Google's ads models have disrupted the classified ads and subscription-based revenues of the news outlets. For example, amid the media industry disruption, some of the Canadian news outlets had recently called for tax and regulatory changes. Some of these news outlets include the National Post of the Postmedia, Toronto Star, SaltWire Network, and the CBC of the Torstar.[17] In coping with digital waves, according to Forbes 2019 Insights survey of 700 executives, only 25% of enterprises in the media and entertainment industry made "meaningful" progress in their digital transformation.[18]

Data-driven decision-making is another development in the digital economic system. A significantly large number of global users flood the economic system through their digital presence. According to the UNCTAD 2019 report,[19] there is an estimate of about 150,700GB of global IP traffic per second by 2022. Here, digital footprints of users from the digital world are inputs for the current smart business models. These data are mainly used to understand target customers and markets and further design better and develop customer-centric products.

Ease of doing business as a digital entrepreneur is affected by the area of operation. Local startups in different regions are prone to different rules and regulations and infrastructural developments depending on their areas of operation. UNCTAD's eTrade Readiness Assessments of Land-Locked Developing Countries 2019 report[20] shows that infrastructure, ecommerce strategies, and legal frameworks are the main constraints for digitized economic activities.

At the core of the major developments that backed the smart business models are emerging technologies. Today, the parade of newly emerging technologies such as artificial intelligence, Internet of Things, big data and analytics, machine

---

[17]The National Post on February 19, 2020, reported news stating "'The news industry is in trouble': Canadian media outlets team up to demand tax and regulatory changes," available at https://nationalpost.com/news/canada/the-news-industry-is-in-trouble-canadian-media-outlets-team-up-to-demand-tax-and-regulatory-changes

[18]Forbes, September 12, 2019, www.forbes.com/sites/awsmediaandentertainment/2019/09/12/how-to-thrive-in-todays-disrupted-media-markets/#752eac2370ed

[19]UNCTAD Digital Economy Report 2019

[20]https://unctad.org/en/pages/PublicationWebflyer.aspx?publicationid=2590

learning, mobile applications and the Web, autonomous vehicles, and financial technologies, including cryptocurrencies, blockchain, and distributed ledger technologies, and robotics are reshaping the business world. Personalized and customized services, tailored applications, and data-driven decision-making are now shaking the business tree that was long rooted with rotten and outdated business applications.

At this stage, some of them are in experimental phases without mass adoption. On the other hand, some of the emerging technologies are a breakthrough in the business world. For example, McKinsey reported that, by 2030, AI adoption is expected to raise global GDP by about $13 trillion.[21] The report also highlighted that industries actually are less than 40% digitized in which there still are further developments to see in the digital economy as the mainstream emerging tech solutions are adopted at a scale. The potentials, however, are immense and exhilarating that these technologies are disruptive to the legacy system. A typical example of AI solutions includes the IBM Cognos Analytics,[22] Aviso,[23] Beyond Limits,[24] and more.[25] A number of businesses are now deploying the IBM Cognos Analytics, AI-enabled business intelligence platform that visualizes and analyzes data and provides insights. The solutions such technologies provide to your business create innovative opportunities to tap into new potentials. Thus, identifying how these emerging technological solutions could fit into your business is a strategic decision to make in digital transformation or a formation of new businesses today.

Summing up, the prominent smart business model tools include

- Digital platforms and marketplaces including mobile applications and the Web

- Digital footprint—big data

- *Emerging technologies*: Fintech, data analytics, artificial intelligence, autonomous vehicles, 3D printing, robotics, Internet of Things, and Internet of People

- Cloud computing

---

[21]See McKinsey Global Institute's briefing, January 2019, on Navigating a world of disruption, available at www.mckinsey.com/featured-insights/innovation-and-growth/navigating-a-world-of-disruption
[22]www.ibm.com/products/cognos-analytics
[23]www.aviso.com/
[24]www.beyond.ai/
[25]See Tech Times for the details on the Top 5 Best AI Solutions In 2019, available at www.techtimes.com/brandspin/243818/20190919/top-5-best-ai-solutions-in-2019.htm

Trust and Reputation: The Currency of the Digital Economy?

Trust, in the business context, refers to the act of value exchange fairly and equitably stating the level of confidence an individual puts on their business partner. This implies that a business confidence, trust, emanates from a robust bridge of asymmetric information, which is built through a repeated interaction. Generally speaking, trust depends on the degree of risk involved in a particular set of transactions. This can be supported by the reputation of the business partner regarding trustworthiness. A simple example could be the two-sided rating scheme in the ride-hailing platforms like Uber and Lyft, where riders or drivers with poor ratings were those with a rough ride-share experience and in some cases subject to criminal acts.[26] On May 29, 2019, The Verge reported that Uber had taken a measure toward deactivating accounts of riders with below average ratings.[27] Accordingly, reputation is one of the most highly valued assets in the current era of the digital economy, and it is considered as the currency of the digital ecosystem (Owyang et al., 2013). In an eBay-like online marketplace, sellers' reputation affects the demand for their products and acceptance rate of the BIN price (buy-it-now price) offered by them, in which case highly reputed sellers have more acceptance by the buyers than the less reputed ones. For instance, let's say there are two sellers who are selling the exact brand of toaster you want to buy. One seller has a five-star rating with 1000 positive reviews. The other seller has a three-star rating with 500 reviews. You would probably choose to buy from the five-star seller over the three-star. Likewise, buyers' credibility both in their bids and customer loyalty depends on their reputation in the market. Economic theories with a motive to capture the dynamics of trust construction between collaborating agents have suggested many game-theoretic analyses (e.g., Fudenberg and Levine, 1992; Friedman and Resnick, 2001; and Dellarocas, 2003). See Figure 1-4.

---

[26]www.theguardian.com/us-news/2020/feb/06/uber-rideshare-lyft-safety-crime
[27]www.theverge.com/2019/5/29/18644143/uber-deactivate-rider-below-average-rating

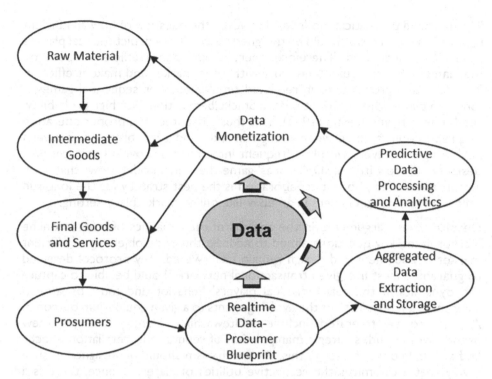

Figure 1-4. Feedback loops in the data-driven economy: prosumers' blueprint to data monetization in supply chain

In game theory, reputation games generally fall under the umbrella of the repeated game (due to the repeated interactions) and Bayesian game structure, with the information asymmetry (where one party has more or better information than the other) and uncertainties underlying this type of interaction. This concept has great importance in today's online marketplaces and the crowd-based business models, where information asymmetry and uncertainties are one of the key problems. Online marketplaces like eBay, Yahoo! Auctions, Alibaba Group, Amazon.com, LendingClub, Kickstarter, Prosper Marketplace, and so on suffer from significant issues of trust. These markets are commonly characterized by a repeated transactional interaction between a number of rational long-run (mostly sellers) and short-run players (buyers with mostly one-time transactions with a single seller) in a sequence of continuous transactions.

In online communities, giving feedback is commonly voluntarily. Since feedback is privately examined and subjectively valued, it is one of the underprovided economic goods. Provided this, some reputation models utilizing game-theoretic modeling approaches have been proposed, with an assumption that player's types are defined by their past record and, hence, committed to honesty (Stackelberg action) with the expectation of their future reputation.

This is sound theoretical modeling. However, the question of how an efficient reputation mechanism should be designed so that it can depict the real player's type is not addressed. Therefore, there should be an efficient reputation mechanism that can guarantee trust within the market and make it efficient. The literature proves that, in repeated simultaneous or sequential games, a long-run player who is patient takes a Stackelberg action with high probability; see Fudenberg and Levine (1992). This thus guarantees the proper operation of a reputation game between a long-run and a short-run player (or between both long-run players with less frequent interactions) provided that it is well designed. In line with this, Dellarocas' game-theoretic model shows that, with a reputation effect, honest collaboration is the best strategy for the long-run sellers and short-run buyers in an eBay-like online marketplace setting.

Despite several arguments in the analysis of the dynamics of trust in online marketplaces, key questions aimed to address the prior objective of efficient market development and design remain unanswered. Any protocol designed to guarantee trust in a given transactional network should be able to capture the dynamics in the real individual players' behavior and must be attack-tolerant in a way that sticks the evolving agents to a given equilibrium outcome. Attacks to be tolerated include whitewashing, identity changes (new pseudonym), fraud, strategic manipulation of reputations, retaliation effects, and so on. In order to attain this, the mechanism should be designed in such a way that it optimizes the respective utilities of players. Hence, there is a need for defining case-specific reputation mechanisms and adapting efficient incentive/punishment schemes that commit all the players to collaborate in a self-enforcing and decentralized way.

To sum up, even if the collaborative economy is a promising economic system in a robust and cost-effective utilization of scarce resources, the effectiveness in its undertakings still is questionable. In this regard, being commonly operated in the form of web-based collaborations, the issue of building trust between the collaborating agents is one of the open areas of research as the collaborative economy grows and expands its applications. We'll take a deeper look at the underlying business models of the collaborative economic system in Chapter 2.

Reputation Management in Online Transactions

In this era of collaborative economy, reputation is a highly valued asset that can be considered as the currency of peer-to-peer systems. Information asymmetry is one of the underlying factors that calls for an efficient reputation mechanism that narrows the information gap between collaborating agents. However, the nature, reliability, and dissemination mechanism of information define the efficiency of a reputation protocol to be adopted for a given network. Chen et al. (2004) compared in their experimental study different reputation mechanisms based on the level of information and self-reporting. Accordingly, they defined a trust value in a range [0, 1], where trust values of 1, 0, and 0.5 represent complete trust, distrust, and uncertainty, respectively. Buskens (2002), on the other hand, argues that the number of links in a network explains why agents trust more one network than another, while the number of links of an agent explains why another agent trusts this agent more than the others in the same network. These metrics allow developing control and learning behavior on the agents that continually interact.

Many other scholars have suggested a mechanism for building trust in a given network (ranging from Kamvar et al. (2003) to Collier and Hampshire (2010) and Donato et al. (2007)). More recent work by Domingo-Ferrer et al. (2016b) suggests a distributed and co-utile way of computing the agents' reputation. This mechanism has the attractive properties of being attack-tolerant, anonymous, cost-effective, and computed in a self-enforcing decentralized way. The reputation mechanisms currently at play in the market are subject to tampering attacks and can be personalized to the peers' benefit, rather than truthfully reporting on a target agent. Because P2P lending implies the interaction between rational agents, the reputation protocol that operates in the market should be self-enforcing in order to be rationally sustainable; in this way, each agent would have incentives to compute values in such a way that it can truly measure the creditworthiness and honesty of all other agents. Hence, making a reputation protocol self-enforcing and beneficial for all involved agents will guarantee that it is in the best interest of each agent in the system to compute another agent's reputation as accurately as possible. A further direction of work in designing a reputation protocol is to take a stride toward merging the outcome-based reputation and also the social reputation (using state-of-the-art social media, like Facebook, Twitter, Instagram posts, or LinkedIn connections in which a bunch of personal data are available) and market-related reputation (such as Amazon or eBay purchases and credit card expenses, or length of phone calls).

For example, one of the key problems underlying the ecommerce market is the lack of trust between transacting agents. This is due to the uncertainties and information asymmetry problems underlying these marketplaces. As a result, these platforms employ various feedback mechanisms that help build trust between the transacting agents. Nevertheless, these reputation mechanisms have their pitfalls apart from being managed in a centralized way. In the eBay reputation system, there is evidence of the correlation between buyer and seller feedback, suggesting that the players reciprocate and retaliate (i.e., a bad review from a buyer will lead to a bad review from the seller in return and vice versa); see Bolton et al. (2013), Cabral (2012), and Resnick and Zeckhauser (2002). The question is, how exactly can an eBay bidder use a seller profile to determine how much to bid, and whether to bid for it at all? In this regard, Aberer and Despotovic (2004) argue that game-theoretic reputation systems, which give the equilibrium of the feedback game, can help handle the problem of seller identification, provided that the players are rational utility-maximizing agents. However, this method of modeling is limited in capturing the dynamics of online platforms, because there is commonly an interaction of a long-term player (e.g., seller) with multiple short-term players (e.g., buyers). Thus, due to its practical limitations in capturing the reality on the ground and quantifying players' discount factors and the discounting criteria, it is not standardized.

The subjective nature of feedback is commonly avoided by a scoring method based on a set of values for random variables representing the feedback (eBay feedback score and the detailed seller ratings). Another method suggested is clustering and filtering of the feedback scores according to their common features in order to capture the heterogeneities among individual raters (e.g., Amazon feedback and ratings). Yet collusive behavior, Sybil attacks (a malicious multiple pseudonym creation to subvert a reputation system through a majority rule) and biased ratings deviate online ratings. As a result, the reputation score aggregation mechanism for the online markets is an open research question. Moreover, cross-validating malicious reporting and whether enough feedback is solicited depends on the underlying incentive scheme under the feedback mechanism.

Feedback systems in ecommerce marketplaces are important, especially with the underlying information asymmetry and market-related risks. They help create a fair and efficient marketplace. Hence, an efficient reputation mechanism can allow us to sort out malicious buyers/bidders and sellers within the transactional network of this market. The reputation mechanism helps sort out malicious buyers/bidders by imposing buyer requirements in the marketplace to those with policy violations, retaliation feedback motive, unpaid items (after placing a winning bid or purchase order), or fraudulent payments. An incentive scheme for the buyers is that being positively reputed helps them to be identified and benefit from the loyal customers' benefit and rewards. A buyer with a negative reputation can encounter limits on account privileges (such privileges in the eBay, e.g., include eBay Money Back Guarantee and discount and reward offers, Gift Cards & Coupons, non-cash eBay Bucks customer rewards program (greater or equal to $5 in the form of an eBay Bucks Certificate to qualifying buyers)) or the Amazon Prime (a paid service that gives buyers a few distinct advantages like free shipping). The reputation mechanism should be designed in such a way that it clearly identifies loyal customers in the transactional network with these incentive schemes under consideration. Negative ratings result in a limit on these privileges or overall buying activity and account suspension in the extreme case. On the other side, selling performance measures can be used to rate the reputation scores of the sellers in the transactional network. These measures include defect rate (item description accuracy), late shipment rate (item delivery), shipping and handling charges, communication, and cases closed without seller resolution.

For example, let us have a look at eBay's rating mechanism (Table 1-3). eBay employs two main feedback mechanisms to bridge the gap resulting from the information asymmetry and build trust between transacting individuals in the network. These are the feedback score (FS) and the detailed seller rating (DSR) The FS method uses aggregation of positive, negative, or neutral rating values for sellers and positive rating values for buyers which later are aggregated to compute each individual seller's/buyer's reputation from the transaction records in every one week. On the other hand, DSR is used as a descriptive index of individual seller's reputation which is computed one star (lowest) to five stars (highest) and the average ratings for a seller are computed once every 12 months for each seller with a minimum of five rating records for the months under consideration.

Table 1-3. The eBay stars and their ratings

Seller's Star Rating	Number of Feedback for a Seller
Yellow star	10 to 49
Blue star	50 to 99
Turquoise star	100 to 499
Purple star	500 to 999
Red star	1000 to 4999
Green star	5000 to 9999
Yellow shooting star	10,000 to 24,999
Turquoise shooting star	25,000 to 49,999
Purple shooting star	50,000 to 99,999
Red shooting star	100,000 to 499,999
Green shooting star	500,000 to 999,999
Silver shooting star	Over 1 million positive feedback

In the eBay rating scheme, the feedback score is positively correlated with the number of positive ratings indicated by the color of the star from yellow star (for aggregated score of 10–59) up to a silver shooting star (for an aggregated score greater than 1 million). Yet, as the feedback score is an aggregation of all the negative, positive, and neutral scores a player in the market has, this way of rating can be biased with size of the transactional network a player in the market has. For instance, consider that two different sellers A and B have 1000 and 100,000 number of transactional networks, respectively. Assume that from all the transaction records, each has 10% negative ratings and 90% positive ratings. According to eBay's feedback computation, even if both sellers have a proportional record of feedback, seller A will be a purple star, while seller B will be a purple shooting star with the scale effect. The other limitation with this method of computation is that it takes longer time to update every transactional outcomes, aggregating every week's transaction record with one individual into one feedback score regardless of the number of transactions in that specific week. Hence, this reputation mechanism fails to capture the real transactional behavior of the players in the network.

Given the strategic nature of feedback giving, in which users retaliate and reciprocate, a co-utile reputation mechanism could be more efficient (Turi et al., 2017). A co-utile reputation mechanism is different from the conventional method of sequential approach in eBay or the simultaneous or blind feedback giving method proposed by Bolton et al. (2013). This mechanism helps compute individual user's reputation fairly based on a global reputation, which is derived from the normalized weighted local reputation scores. Turi et al. (2016) argue that reciprocity equilibrium can lead to a co-utile outcome for positive reciprocity, provided that the outcome is Pareto-optimal and results in strictly greater payoff to the players. Therefore, reciprocal feedback can be co-utile feedback. Yet, favoring one another in a reciprocal setting might lead to a biased reputation system at an aggregate level. Hence, the aggregation mechanism should be designed in such a way that it gives weight for each individual transaction in the network.

Some of the common problems in the online market is that it is global in nature and hence difficult to enact global standard rules and regulation and as a result hard to make efficient contractual agreements. The other is information asymmetry and hard for identification with a volatile and possibly unstable pseudonym operation. Zero marginal cost pseudonyms complicate transaction in the online marketplaces. Friedman and Resnick (2001) proposed two mechanisms to cope with this problem: (1) cryptographic verification of unique identities of each member with a protocol that uses blind signatures and (2) a transactional network structure with unprofitable exit and re-entry setting through a new entry fee (or implicit cost of an initial reputation building) that offsets the gain from any potential exit and re-entry. The co-utile reputation mechanism proposed in Turi et al. (2017) employs the second mechanism by setting zero reputation scores for all new and malicious players with an intention to disincentive whitewashing. Setting zero reputation (the worst possible reputation) to new entrants in online marketplaces is proved to be the most reasonable mechanism to punish malicious players re-entering the market with a new pseudonym (see also Dellarocas, 2003a).

Hence, from our discussion, we see that the digitization of everything in the collaborative economy including finance, service delivery, and goods and services trading and understanding this dynamics doesn't merely rely on traditional economic theory-based analysis. Instead, a multidisciplinary approach, including computer science, information systems, management science, and psychology, has to be in place. The science of building trust calls for varied insights from computer science, information systems, management science, and psychology beyond the conventional microeconomic and game-theoretic human behavior modeling.

Some Digital Companies and Their Business Models

The most common business models for digital companies include commission or brokerage fees, subscription plans, service usage–based fees, selling and rental of goods and services, ads display (web advertising model), and license sells for software products.[28]

In this section, we'll discuss a selection of digital platforms and their business models, including retail ecommerce platforms, hospitality and transportation platforms based on Uberification, search engine companies like Google, and startups based on Fintech solutions.

Retail Ecommerce Platforms

Ecommerce has allowed the sale of goods and services online across geopolitical borders. In 2019, about $3.5 trillion is globally spent in ecommerce transactions (see Table 1-4).

Table 1-4. Ten of the largest ecommerce in 2019, by region[29]

Region	Volume of Transaction in 2019
China	$740 billion
United States	$561 billion
United Kingdom	$91 billion
Japan	$87 billion
Germany	$77 billion
South Korea	$69 billion
France	$55 billion
Canada	$44 billion
Russia	$19 billion
Brazil	$16 billion
Africa and the Middle East	$18.6 billion

---

[28]Visual Capitalist at www.visualcapitalist.com/startups-improve-odds-unicorn/, accessed on May 22, 2020.

[29]Based on data fetched from Statista, www.statista.com/outlook/243/100/ecommerce/worldwide

Amazon, eBay, Alibaba (BABA), BigCommerce, Shopify, JD, PinDuoDuo, 3dcart, WooCommerce, Volusion, PrestaShop, Weebly, Jumia, Takealot, Zando, Bol, Coolblue, Squarespace, Zalando, and Magento are some of the players in the ecommerce digital industry space. In this section, we will have a closer look at the business models of three sample ecommerce marketplaces (Amazon, Alibaba, and Shopify).

Amazon

Amazon is an online retailer of goods and services. To generate revenue, Amazon relies on a hybrid business model of commission or brokerage, subscription plans, selling and rental of goods and services, and advertising. According to Statista,[30] the company generated total net sales of about $87.44 billion during the fourth quarter of 2019.

Amazon sells goods online with inventory in its local warehouses. The company also operates by providing an online platform for selling new and used goods and services with other partner retail companies and retains commission for listings on its platform.

In its cloud business, Amazon Web Services (AWS), the company provides on-demand cloud computing platforms and APIs to individual and institutional customers. Virtual computers (Amazon Elastic Compute Cloud) is one of the services provided by AWS. AWS accounted for 13% of the company's revenue in the first quarter of 2019. Also, it hosts advertising services on its highly visited site.

Another revenue source is from its Kindle Store for eBooks. With the growing independent eBook publishing market, the company has managed to generate significant revenue from the sales of eBooks on Kindle. This business model has helped the company to be a dominant player (with 67% market share in 2019[31]) in the eBooks market.

Through its Amazon Prime service, the company also uses subscription plans that allow members to stream movies, TV shows, and music via the Internet, exclusive shopping deals, and fast product shipping.

The company charges a subscription fee of $39.99 per month for a professional selling plan and free individual subscription plan. In its selling fees, it charges 6% for PCs and 45% for Amazon device accessories. On its per-item fees, it charges a $0.99 fee for each item sold by individual sellers and free for

---

[30]www.statista.com/statistics/273963/quarterly-revenue-of-amazoncom/
[31]About eBooks at https://about.ebooks.com/ebook-industry-news-feed/, accessed on May 22, 2020.

professional sellers. Sellers also pay a referral fee on each item sold on the site. See Selling on Amazon Fee Schedule for the details.[32]

The company has secured a competitive advantage in its core business lines. Brick-and-mortar stores, Alibaba, eBay, and other ecommerce marketplaces and video streaming sites, like Netflix, are some of the competitors in its different lines of business. In fostering its competitive advantage in each sphere of business, the company makes a massive investment in new technologies, research and development, partnerships, and acquisitions. The company has acquired or invested in about 128 companies in AI, clothing and accessories, financial services (fintech), media production and entertainment, publishing, transportation, and logistics.[33] In 2018, the company invested $753 million to acquire online pharmacy, PillPack. With interest in healthcare, Amazon has partnered with Berkshire Hathaway and JPMorgan Chase. In transportation, self-driving car investments have been reported[34] (e.g., startup called Aurora, electric truck startup Rivian). With its project Kuiper, Amazon plans to set up to offer broadband access from orbit with 3236 satellites to expand a global high-speed Internet access.[35]

Alibaba

Alibaba is a dominant ecommerce player in China, with about 58% market share. Alibaba has four business models which we will briefly discuss in this section. It operates through its three main web portals: Alibaba.com, Taobao, and Tmall, to facilitate transactions between buyers and sellers. As of June 2019, the company has 674 million users.[36]

The first business model is through its Alibaba.com marketplace, where the company focuses on a business-to-business (B2B) business model of a transaction between wholesale suppliers and global retail distributors. The second business model is through its Taobao marketplace, where the company utilizes eBay and Amazon-like business-to-consumer (B2C) or consumer-to-consumer (C2C) business model. The third Alibaba's business model is through its Tmall marketplace, where the company facilitates B2C online retail of multinational brands (like Gap, Nike, and Apple) for China's middle class. Advertising fee of Taobao sellers ranking in the Alibaba's internal search

---

[32]https://sellercentral.amazon.com/gp/help/external/200336920?language=en_US&ref=efph_200336920_cont_201822160, accessed on December 15, 2019.
[33]Inc at www.inc.com/magazine/201705/zoe-henry/will-amazon-buy-you.html
[34]www.wired.com/story/amazon-aurora-self-driving-investment-funding-series-b/
[35]TJI Research, https://this.just.in/amazon-developing-new-space-and-satel-lite-services/, accessed on May 22, 2020.
[36]www.alibabagroup.com/en/news/press_pdf/p190815.pdf

engine, deposits, annual user fees, and sales commissions on each of its portals are its revenue sources. The fourth business model of Alibaba is through its financial service, Ant Financial.

AliExpress and 1688 (online retail), Alimama (advertising platform operating search marketing, display marketing, promotion commission, and real-time bidding utilizing big data), Aliyun (in cloud computing), and Cainiao Network (Chinese Smart Logistics Network) are the other subsidiaries of the company. According to the Macrotrends, the company's annual revenue for 2019 was $56.152 billion, a 40.74% increase from 2018.[37]

Shopify

Shopify is a Canada-based ecommerce marketplace that enables sellers to commercialize their products on its cloud-based platform. It uses a subscription-based business model. As of early 2020, sellers pay a monthly subscription of basic ($29), Shopify ($79), and advanced ($299) plans to access the Shopify tools and resources. Unlike Amazon, eBay, or Alibaba's business models, the Shopify platform is a specialized ecommerce platform that provides sellers with the tools to build and promote their web-based stores of a unique brand. This mimics the traditional shop rentals in a commercial building. As of 2019, the platform hosts about 820,000 online stores (SimilarTech, 2019). Its business model is ideal for unique branding of any size (e.g., Tesla and Red Bull are some of the big brands with online stores on Shopify).

In addition to the subscription fees, it has third-party apps in its App Store. Adding third-party apps can increase your monthly costs.

Shopify also supports a payment gateway called Merchant e-Solutions, which provides a global payment processing offering an automated billing, mobile payment, real-time transaction results, web-based reporting, PCI compliance, and fraud management.[38] In the third quarter of 2019, Shopify Merchant Solutions generated about $225.0 million in revenue from payment processing fees of Shopify Payments, Shopify Shipping, Shopify Capital, transaction fees, referral fees, and sales of point-of-sale hardware.[39] According to Investors. shopify, the company generated a total of $390.6 million revenues in the third quarter of 2019, of which $165.6 million is from the subscription solutions.[40]

---

[37]Macrotrends, www.macrotrends.net/stocks/charts/BABA/alibaba/revenue, accessed on March 20, 2020.
[38]www.shopify.com/payment-gateways/united-states/merchant-e-solutions
[39]Marketplace Pulse, www.marketplacepulse.com/stats/shopify/shopify-mer-chant-solutions-revenue-131, accessed on May 22, 2020.
[40]Shopify financial data available at https://investors.shopify.com/Investor-News-Details/2019/Shopify-Announces-Third-Quarter-2019-Financial-Results/default.aspx, accessed on March 20, 2020.

Uberification

The millennial era is characterized by an intense usage of mobile devices and increased screen times. A survey on the screen time shows that, on average, people in the United States check their phone every 12 minutes.[41] According to the Statista, as of 2019, there are 3.2 billion global smartphone users[42] and that by 2023 the global mobile app revenues are expected to hit $935.2 billion.[43] The ride-sharing company, Uber, took the mobile web revolution a step forward by redefining the transportation service through on-demand service provision based on mobile applications. Uberification refers to the provision of services based on Uber's business model of app-enabled mobile services. Without the need to own the product, Uber and similar companies (like Airbnb) have derived a massive chunk of revenue by creating digital platforms that connect service providers and customers. Similarly, online food orders and delivery platforms like Uber Eats and SkipTheDishes facilitate instant access to food orders and delivery from local restaurants. The mobile app-enabled business model is booming. According to App Annie, there were about 194 billion App downloads in 2018.[44] Thus, in today's competitive business environment, capturing the customer base of mobile users by building a mobile app is a vital business strategy as building a website. To help us understand the core of this business model, we will have a closer look at two of the biggest companies utilizing this, Uber and Airbnb.

Uber

Through its online platform and smartphone App, Uber, Uber Technologies facilitates on-demand service between users and service providers. The company started as a ride-sharing company. Over the years, the tech company has diversified its products, including Uber P2P ride-sharing (UberPOP), ride service hailing (UberPool), food delivery (Uber Eats), electric bikes and scooters, carrier shipping (Uber Freight), aerial electric ride-hailing, air flights (uberAIR/Uber Elevate), and helicopter rides (UberCHOPPER). Founded in 2009, the company is one of the disruptive companies in the last decade.[45] Uber is further powered by its key technologies like AI, machine learning, robotics, and self-driving vehicles. The San Francisco-based company, Lyft, is one of its competitors. As of 2019, the company has about 30,000 employees.[46]

---

[41]https://nypost.com/2017/11/08/americans-check-their-phones-80-times-a-day-study/

[42]www.statista.com/statistics/330695/number-of-smartphone-users-worldwide/

[43]www.statista.com/statistics/269025/worldwide-mobile-app-revenue-forecast/

[44]www.appannie.com/en/insights/market-data/the-state-of-mobile-2019/

[45]CNBC ranked Uber second from the list of 2018 CNBC Disruptor 50 companies, Disrupting: Public transportation, taxi, and limousine services, www.cnbc.com/2018/05/22/uber-2018-disruptor-50.html, accessed on May 22, 2020.

[46]https://pitchbook.com/profiles/company/51136-75

However, the Uberification business model has been questionable, mainly due to the employment package such companies offer. On May 8, 2019, Uber and Lyft drivers conducted a strike against low wages and lack of full-time employment benefits, long hours of work, and working conditions.[47] The drivers were classified as independent contractors, which assumes the company is free riding to generate its huge chunk of revenue. As of the third quarter of 2019, the company generated revenue of $3.8 billion.[48]

In April 2019, Driverless cars, which is the company's self-driving unit got a $1 billion investment from SoftBank and Japan's auto industry (The Verge).[49] However, there still are controversies around driverless cars. One of the major incidents around this, the autonomous vehicle crash of Tempe, Arizona, in March 2018, has made the company questionable regarding this service. Further, major regulatory issues arise around driverless cars, one of which is the issue of liability in the case of crashes.[50]

Airbnb

Airbnb facilitates access to local homes by connecting guests with hosts through its online platform. It operates in more than 190 countries, with 31 offices around the world and 13,000 employees. In 2018, the multibillion hospitality tech company is valued at about $38 billion.[51]

The company follows a crowd-based business model for a hospitality service where a community of interested individuals interacts over its digital marketplace. Potential hosts make a listing of places or events on the Airbnb platform where guests can make a booking/reservation. The company generates revenue from fees for booking accommodations and Airbnb experiences and also charges VAT on service fees.[52] Guests are charged a guest service fee (0–13% depending on the location) for a completed booking through its platform. In addition, hosts are charged host fees (3% or more depending on the location) for property or event listing with a completed

---

[47]https://globalnews.ca/news/5254600/uber-lyft-drivers-strike-declining-wages/

[48]https://investor.uber.com/news-events/news/press-release-details/2019/Uber-Announces-Results-for-Third-Quarter-2019/, accessed on March 20, 2020.

[49]www.theverge.com/2019/4/18/18507049/uber-atg-self-driving-autonomous-car-investment-softbank-toyota-denso

[50]See ABC for some points on Legal Implications of Self-Driving Vehicle Technology, available at www.americanbar.org/groups/litigation/committees/business-torts-unfair-competition/practice/2018/top-8-legal-implications-of-self-driving-car-technology-litigation/, accessed on May 22, 2020.

[51]www.statista.com/topics/2273/airbnb/

[52]See Airbnb service fees at www.airbnb.ca/help/article/1857/what-is-the-airbnb-service-fee?locale=en&_set_bev_on_new_domain=1577510813_vPS6N-5PQtaytKsO3, accessed on March 20, 2020.

transaction. The platform also offers a host-only fee to allow service providers the control over final prices.

Since its inception in 2008, over 400 million global guests have used the accommodation service through the Airbnb platform.[53] Like all other business of the collaborative economy, Airbnb's business model is far from perfection. Some of the issues around the company's business model are local rental shortages with preferences for Airbnb listings, illegal subletting and safety, and security concerns resulting from home-sharing services with strangers.[54]

Google

Google is one of the tech giants who free rides the Internet through its online ad-based business model. The company's hybrid business model aggregates multiple business lines across sectors of publication, mail, music, and broadcasting industries beyond its advertising networks and cloud services business. The company's prominent business model is the bundling of online advertising technologies with its search engine service. In its search engine, the company has formed a co-utile form of value creation. That is, global users can access its search engine for free whose data then becomes the input for the targeted ads. It leverages its search algorithm to process queries and aggregate users' data.

Data-driven decision-making is at the core of today's knowledge-based economy. The global IT spending for 2019 is about $3.76 trillion with data centers and enterprise software spending.[55] Users' psychographic and behavioral data, which are fetched and aggregated, are also used for intelligent business decision-making and understanding of markets by businesses. This has a significant effect on the understanding of customers and markets, design communications, product development, and branding strategies (Caulkins et al., 2018; Kregor et al., 2018; and Sleep et al., 2019).

Beyond its ad-based business model, Google also provides cloud computing (a.k.a. on-demand computing) and data storage services for users and enterprises. The tech giant is one of the most prominent cloud vendors like Amazon Web Services, Microsoft Azure, and IBM. AI, IoT, and analytics are the leading technologies the company relies on. Furthermore, Apps, in-app purchases, Google Play Store contents (music, books, movies, TV shows, news, and magazines), and software and hardware products are the other

---

[53]www.alltherooms.com/analytics/airbnb-ipo-going-public-revenues-business-model-statistics/

[54]A survey on 1021 Airbnb horror stories shows uncovered various unchecked dangerous loopholes and scams around the short-term rental platform, www.asherfergusson.com/airbnb/, accessed on May 22, 2020.

[55]www.gartner.com/en/newsroom/press-releases/2018-10-17-gartner-says-global-it-spending-to-grow-3-2-percent-in-2019

revenue sources of Google. The multibillion tech giant generated about $45.8 billion in revenues in the fourth quarter of 2019, of which the majority comes from its ads business.[56] In 2018, its Google website revenue alone was $136 billion, which is the largest share of the revenue of its parent company, Alphabet.[57]

Data privacy and security, antitrust, search result manipulations, and censorship are some of the issues around its business environment. Still, with less sophisticated users of the Web, the data privacy issue remains a dilemma. The black box problem around the AI tech it uses for decision-making is another concern which the company pitched to resolve through Explainable AI:[58]

> *People say they want privacy, but their actions indicate that they do not really care about it. Although many people say they dislike companies tracking their locations, "everyone loves this feature of Google Maps that tells you how long it will take to get home."*
>
> —Hal Varian, Google's chief economist [59]

Fintech

Fintech refers to technological solutions for financial services. Some of the major services offered with these technological solutions include underwriting, lending, transaction banking, asset management, mortgages, financial planning and management, and portfolio management, payments, currency exchanges, insurance, credit rating, digital currency, capital management, investment, and more. AI, machine learning, distributed ledger technologies (such as Blockchain), and data analytics are at the core of fintech developments. Fintech solutions also power online businesses and ecommerce. These technological solutions, mostly run by startups, are disruptive to the traditional banking and financial sectors. Annual review by McKinsey (2015) reported that 60% of global banking profits, mostly, consumer finance, mortgages, SME lending, retail payments, and wealth management, are at risk from these market entrants with disruptive technologies. By 2023, the market is expected to reach $305.7 billion, of which payment/billing solutions take the highest share.[60] There are about 12,211 global fintech startups with a high concentration in the United States.[61] Some of these fintech companies include Betterment and Wealthfront, Venmo, Robinhood, Ant Financial, Motif Investing, Xoom,

---

[56]www.statista.com/statistics/267606/quarterly-revenue-of-google/
[57]www.statista.com/statistics/266206/googles-annual-global-revenue/
[58]www.bbc.com/news/technology-50506431, accessed on May 22, 2020.
[59]https://fortune.com/2018/10/30/data-regulation-tech-industry/, accessed on May 22, 2020.

2iQ Research, ZestFinance, Credit Karma, CommonBond, Kabbage, Tesorio, iDGate and QxBranch, SoFi, Square, Stripe, LOYAL3, Atom Bank, and MaxMyInterest. In addition, already-established IT companies like Facebook, Apple Pay, Android Pay, and Google Wallet are also actively involved in the money transfer markets and mobile payments. Here, the top 48 venture capital-backed fintech companies are valued at about $187 billion.[62] The top ten of the leading Fintech innovators for 2019, according to KPMG, are Ant Financial (China), Grab (Singapore), JD Digits (China), Gojek (Indonesia), Paytm (India), Du Xiaoman Financial (China), Compass (United States), Ola (India), Opendoor (United States), and OakNorth (United Kingdom).[63] Mobile technology, digital transformation, and users' digital preference have contributed to the fintech innovation diffusion. According to Ernst & Young, 64% of global consumers have at least once used fintech-powered platforms, and 96% of them are aware of at least one fintech service.[64] The market is growing at a fast pace, with significant investments across different sectors. Partnering with fintech startups and embedding fintech solutions into a business has become a vital competitive strategy for businesses. In 2018, there were a total of $111.8 billion global funding deals for fintech,[65] and in the second quarter of 2019, fintech investment topped about $8.3 billion.[66]

Digital Economy in the Developing Regions

About 50% of the world's population doesn't participate in the digital economy at all (WEF), of which the dominant share goes to the developing regions. In order to have a look at the digital economic system from the developing regions' perspective, we will pick Africa's nascent digital economy landscape. In this case, we will discuss the issue of digital financial inclusion in the lens of the developing countries, specifically Africa, where there is a significant share of the unbanked population.

---

[60]www.globenewswire.com/news-release/2019/04/09/1801702/0/en/Global-Fintech-Market-2018-2023-Market-Set-to-Reach-USD-305-7-billion-by-2023.html
[61]www.statista.com/statistics/893954/number-fintech-startups-by-region/
[62]www.cbinsights.com/research/report/fintech-trends-q2-2019/
[63]https://home.kpmg/au/en/home/insights/2019/11/2019-fintech-100-leading-global-fintech-innovators.html
[64]https://assets.ey.com/content/dam/ey-sites/ey-com/en_gl/topics/banking-and-capital-markets/ey-global-fintech-adoption-index.pdf
[65]https://home.kpmg/xx/en/home/media/press-releases/2019/02/global-fintech-investment-hits-record-in-2018.html
[66]www.cbinsights.com/research/report/fintech-trends-q2-2019/

Africa's Nascent Digital Economy: Digital Financial Inclusion

The share of adults using mobile phones in Sub-Saharan Africa doubled over the last 5 years, of which a significant amount is unbanked. The region accounts for the highest mobile money usage in Africa. The barriers to financial service include lack of ID, little money for banking, and cost and geographic constraint to access banking services. Moreover, lack of confidence in traditional financial institutions is one of the other issues.

Reports show that about 66% of Sub-Saharan Africa is unbanked (the Global Findex Database, 2017,[67] and World Bank[68]). This gap is a potential niche for mobile payments like the Kenyan M-Pesa, Nigerian Moneywave, and other fintech solutions. Moreover, the fast pace of mobile subscription allows for a potential expansion of digital financial inclusion through virtual financial services.

Key drivers of digital financial inclusion in Africa are mobile payments, micro-credit, and crowd-based digital business models, DLTs, and cryptocurrencies. Fintech waves have brought tech and telephone companies in the credit market. Social lending apps through smartphones hold a significant potential in redefining and transforming the microfinance funding models in remote rural areas and crowded cities of the continent.

In the past 5 years, Africa's digital entrepreneur ecosystem through incubators, accelerators, and tech hubs has grown tenfold (World Bank). The continent has the highest rate of mobile subscriptions with about 50% of subscriptions in Sub-Saharan Africa. This implies the potential for leapfrogging fintech solutions. Mobile-enabled and web-based platforms by local tech startups are increasing in the continent. Only 27% of Africa's population has access to the Internet, which is only 10% of the global online population (World Bank). Digitizing government payments, remittances, SME payments, and value chain payments enables participation in the digital economy and drives progress to the goal of universal financial access (World Bank).

Fintech solutions are playing key roles in extending financial and banking services to the underserved, thus significantly adding to the global agenda of financial inclusion. These digital solutions allow affordable and accessible financial services to everyone. The innovation diffusion of fintech is significant in emerging economies (e.g., Indonesia, China, and Kenya). In addition to convenience, the following features make fintech solutions appealing in emerging economies:

- *Growing mobile subscription and built-in applications*: Mobile money sector coverage in Western Africa is 13 times larger than the local banks. Flutterwave, the Nigerian

[67]https://globalfindex.worldbank.org/sites/globalfindex/files/2018-04/2017%20Findex%20full%20report_0.pdf

[68]http://documents.worldbank.org/curated/en/719111532533639732/pdf/128850-WP-AFR-Digital-Access-The-Future-of-Financial-Inclusion-in-Africa-PUBLIC.pdf

mobile payment system, recently partnered with the Chinese tech giant Alipay for receiving payments for transactions with its users. This creates the opportunity for the Nigerian merchants to participate in cross-border digital economic system.

- *Reduced service and transaction costs*: For example, the mobile money, M-Pesa, allowed the virtual transfer of payments and reduced travel and wait times. This payment solution has increased the rural household incomes of Kenya by up to 30%.

- *Ease of access to credit for SMEs, unlike credit rationing biases and high costs of credit in traditional funding models*: For example, Alipay provides credit for vendors operating on the Alibaba ecommerce platform. Through service bundling across its platforms, the Chinese tech giant uses users' real-time data; it has built an efficient risk pricing and functioning financial services. Ant Financial operates as a virtual financial institution that is subject to regulations.

- *Growing mobile phone subscription and Internet service coverage*: For the unbanked, mobile subscription alone has replaced the bank account function of basic financial services like the virtual credit market access to remote rural areas.

- Data access for rating and pricing risk and surpassing the geographic constraints through virtual institutional presence put fintech solutions at advantage over the traditional financial services in banking the unbanked. Recently, the African Development Bank launched the African digital financial inclusion facility which allows credit scoring using geolocation data, contacts, phone call frequency, and call logs. However, this system of credit custody comes at the cost of an invasion of users' privacy.

- *A complementary monetary system*: The recent Zimbabwean hyperinflation of 300% (IMF[69]) is a good example of a fiat currency collapse. This has led to a multicurrency system and a near fully digital monetary system. About 90% of the country's adults are users of EcoCash, the

---

[69]www.imf.org/en/News/Articles/2019/09/26/pr19355-zimbabwe-imf-staff-concludes-visit-art-consult-discuss-1st-rev-staff-mon-program

Zimbabwean digitized payment system (Techzim[70]). However, mobile money like EcoCash has been criticized for exacerbating financial instabilities in countries with a poor monetary system. EcoCash drained the foreign currency in the hands of the people at a time and misused the cash-in, cash-out, and cash-back services for selling foreign currencies in demand, resulting in financial instability concerns in the country (the *Financial Times*[71] and *Quartz Africa*[72]). There is a similar concern around M-Pesa's disproportionate charges on the smallest transactions and transaction fee of up to 31% on cross-border payments (usury laws need to be in place). M-Pesa is a typical example for digital financial inclusion of the unbanked, where it helped to increase Kenya's financial inclusion to 83% from about 27% prior to its inception (2019 Financial Access Household Survey[73]).

On the regulatory sphere of the digital economy, P2P regulatory frameworks of quota restriction requirements and minimization of operational risks and customer protection (segregation of platform user money, well-ordered platform cessation, default and debt management, transparent and informative lending process) are at play. One of the regulatory requirements (e.g., Ethiopia) to operate a P2P lending market is a partnership requirement with traditional banks and credit agencies facilitating the lending process. Potential risks of credit default, financial regulation, and supervision, data protection, technology risk, and reputation risk are at the core of concerns around such virtual trade and credit services. Financial tech solutions alone are not enough to increase financial inclusion. Rather, a well-functioning payment system, physical and institutional infrastructure, economic stability (e.g., moderate inflation with stability in fiat currencies), robust supervisory and regulatory policies, and viable consumer protection are required.

More specifically, issues to consider in scaling the digital economy in Africa are pointed out as follows. Primarily, policy reforms to lower entry barriers (e.g., telecom, encourage competition and investment) and ensuring competition and efficiency through fair access to credit are still works to be done. A significant barrier to entry and red tape are some of the constraints tech startups face in Africa. For example, in 2018, Nigeria drafted a policy proposal

[70]www.techzim.co.zw/2019/10/ban-on-cash-in-cash-out-affects-onemoney-and-telecash-more-than-ecocash/

[71]www.ft.com/content/2078bf62-f9ab-11e9-98fd-4d6c20050229

[72]https://qz.com/africa/1321152/zimbabwes-ecocash-mobile-money-crash-has-people-worried/

[73]https://fsdkenya.org/publication/finaccess2019/

of shareholder funds that range between $275,000 and $14 million for fintech startups licensing. Uganda's free zone for developments around digital solutions, on the other hand, is a step forward in facilitating the innovation diffusion of fintech solutions. Furthermore, poor infrastructural developments have lagged the continent behind the fast-growing global digital economy space. Global access to digital financial services, continental payment infrastructure, and platforms could allow the population to participate in the global and continental digital economy space. However, only a few governments are investing in developing digital infrastructure (universal Internet network coverage, affordable Internet, and broadband connectivity), services, skills, and digital entrepreneurship. Besides, supporting the demand side for higher innovation diffusion is vital. Digital literacy and curriculum design for the lower-end infrastructural development through innovation hubs and ICT centers will allow seizing opportunities in the digital world. In the continent where the majority of the population use mobile and web technologies only for checking email, making phone calls, and social media presence, human capital investment enhancing digital skills of workers and entrepreneurs is vital to adopt the digital economy at a full scale. Moreover, smartphones are smart by algorithm, not smart by heart to safeguard users and help in decision-making. Thus, digital financial literacy is also an issue to be given a huge concern.

To ensure a smooth and robust digital transformation is another issue to consider. In the dynamic digital era, we are adopting the rapid changes and developments; thus, every company is an education center to continually train employees for digital skill readiness and effective digital transformation. When it comes to our global village of the Internet era, thinking big through a digital single market that resolves regional fragmentations and interoperability of policies across the continent could help in enhancing the nascent digital economy space. A well-structured consumer protection system is also important in the digital economy. For example, in the digital financial markets, less sophisticated investors and creditors with the urge of access to loans participate in financial services of this form. In this regard, there is evidence of increasing debt with the ease of access to virtual credits at speed. As it has been the case with the 2008 financial crises of sub-prime lending, banking the unbaked comes at a cost. Besides, the commodification and monetization of data is against data privacy and ownership of users. In this regard, Kenya has passed the EU's GDPR-inspired laws, while Google has set a limit on lending apps with a loan repayment period of a month or less.

In summary, Africa's digital economy is a very early stage of development. Yet, it's expected that the continent's growing digital native generation with locally developed digital solutions and tech startups will make the difference as it adapts to the new developments in this economic system.

The Advent of the Digital Era and Global Regulatory Frameworks

Digital transformations in the global economies have called for reviewing and developing new regulatory frameworks. In this section, I will discuss the main regulatory practices in the digital economy space. Together with the support of the developments of the digital economic system, regulatory institutions are responsible for the advancement of the ICT sectors. Thus, in this disruptive phase of the digital space, to ensure a fair, competitive, and innovative business environment is one of the main goals of governments. To date, there are various rules and regulations in place for the digital economy. As a result, many tech companies have been subject to fines and penalties for violating the digital economy rules and regulations in place. Table 1-5 presents selected digital frauds, data breach fines, penalties, and settlements during the past two years.

Table 1-5. Selected digital frauds, data breach fines, penalties, and settlements in 2018 and 2019

Company	Issue	Fine	Regulatory Institution	Year
Facebook	Cambridge Analytica scandal	$5 billion	Federal Trade Commission	2019
Facebook	Social network's handling and misuse of users' data	$100 million	The US Securities Exchange Commission (SEC)	2019
Uber	600,000 driver and 57 million user accounts' data breach in 2016	$148 million	A multi-state settlement with 50 US states and Washington, DC	2018
Yahoo	Failure to disclose a massive security breach in 2013	$35 million	The US Securities Exchange Commission	2018
Google	Lack of transparency, information, and valid consent regarding ads personalization (for two main GDPR violations)	$57 million	French data protection authority (CNIL) under the EU's data privacy law	2019
Google and YouTube	Kids' personal information collected through YouTube channels without parental consent	$170 million	Federal Trade Commission	2019

(continued)

Table 1-5. (continued)

Company	Issue	Fine	Regulatory Institution	Year
LendingClub	Securities Exchange Commission fraud charges of improper usage of funds to benefit LCA's parent LendingClub	$6 million	The US SEC and Department of Justice	2018
O2 Advertising	Lack of data protection and improper data retention	$10,000	Personal Data Protection Commission of Singapore	2019
British Airways (BA)	BA through its website redirected customers to fraudulent site compromising users' data against the EU's GDPR	$228 million (£183 million)	United Kingdom's Information Commissioner's Office (ICO)	2019
1&1 Telecommunications (Internet and mobile service provider)	GDPR violation with a weak technical and organizational protection of customer data	$10.6 million (€9.55 million)	Germany's Federal Commission for Data Protection and Freedom of Information (BfDI)	2019

In the information society we live in, most of the digital platforms are used by non-privacy-conscious users. Marketplaces are also filled with many less sophisticated buyers and investors. Digital frauds, scams, unethical practices, digital market manipulation and deceptions, fake news, privacy, and security concerns are some of the issues in the digital economy.[74] In addition, whenever vulnerable people are involved in a value creation process, the law needs to intercede. Countries follow different approaches to deal with the issues that arise in this economic system. An initiative called e-consumer.gov has been launched in an effort to protect global consumers and foster fair trade practices in the digital economy. Table 1-6 shows the top ten complaint reports between July 1 and September 30, 2019, for companies based in the United States, China, United Kingdom, India, Canada, Hong Kong, France, Spain, Poland, and Germany (e-consumer.gov[75]).

---

[74]. The issue of illegal sale of human kidneys for auction had been a topic of discussion around the ecommerce marketplaces, late in 1999. The kidney that was listed on eBay had reached a bid of $5.75 million until it was removed by eBay. See www.nytimes.com/1999/09/03/us/auction-for-a-kidney-pops-up-on-ebay-s-site.html

[75]https://econsumer.gov/en/ComplaintTrend#crnt

Table 1-6. Top complaint reports for the
e-consumer.gov (July 1–September 30, 2019)[76]

Product or Service	Total # of Reports
Shop-at-Home/Catalog Sales	6422
Imposter: government	1360
Imposter: business	904
Travel/vacations	416
Employment agencies/job counseling/overseas work	310
Telemarketing practices	300
Romance scams	286
Internet Information Services	271
Prizes/sweepstakes/lotteries	270
Investment scams	198

With the fast pace of growth in the tech space and digital transformations, there are still loopholes in international regulatory practices. In order to effectively capture the digital economy, revisiting the existing regulatory frameworks is vital. Such a revision should consider private capital, competition, global and regional interoperability, consumer and data protection, security, legal intercept, taxation, a public interest, and freedom of innovation (see ICC Policy Statement, 2016[77]).

One example of the gap in the digital economy's regulation is the lack of robust taxation systems. Multinational company digital tax dodging and base erosion and profit shifting (BEPS) in the digital economy are common mainly in developing regions (e.g., Africa, Etter-Phoya et al., 2019) where the tech giants operate. According to the EU Commission, on average, digital multinationals pay only 9.5% effective tax rate, which is significantly lower than the traditional multinationals that pay 23.2%.[78] To harness a fair share of the growing revenues of digital multinationals, the EU Commission proposes a digital single market and interim taxation. In developed countries, new taxation systems are underway for tech companies whose revenue bases are reliant on their citizens. A digital service tax on digital service provision to

---

[76]Source: e-consumer.gov
[77]https://iccwbo.org/publication/icc-policy-statement-on-regulatory-modernization-in-the-digital-economy/
[78]https://ec.europa.eu/taxation_customs/sites/taxation/files/factsheet_digital_taxation_21032018_en.pdf

citizens has now started to be imposed in some countries like Austria (5%), Canada (proposed 3%), France (3%), Turkey (7.5%), and the United Kingdom (proposed 2%).[79]

With a significant concentration of the tech companies in the United States, the digital taxation system has faced backlashes from the US government which claims the act an unfair trade practice in defending its tech giants like Apple, Facebook, Google, and other American tech companies.[80] There also is growing digital taxation in Africa, where countries like Benin, Kenya, Tanzania, Uganda, and Zambia imposing taxes on the use of social media[81] with expected reforms to levy a tax on revenues of the multinational tech giants as well.[82] Digital taxation on users is claimed to reduce connectivity, especially in Africa.[83] A framework for international digital taxation can reduce the opportunities for a tax haven in the digital economy. The recent framework on the international agreement for a unified approach for digital taxation proposes new rules to tax multinational digital companies.[84] Here, tax differentiation across business lines, double taxation, enforcement, and difficulty of collection of taxes from digital multinationals and the absence of physical presence of some digital businesses are some of the challenges for digital taxation. On the other hand, the United States has become a watchdog for its tech giants as nations press onto the digital service tax.[85]

The other recent developments in the regulatory sphere of the digital economy are the General Data Protection Regulation (GDPR). The GDPR applies to the 28 European countries calling for a transparent and informed data access policy. Companies violating the GDPR are subject to a sanction of up to 4% of their global annual revenues or 20 million euros, whichever is greater. Until the end of 2019, a total of about $476,401,336 fines have been

---

[79]See the Digital Services Tax: response to the consultation, 2019, available at https://assets.publishing.service.gov.uk/government/uploads/system/uploads/attachment_data/file/816389/DST_response_document_web.pdf

[80]www.nytimes.com/2019/07/10/business/us-france-tariffs.html

[81]https://webfoundation.org/2018/11/how-some-african-governments-are-keeping-millions-of-citizens-offline/?mc_cid=8c91bc4943&mc_eid=875484373f

[82]"Uganda Plans Reforms to Tap Facebook, Google Advertising Revenue," Bloomberg Tax, October 24, 2019, available at https://news.bloombergtax.com/daily-tax-report-international/uganda-plans-reforms-to-tap-facebook-google-advertising-revenue

[83]See 2019 Affordability Report at the Alliance for Affordable Internet (A4AI), available at https://news.bloombergtax.com/daily-tax-report-international/uganda-plans-reforms-to-tap-facebook-google-advertising-revenue

[84]See the Public Consultation Document Secretariat Proposal for a "Unified Approach" under Pillar One, 2019, available at www.oecd.org/tax/beps/public-consultation-document-secretariat-proposal-unified-approach-pillar-one.pdf

[85]The New York Times, "As Nations Look to Tax Tech Firms, U.S. Scrambles to Broker a Deal," July 12, 2019, at www.nytimes.com/2019/07/12/business/economy/tech-company-taxes.html

charged on 134 violations across the member states (GDPR Enforcement Tracker[86]). The United Kingdom, France, Germany, Austria, and Bulgaria are the top five countries with the highest fines since the implementation of the GDPR, as of December 2019.

On the other hand, there are some disparities in the regulations of the US digital economy. Here, the digital economy rules and regulations for data privacy, taxation, and net neutrality are not uniform across states. For example, while 27 states in the United States levy a digital sales tax of 1% to 7%, 23 other states do not levy any.[87] The California Consumer Privacy Act (CCPA), effective January 1, 2020,[88] is the act for the protection of consumers based in California. The Act applies privacy and transparency requirements for consumer data. Unlike the GDPR, the CCPA is not applicable at the federal level.

Moreover, there is discriminatory taxation across digital goods and services. Accordingly, a framework for digital single market that fosters a non-discriminatory and uniform regulation of the digital economy across the states is crucial (McQuinn A. and Castro D., 2019). China follows a digital protectionism approach with data localization and blocking of foreign digital platforms (including Facebook, Google, and Dropbox). This has protected the Chinese tech giants from the potential competition of the global digital economy space (e.g., Baidu, Alibaba, and Tencent).

To survive the dynamic digital business environment, tech companies also need to apply various non-market strategies. One of these is lobbying. In this regard, lobbying expenses have dramatically increased over the past few years amid regulatory changes. In order to communicate strategic information to government officeholders, the tech giants spend billions of dollars in lobbying. In 2018, Google spent $21.7 million on lobbying.[89] According to the Center for Responsive Politics, in the second quarter of 2019, three of the biggest tech companies (Amazon.com, Facebook, and Alphabet Inc.) joined the top lobbying spenders, spending $4.15 million, $4.11 million, and $3.15 million in lobbying, respectively.[90] The lobbying cost has been dramatically increasing over the years as regulatory interventions in digital platforms increased.

---

[86]www.enforcementtracker.com/

[87]See a blog post by Victoria Venn, November 11, 2019, Sales Tax for Digital Goods in the U.S., available at https://quaderno.io/blog/sales-tax-digital-products-us/

[88]National Law Review, available at www.natlawreview.com/article/2019-year-ccpa-infographic

[89]CNBC, www.cnbc.com/2019/06/09/google-is-techs-top-spender-on-lobbying-but-facebook-amazon-also-up.html, accessed on May 22, 2020.

[90]See OpenSecrets.org at www.opensecrets.org/news/2019/07/facebook-google-amazon-up-lobbying-game/, accessed on May 22, 2020.

The four big techs (Amazon, Apple, Facebook, and Google) spent a total of $27.4 million on lobbying combined in 2016, and this spending doubled in 2018 to about $55 million.[91]

Summing up, a digital business model that operates over the Web and utilizes cloud infrastructures should consider and implement the rules to operate in the dynamic digital non-market environment. Moreover, such business models should consider data access and processing policies, privacy, and security by design. On the users' side, formation of user data unions could help protect the data rights of users in the digital economy space and compensate or reduce free riding over the monetized user data. The last note is on the choice of the location of cloud server hosts, which is highly dominated by the US-based web hosts, and the accompanying rules in the host and source countries.

Summary

This chapter took a deep look into the digital economy. The digital economy takes many varied forms, and information technology plays a pivotal role in enabling most of the sharing economy. Various online platforms enable connections between people, organizations, and ideas more efficiently than the traditional ways of communication. This results in new economic, social, and financial models that further enhance the sharing economy. Information technology and social media, population growth, growing income disparities, and the increasing global financial, environmental, and social crises are some of the driving forces behind this system. Hence, through the collaborative economic setting and mainly through the Internet, a means to share and utilize limited resources in a collaborative way is created.

In its raw sense, the digital economy system is governed by the following core principles: collaboration, empowerment, transparency, humanity, and altruistic sharing for the common well-being. This economic system is characterized by the underlying key economic features of sharing, leasing, swapping, selling and buying, lending, giving, and bartering. With these key transactional features, it unlocks the idle capacity in the utilization of the scarce economic resources mainly using, but not limited to, the Internet. Various online platforms enable connections between people, organizations, and ideas more efficiently than the traditional ways of communication. This results in new economic, social, and financial models that further enhance the sharing economy. Financial technologies, including the business lines of peer-to-peer (P2P) transactions, crowdfunding and crowdsourcing, innovation, and educational marketplaces, are some of the common structures of this economy. The collaborative

---

[91]See Center for Responsive Politics at OpenSecrets.org.

economy paradigm revolves around the core principles of *collaboration, empowerment, transparency, humanity*, and that of altruistic sharing for the common well-being, which results in efficiency with no hyper-consumption. The emergence of irreversible consumer behavior is one of the catalysts for a widespread replication of this system all across the globe. This implies a preference shift of the digital society to a new form of utilization of goods and services. Moreover, the significant insights underlying the digital economic system have facilitated (and benefit from) big data processing.

In addition, the Uberification of services across different sectors of the digital economy following Uber's business model of app-enabled mobile services has greatly facilitated instant access to economic resources. Equal to the collaborative system the digital economic system enabled, as discussed in this chapter, this economic system has also created fat tech companies which exploit the honeypot at a scale. Rifkin (2014), in his book *The Zero Marginal Cost Society*, presents the paradox in the capitalist system and that the invisible hand that has been responsible for capitalism's success has led to a new successor paradigm called the collaborative economy. He describes this collaborative system as a "zero marginal cost society." Nevertheless, some of the new business models we came across with this trend have elements of altruism and interest combined, which has diverted the core principle underlying the sharing economy with a seed of capitalism embodied in it. In line with this, some scholars argue that the collaborative economy, which has initially manifested itself in the form of sharing economy, has the tendency to be pure capitalism.

This economy is characterized by abundant liquidity. PricewaterhouseCoopers estimated that, by the year 2025, transactions under this economy are expected to generate about $335 billion at a global level. Despite its abundant liquidity, the collaborative economy has posed many challenges to the incumbent traditional players of the respective sectors. Some of these challenges include disrupting the incumbent customer base of traditional sectors and also making their business models and services obsolete. Furthermore, the service sector of this economy is booming with the catalyzing advancements in digital technology. In the e-education service provision, for example, video conferencing and streaming and online collaboration portals without a need for face-to-face contact have eased the access for global supplies and demand in the sector. Also, in the e-health sector, the traditional business is hard hit by this wave, in which remote diagnosis, advertising of drugs and other treatments, and the sharing of patient experience through electronic health records are made easy. The same trend is true in the broadcasting and media sector, where a vast amount of social media networks and user-generated content is flourishing. On the other way round, with the new business models, new risks to the collaborative economy itself arise. These new models are exposed to new challenges and uncertainties unique to their individual setup. This is mainly due to the dynamic and hasty evolution of the business models in order to cope with the new regulatory and legal codes and the latest technology-based competition from their fellow players. Furthermore, this economy, being in its infant stage of development, poses a challenge to the government, because it is difficult to enact new rules and regulations coping with the dynamics of the collaborative business models. This will disrupt the government's revenue also with a paramount transformation of the incumbent market players before new rules are enacted. Another critical thing to point out in this trend of the new economy is the problem of mistrust between the players within the system itself. This results from the uncertainties and asymmetric information that exist in most of the transactions of the digital economy models.

The topics covered under this chapter are far from addressing all the issues arising in the digital economy. The aim here, in general, is to foster the application of the digital economy and its core principles through a closer analysis of the underlying business models. Detailed analyses and presentations of the main business models and technologies for digital entrepreneurship are given in the subsequent chapters.

Crowd-Based Digital Business Models

Crowdfunding, Crowdsourcing, and P2P Online Lending

The chapter presents an in-depth discussion of the value creation in the platform-based businesses of the Web, including crowdfunding, crowdsourcing, and peer-to-peer (P2P) online lending market. Moreover, solution concepts that resolve potential issues of trust and fear, mainly in crowdfunding and P2P online lending, will be presented. Through intriguing facts, up-to-date data on the existing platforms, and illustrative examples, the chapter will help you understand the current state of the art. This is to equip the reader with the techniques on how to effectively participate in crowd-based businesses as a digital entrepreneur or investor. The chapter is organized as follows. The first section focuses on crowdfunding, examining the crowdfunding models, underlying problems, proposed solutions, and the implication for crowdfunding.

© Abeba N. Turi 2020
A. N. Turi, *Technologies for Modern Digital Entrepreneurship*,
https://doi.org/10.1007/978-1-4842-6005-0_2

The second section looks at the crowdsourcing market, highlighting the value creation process between the crowd community and requesters. The third section dives into the P2P online lending market with a detailed discussion on the value co-creation in P2P lending and the underlying problems and a distributed reputation mechanism for P2P online lending. We will discuss some of the business models at the core of the digital economic system, ranging from crowdfunding to P2P online lending markets.

Crowdfunding

A growing number of individuals motivated by profit, philanthropy, or any other reasons are engaged in the crowdfunding industry. This industry is experiencing fast growth as indicated in a recent report.[1] As of January 18, 2020, a total of $6 billion has been globally raised from about 62 million backers across different platforms.[2] By 2025, the global crowdfunding market is expected to generate up to $28.8 billion.[3] The largest crowdfunding regions are North America and Asia. A wide range of online third-party market platforms link entrepreneurs, investors, and philanthropists to facilitate investing in social enterprises. Currently, there are a number of diverse crowdfunding platforms with different application areas and methods of funding. These include Kickstarter, Sellaband, AngelList, Betterplace, JumpStart Africa, VereinRespekt.net, c-crowd, Seedups, Thundafund, Prosper, Funding Circle, LendingClub, and so on.

---

[1]http://research.crowdsourcing.org/2013cf-crowdfunding-industry-report
[2]www.thecrowdfundingcenter.com/data/
[3]www.statista.com/topics/1283/crowdfunding/

Histogram

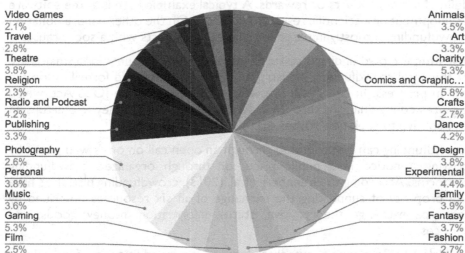

Video Games 2.1%	Animals 3.5%
Travel 2.8%	Art 3.3%
Theatre 3.8%	Charity 5.3%
Religion 2.3%	Comics and Graphic... 5.8%
Radio and Podcast 4.2%	Crafts 2.7%
Publishing 3.3%	Dance 4.2%
Photography 2.6%	Design 3.8%
Personal 3.8%	Experimental 4.4%
Music 3.6%	Family 3.9%
Gaming 5.3%	Fantasy 3.7%
Film 2.5%	Fashion 2.7%

Figure 2-1. Percentage of global successful projects by category (January 1, 2014–March 12, 2020)[4]

What Is Crowdfunding

Crowdfunding is shaping the collaborative economy by creating a financial market that operates as an accelerating catalyst for a wider range of investor-entrepreneur relations.

Crowdfunding can generally take the form of investment crowdfunding (which can follow debt-based, equity-based, profit-sharing, or hybrid models) or donation crowdfunding. In investment crowdfunding, project initiators and funders interact on the basis of expected returns. For example, in equity crowdfunding, several types of capital and creative projects are sold to a crowd of potential shareholders in the form of equity, while in debt crowdfunding, the crowd investors finance the debt and receive a debt instrument that pays interest return. Note that equity-based crowdfunding is one of the potentially co-utile markets in the crowdfunding industry, because it is a win-win game both for the entrepreneur who gets new financing sources and an investor backing this entrepreneur which gains by being a stakeholder of a potentially growing startup company. A special form of investment crowdfunding is reward-based crowdfunding in which the returns are non-financial. In reward-based crowdfunding, the crowd collaboratively donates,

---

[4]Source: Author's extraction based on data from The Crowdfunding Center at www.thecrowdfundingcenter.com/data/categories

pre-purchases products, or buys unique expertise experiences in return for a defined set of products or rewards. A typical example here is a free software development or a scientific research project.[5, 6] On the other hand, a donation crowdfunding is mostly initiated for charitable projects with a social cause.

Investment crowdfunding is still in its infancy: it only accounts for a small share of the total crowdfunding industry, and its legalization and formalization are still in progress. In late 2012, President Obama signed the JOBS Act, which legalizes equity financing through crowdfunding as seed money to startups, in an initiative to seek new routes that stimulate the economy.[7]

Crowdfunding can be promoted through an open call on one's web page,[8] by posting a notice in a public place, or through organized crowdfunding platforms. According to Greenberg et al. (2013), crowdfunding platforms have the property of supporting the exchange of all six resources described by resource exchange theory: love, status, information, money, goods, and services.

Mollick (2013) pointed out that, beyond or in addition to fund-raising, crowdfunding is used by entrepreneurs to demonstrate/estimate the demand for a proposed product (hence operating as a signal for the traditional form of funding), to pre-sell and introduce a new product (marketing purposes), to create interest in new projects in their early stages of development, to attract the attention of the media, and so on. According to Gerber et al. (2012), requesters/entrepreneurs take part in the crowdfunding market to raise funds, establish relationships, receive validation, replicate successful experiences of others, and/or expand awareness of their work through social media. On the other hand, these authors also identified the motives for funders to participate in this market as seeking rewards, supporting entrepreneurs, or engaging and contributing to a trusting and creative community; they concluded that the weight attached to each of these motives varies across different players. In this regard, Pazowski et al. (2014) also argue the same as the aforementioned scholars and further discuss the disincentives for both entrepreneurs and funders. Along the same line, Lehner (2013) stated that the crowd behaves in unpredictable, chaotic, and multifarious manners and reacts in a hyperbolic way to any actions by the funded project.

---

[5]See, for example, Experiment, a crowdfunding platform for scientific research at https://experiment.com/. The platform follows an all-or-nothing crowdfunding model, in which initiators collect the funds if the project meets its funding goal during the specified timeline of the campaign.

[6]www.weforum.org/agenda/2019/02/crowdfunding-money-for-research-levels-the-playing-field/

[7]www.masscatalyst.com/news/what-is-title-iii-equity-crowdfunding

[8]For example, the movie *Hotel Desire* raised €170,000 in 80 days at its own website www.german-films.de/filmarchive/browse-archive/view/detail/film/hotel-desire/index.html

Personal networks (involving public figures) and extensive social media networks (through Facebook, Twitter, etc.), as well as the quality of the underlying project, have most often been mentioned as key factors to success of crowdfunded projects.

Main Problems in Crowdfunding

There are a number of problems that are inherent to crowdfunding, including issues of coordination and asymmetric information resulting in mistrust and fear effects. Lack of coordination between funders is one of the key deterring factors in the crowdfunding effort. An experiment on a simulated donation-based crowdfunding platform by Solomon et al. (2015) indicates that a leadership approach is a better strategy to donate for a project of one's interest (i.e., to back a project on which you have confidence in order to signal for other potential donors) provided a time frame for a project to be funded. In contrast, the wait-and-see approach is a better strategy for funders with small payouts and relatively weak preferences (wait and make a small contribution at the end). In addition to this, both intentional and unintentional free riding may occur in the crowdfunding market.

Let's say you have a non-exclusive civic project and that you rely on crowdfunding to run the project. As it is common for public goods (a common word in economics for non-excludable and nonrivalrous goods), potential backers can free ride on other actual backers' contributions, in which case you cannot exclude the expected benefits. Another example is open source projects (e.g., codes and applications) like the ones through the community-raised funding on the Linux Foundation.

According to Wash and Solomon (2014), crowdfunding entails some element of public good. Clearly, if funds are raised for schooling, healthcare, and so on, this is public good in the obvious sense. Yet, a subtler form of public good occurs no matter the nature of the new product being funded, because the funding crowd makes that product available to the market for everyone to use *ex post*.

Being an interaction between anonymous players, the crowdfunding business model suffers from the information asymmetry problem. As Wash and Solomon (2014) stated, crowdfunding markets do not guarantee a stable match and there exists mistrust by the funders (is the entrepreneur trustworthy?), while on the side of the entrepreneur/requester, there is a fear of failure and a fear of public disclosure of the project idea and its details (with the subsequent loss of intellectual property). Belleflamme et al. (2014) also identified uncertainties and information asymmetries between the entrepreneur and funders in the pre-ordering and profit-sharing forms of crowdfunding. They recommended the formation of strategic ties between the entrepreneur and investors/consumers by creating a sense of belongingness, membership to the community, and the rights of control and vote. The latter rights can be realized in some cases by involving the crowd in some strategic decisions about the design and nature of the product. Mollick (2013) identifies delay in payment of pre-agreed rewards to the funders and failure as a result of a fraud or an overambitious project as some other challenging uncertainties in crowdfunding (see also Cumming and Johan, 2019).

Hildebrand et al. (2014) found that there exist perverse incentives for the group leaders in peer-to-peer lending systems. This implies incentive manipulation through a potential bribing attack in which group leaders get rewards for a signaling effect. As a result, they suggested that the leader take a significant share of the loan and defined the cutoff criterion in effect. According to them, this will lead to lower interest rates and lower rates of default.

Reputation and signaling mechanisms are proposed for most of the crowdfunding markets through centralized platforms. Another recent form of digital financing relies on a purely distributed network built on blockchain and distributed ledger technologies. Such crowdfunding models are under the tokenization business model, which includes the initial coin offering (ICO), initial token offering (OTP), secure token offering, and coinsale (we will discuss further about the blockchain-powered decentralized applications and funding models in Chapters 3 and 4 of this book). A typical example of the recent failures in the crowd-based digital business models of this form is the DAO attack (the attack on the decentralized form of crowdfunding based on the blockchain platform).

The decentralized autonomous organization (DAO) was a smart contract (a ruleset in blockchain tech language[9]) built for automating organizational decision-making and business rules through decentralized network on the Ethereum blockchain platform. It used crowdfunding (crowdsale, or an initial coin offering (ICO)) in tokenizing the service. Unlike marketplace crowdfunding, the DAO was not owned by any individual, but rather it belonged to the distributed network of people governed by a consensus mechanism. In May 2016, following its deployment, the DAO raised about $150 million through crowdfunding coinsale. This coinsale was one of the largest crowdfunding in the history of the digital crowd-based business models. However, the DAO crowdfunding was attacked by a malicious smart contract that withdrew

---

[9]Discussed in detail in Chapter 3 and 4 of this book.

about one third of the funds (12 million ETH) from the DAO. As Vitalik Buterin announced on June 17, 2016:

> An attack has been found and exploited in the DAO, and the attacker is currently in the process of draining the ether contained in the DAO into a child DAO. The attack is a recursive calling vulnerability, where an attacker called the "split" function, and then calls the split function recursively inside of the split, thereby collecting ether many times over in a single transaction.... The development community is proposing a soft fork, (with NO ROLLBACK; no transactions or blocks will be "reversed") which will make any transactions that make any calls/callcodes/delegatecalls that execute code with code hash 0x7278d050619a624f84f51987149ddb439cdaadfba5966f7cfaea7ad4 4340a4ba (ie. the DAO and children) lead to the transaction (not just the call, the transaction) being invalid, starting from block 1760000 (precise block number subject to change up until the point the code is released), preventing the ether from being withdrawn by the attacker past the 27-day window. This will later be followed up by a hard fork which will give token holders the ability to recover their ether.[10]

The funds were recovered through a soft fork[11] and hard fork[12] that drained the attacker.[13]

Crowdfunding Models

The fund-raising projects from the general public through the online platforms commonly rely on two basic models or a mixture of them. The two models are "all or nothing" or "keep it all."

The all-or-nothing (a.k.a. return rule method) model is when the fund-raising period is over, money is only collected from the contributors if a predetermined minimum amount of money has been pledged; if the target amount is not reached, no money is collected. This method is better for projects whose success critically depends on a certain minimum budget (Wash and Solomon, 2014).

---

[10]https://blog.ethereum.org/2016/06/17/critical-update-re-dao-vulnerability/
[11]A soft fork is a blockchain (a distributed digital ledger technology) term which refers to a fork to a blockchain that invalidates all prior transaction records/blocks, thus building over the same history of records under a given protocol.
[12]A hard fork is a blockchain term for a change in either the consensus rules or protocol and building of a different history of records.
[13]https://blog.ethereum.org/2016/07/20/hard-fork-completed/

The keep-it-all (a.k.a. direct method) model is where all the funds collected over that specified fund-raising period are handed over to the requester (entrepreneur), whether the target amount is reached or not. This model is convenient for continuous projects in which any amount of funds raised can still be used to keep the project in progress.

The bounty model, in which a reward is raised for the entrepreneur completing a certain task, can be viewed as having some elements of the previous two models. According to Wash and Solomon (2014), the all-or-nothing method in the donation-based crowdfunding increases the donors' willingness to donate; further, it leads them to donating according to their preferences rather than relying on the projects that signal high funding preference by other funders; however, it disincentivizes coordination. On the other hand, according to the same authors, the keep-it-all mechanism encourages coordination, with a less efficient outcome. See, for example, Figure 2-2 depicting the number of successful projects across selected crowdfunding sites by category. Note that each of the platforms has its own funding model.

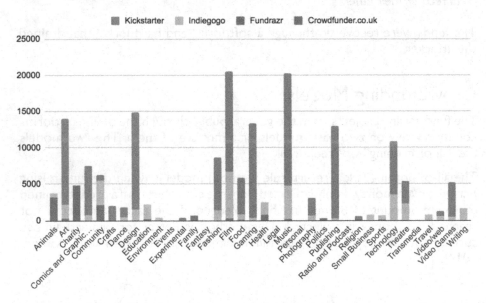

Figure 2-2. Fully funded projects across crowdfunding platforms by category (January 1, 2014–March 14, 2020)[14]

---

[14]Source: Author's extraction based on data from The Crowdfunding Center, available at www.thecrowdfundingcenter.com/data/categories

Investment Crowdfunding

In line with the theme of the text, I will narrow down the discussion in the remaining sections into investment crowdfunding that involves entrepreneurial and investment decision-making, unlike the donation crowdfunding. More specifically, by taking equity-based crowdfunding, I will present a detailed analysis of the underlying business model.

Investment crowdfunding can follow debt-based, equity-based, profit-sharing, or hybrid models. It is one of the examples of a potentially co-utile market, in which two or more agents with different motivations interact. The case we analyze here in detail is a specific type of investment crowdfunding, debt-based crowdfunding, which can be extended to equity crowdfunding through convertible notes. Like in crowdsourcing, anonymity in the crowd and asymmetric information between the crowd and the entrepreneur are key features in this industry. As stated by Romer (2011), such asymmetric information between the two dealers can distort investment choices more than would be the case for decisions based on only interest rates or profits. In this market, both agents (funder and entrepreneur) are rational and take part in the market to optimize their respective expected utility ("profit").

Investment crowdfunding is in its infancy, and it represents only a very small share of the total crowdfunding volume. In addition to the legal constraints imposed on the market, other factors (including mistrust and fear of disclosure, as described earlier) deter individual players from taking part in such forms of investment. These factors still keep drawing the market back, despite the approval and legislation enhancing such open funding. For this reason, a co-utile protocol whereby both agents mutually benefit and derive their optimal utility would be very useful. In this sense, we aim at neutralizing the potentially deterring factors through incentive mechanisms in order to ensure the co-utility of the protocol.

An efficient crowdfunding decision under financial market imperfection can be developed through a robust mechanism design, including reputation system and cryptographic solutions (Turi et al., 2017). Unlike the traditional form of investment, further consideration in crowdfunding is a case in which the crowd investor may end up with negative returns (loss of the principal invested plus verification costs). This is an extreme scenario in case the crowdfunded project fails or happens to be a fraud.

It is important to note the following key points about equity crowdfunding:

- Being the owner of the project, the entrepreneur has much more information about her investment project (return, actual output, risk, actions of the entrepreneur, etc.) than the potential crowd investors.

- The investor incurs a verification cost to gather enough information on the project details to make an investment decision; this verification cost is assumed to be compensated by the entrepreneur (see Romer, 2011).

- The project financing can wholly rely on crowdfunding (as a special case of Romer's financial markets' imperfection analysis, the entrepreneur's wealth invested in such a project is zero) and has an expected output which might be different from the actual output.

- There are a large number of crowd investors, and there exists competition among them.

- The investors are risk-averse in their investment decisions of projects listed on crowdfunding platforms. That creative idea you seek for funding should prove confidence in the eyes of your potential backers. Here, the campaign strategy you use and the project display to pitch your idea have to be robust.[15] Entrepreneurs in online platforms also are risk-averse toward publicizing creative project ideas/products to the anonymous crowd for fear of being copied. Equally important with efficient impeachment is to avoid claiming fictitious (unattainable) products in an effort to win the crowd.

- In equity crowdfunding, the entrepreneur becomes indebted to reward the expected return to the investors. Hence, the entrepreneur's optimal strategy is the one that minimizes the verification cost, given their respective basic returns, at some critical level of debt to the entrepreneur. Note again that, unlike the traditional form of investment, this form of investment may end up with zero return and hence loss to investors even if they pay the verification cost.

Investor's Funding Decision

A potential investor in crowdfunding, or backer, considers a number of things before committing to fund a project. The expected net return to the investor (backer) under a debt contract with the competition and risk of project failure assumptions depends on the level of investment, rate of return, the probability

---

[15]See, for example, a sample most backed successful project, Fidget Cube: A Vinyl Desk Toy, project which raised a total of $6,465,690 from 154,926 backers on Kickstarter. Listing and campaign available at www.kickstarter.com/projects/antsylabs/fidget-cube-a-vinyl-desk-toy?ref=discovery_most_backed

of success for the project, and the proportion of backer's investment to the total debt of the entrepreneur. By implication, the investment decision of the backer depends on the expected net return of the project. Therefore, an investor takes part in the crowdfunding of the project if and only if the required net return is not more than the optimal expected net return. This implies that, in order for her to invest in the project, her return for investing in that project should, at least, match the return of investing in a safe asset. Otherwise, if the latter return is greater than optimal return from crowdfunding investment, she does not take part in the project at any interest rate. Note that this also implies that the risk premium offered by the projects should be substantial enough, depending on the market, to surpass the minimum required level of return which could be attained by investing in a safer asset. Furthermore, it is limited to the extent to which it can offer optimal return to the individual investors. Also, the unobserved risk premium induced in the random interest rate offered by varied projects to be crowd financed should minimally be bound to the market optimal level of return.

Given a crowdfunding debt contract and the proportion of backers' investment, if the project surely rewards the backers and the expected return is guaranteed, then the underlying investment decision depends on the utility a potential investor might derive from this level of return, given the required rate of return. As stated previously, investors in crowdfunding platforms are risk-averse of various degrees based on their level of information, experience with such investment, invested amount, income, and so on. The analysis of this market further considers constant absolute risk aversion and invariant risk in absolute money terms (see Cvitanic and Zapatero, 2004, and Turi et al., 2017). An investor, who is maximizing her expected utility of return, invests in the project if she derives positive utility from the funding, provided that the utility is strictly higher than the utility of the next best alternative safer investment. That is, if the utility she derives by investing in that project is at least as high as the utility she would obtain with a safe asset (local nonsatiation). Therefore, keeping all other factors aside, a risk-averse investor takes part in the crowd investment at the optimal debt contract when deriving higher utility as compared to a safe asset. Another interesting scenario is the case in which the investor might end up with negative returns, in case of fraud or failure of the project. A risk-averse investor also tries to avoid this scenario in her investment decision, reflected in the mistrust effect which we will discuss later in this chapter.

Entrepreneur's Investment Decision

In many cases, entrepreneurs choose crowdfunding over alternative funding options for many reasons, for example, to access a large number of investors or for any other reason like demonstrating the demand for a proposed product, creating interest in new projects in the early stages of development, attracting the attention of the media, marketing, establishing relationships, receiving validation, replicating successful experiences of others through feedback, expanding awareness of work through social media, and so on (see Mollick, 2013, and Gerber et al., 2012). Entrepreneurs broadcast their project for public funding through crowdfunding platforms, if the net return is greater than the market value of the project idea if transferred to a second party (e.g., white labeling or acquisition of fintech startups by established financial institutions). As mentioned previously and will soon discuss in detail, due to the *disclosure fear effect*, the entrepreneur also is risk-averse toward her project being funded through the anonymous crowd. Provided these, a digital entrepreneur goes for crowdfunding if the utility she derives by running the project through seed money financing from an anonymous crowd is at least as high as the market value of her project idea when sold to some buyer and, more generally, if the expected return paid to the outside investors does not result in credit rationing and if the expected net returns to her are higher than what she can earn by refraining from running the project (opportunity cost of investment).

The Effects of Fear and Mistrust in Crowdfunding

From the earlier discussion, we see that to make crowdfunding co-utile, we must deal with negative utilities that deter an individual investor or entrepreneur from taking part in this market. Apart from the net return-based investment decisions highlighted in the previous section, some other factors might discourage the participation of an agent.

One of the main deterring factors is *mistrust by funders* regarding possible frauds (Cumming and Johan, 2019). A study conducted on projects listed on Kickstarter and Indiegogo shows that fraudulent listings are characterized by less crowdfunding engagement history and poor social media presence and provide poorly worded, deceptive, and confusing crowdfunding campaigns (Cumming et al., 2016). For example, in May 2013, a crowdfunding scam claiming to improve traditional beef jerky attracted about $120,000 pledges and got suspended before within minutes of completion on Kickstarter.[16,17] The project was characterized by some negative crowd feedback, no picture or video of founders in the content display, a campaign page from backers with new accounts, and a poor backing records of unsuccessful campaigns and predatory pricing of rewards with significantly small amount of pledge requests as compared to expected rewards (Cumming and Johan, 2019).

---

[16]See the fraudulent crowdfunding campaign "KOBE RED - 100% JAPANESE BEER FED KOBE BEEF JERKY" at www.kickstarter.com/projects/kobered/kobe-red-100-japanese-beer-fed-kobe-beef-jerky
[17]https://money.cnn.com/2013/06/17/technology/kickstarter-scam-kobe-jerky/

Another example, Theranos, a health tech startup, has been charged with wire fraud in its crowdfunding attempt using fictitious blood testing technology claims.[18] The tech startup is one of the top Silicon Valley fraudulent startups of the digital era. Journalist John Carreyrou has explored the multibillion-dollar startup, Theranos, fraud scandal in his book *Bad Blood: Secrets and Lies in a Silicon Valley Startup* (Carreyrou, 2018).

Funders want to be sure that their investment goes to the right project and they want to be guaranteed the promised return. As Lehner (2013) pointed out, the utility functions of equity investors in crowdfunded ventures may differ from those of traditional for-profit investors.

From the entrepreneur's point of view, *fear of failure and imitation or plagiarism with full content disclosure* (loss of intellectual property) are deterring factors for crowdfunded ventures. This element of fear on the side of the entrepreneurs affects the extent they could freely signal quality and preparedness of their project idea to the general public. As a result, the entrepreneur faces a trade-off between a need of raising capital and the threat of their idea being copied by other market participants (Pazowski et al., 2014).

With a larger level of crowdfunding project output and a higher credibility of the project, an individual crowdfunding investor's utility increases, while this is not true if the project has larger output and low credibility. Hence, above the minimum required return with trust, the utility of an individual investor will be the highest possible one under this condition, and collaboration in the crowdfunding takes place with full credibility. On the other hand, with low trust, the credibility of the project fails, and even above the threshold expected return, no collaboration in crowdfunding takes place.

As much as the crowdfunding markets' significance to the digital entrepreneur and investor community, there are various scams and frauds across different platforms. See, for example, The Doom That Came To Atlantic City![19] A board game project on Kickstarter was charged for a deceptive crowdfunding campaign. In 2012, the crowdfunding campaign targeted $35,000 and actually raised $122,000 failing to reward or return the funds to its backers.[20] A similar example on another crowdfunding platform, Indiegogo, is the iBackPack crowdfunding campaign.[21] The crowdfunding campaign was charged by the FTC for failing to use consumer funds to produce high-tech backpacks.[22]

---

[18]The US SEC https://www.sec.gov/news/press-release/2018-41
[19]www.kickstarter.com/projects/forkingpath/the-doom-that-came-to-atlantic-city/comments
[20]The Federal Trade Commission at www.ftc.gov/news-events/press-releases/2015/06/crowdfunding-project-creator-settles-ftc-charges-deception
[21]www.indiegogo.com/projects/ibackpack-wifi-ultra-thin-powerful-batteries#/
[22]The Federal Trade Commission at www.ftc.gov/news-events/press-releases/2019/05/ftc-charges-operator-crowdfunding-scheme

Proposed Solutions

Lack of trust in crowdfunding leads a potentially co-utile market to a non-co-utile outcome. To have a market that works optimally, we must keep the investment crowdfunding strictly co-utile. The following are some possible solutions to the problems of mistrust by investors and fear of intellectual property loss or other project-related fear by the entrepreneur.

Encrypt and Secure Your Ideas to Protect Your Intellectual Property

Entrepreneur should be guaranteed protection for her intellectual property that does not depend on any legal common framework accepted by all investors (protection should be self-enforcing if we want to achieve co-utility). To do so, any individual entrepreneur, before publicly broadcasting her idea, should encrypt it and secure the private key with a decentralized timestamp,[23] where an individual hash tag is generated for each project description in a common basket for all the projects running on a specific platform. Hence, in case of any claim, she can decrypt the document and claim ownership.

Contribute to Projects That Are Promising

A robust reputation system built in a crowdfunding platform can help in filtering credible projects.

Individuals taking part in this market are rational, and investors can diversify the risk by investing in more than one project. Mollick (2013), in his analysis of the crowdfunding industry, has found evidence that funders respond to signals about the quality and creditworthiness of the project, regardless of their expectations for financial return. Signaling can be through peer ratings, where the probability of failure from the past record and poor quality or an infeasible project can be revealed and publicly displayed based on these general public ratings. Such a public rating also allows for experts within the crowd to evaluate the project idea.

Moreover, as Wash and Solomon (2014) stated, individual project funders complement each other because no individual funder can finance the project alone. Thus, each funder prefers to contribute to projects that are promisingly financed by others, so that the project receives enough funds to succeed. Likewise, investments in crowdfunded startups do not rely wholly on one individual investor's contribution, but on an aggregate contribution by the entire crowd. Therefore, equity investments by the crowd complement each

---

[23]Refer to the decentralized timestamp mechanisms in crypto currencies like Bitcoin.

other. This implies that there is a need for collaboration between the agents (either between the investors themselves, or between entrepreneurs, or between investors and entrepreneurs).

Diversify Your Investments

In order to minimize crowdfunding risk, potential investors in equity crowdfunding can invest in more than one unrelated project. This will enable you to minimize risk by replacing a single risk with a large number of smaller, unrelated risks across a number of diverse projects. As is common in financial markets, remember that this technique can help you in minimizing project-specific risk, not market risk.

Proposed Crowdfunding Mechanism

Crowdfunding projects listed on most platforms only pass a basic screening process on whether they meet the platform requirements. Hence, it is up to the potential backers to filter the worthiness of projects to invest.[24] In some of the platforms like Kickstarter, the all-or-nothing funding model helps filter out unattainable projects. Here, a community-based reputation mechanism to rate entrepreneurs and mitigate mistrust by investors will be presented. The following solution concept with a head of special interest (a team lead) and a signaling effect has been proposed in our prior study of the crowdfunding market (Turi et al., 2017).

In our setting, we consider the interdependent utility of the community by maintaining the resource flow within the community with the reputation mechanism. Furthermore, we assume that an individual can form a team and become what we will call the "head" of her team. Hence, in this setting we introduce a team player, where there will be varied teams of different nature and interests within the market. An entrepreneur can broadcast her project idea individually or join a team for a signaling effect. Any individual investor who is interested in any of the teams will join the team to avoid the risk of failure with a membership fee that is proportional to her individual investment capacity. An entrepreneur who wants a signaling effect from such team leaders pays a stimulation fee for the signaling effect of the head and the fee is paid in two rounds: first, before the signal and, second, after a successful campaign with the signaling effect. This will allow for a detailed and closer look at the feasibility of the project by a second party who plays a signaling role.

The key role of the head in this transaction is to bear the risk of failure, with an insider's view assumption, through signaling for a potentially promising project. The head issues protection notes to the members in that it guarantees

---

[24]www.kickstarter.com/blog/accountability-on-kickstarter

potential investors (team members who are supposed to pay continual membership fee) to be paid some percentage of their invested amount as compensation in case of failure of a wrongly signaled project. Furthermore, the signaling also has a spillover effect for other potential investors who are not members of the team.

In the deal between the entrepreneur and the head, the entrepreneur provides the head with additional convincing information on her project far more detailed than the information disseminated to the general public. In order to avoid the project idea being leaked or overtaken by the head, the entrepreneur provides a redacted document, with key content being reasonably suppressed.

We further assume that there will be a defined time frame within the platform in which it is expected to raise the funds for the project. Hence, assuming the debt contract as discussed earlier, when the project is broadcast for crowdfunding, the head pledges some amount of money which will be issued in the form of convertible notes as early as possible to signal the trustworthiness and value of the project. In doing so, she takes into account the net gain she draws from the investment. Her return from the signaling investment depends on the level of risk she takes, which in turn depends on the level of creditworthiness of the project provided the level of generalized information in the redacted document and other detailed information, including the personnel qualifications and general public rating.

Note that the head derives an informational advantage over the general public from directly observing the redacted project idea and other more detailed information. A rational head aims at maximizing her gain by minimizing the possible risk due to the failure of the project. The protection note issued is some percentage of the purchased share. Hence, the possible loss by the investor who is a member of the team in case of failure of the project will be reduced to the interest, the unrecovered proportion of the loan, and the time value of money. Therefore, when responding to the signaling effect of the head, investors should take into account the possible scenarios in which the entrepreneur really signals a potentially promising project.

If a potential investor would like to convert her invested amount C into a share, the outstanding balance of the loan is automatically converted to equity at a discount rate d. In this case, in addition to the expected return on equity, the investor will have a greater share amount over a new individual investing the same amount of money at a given price, p, at the valuation of a later funding round. This difference in return is equal to $\dfrac{dC}{p - dp}$.

For example, suppose an investor invested \$21,000 in a project startup using a convertible note with a discount rate $d=15\%$. Let the stock price, p, at the valuation of the later funding round be \$7 per share. Then, at the valuation of a later funding period, she will have a total of 3529.4 shares weighing to unrealized return amount, $\left(\dfrac{C}{p-dp}\right)p$, of \$24705.8 at \$7 per share. However, a new investor of the same amount of investment will have a total of 3000 shares at the valuation of the later funding round.

The expected total return to the head will be the principal (the invested amount by the head), the interest on the invested amount, the service charge for membership to the group, the stimulation fee for the signaling effect, and the risk taken by the head (in two forms, fixed rate of prepayment, followed by up on fulfillment fee, which is some percentage of the pledged amount by the head and total money for the protection note).

As long as the project to invest in is successful through the signaling effect, all the parties (investor, head, and entrepreneur) benefit. Furthermore, in order to avoid false signals from their investment decisions, there should be a clear-cut criterion which filters reasonable signaling with a sufficiently large share of investment by the head (commonly referred to as *sufficient skin in the game*).

In case of systemic signaling to a potentially failing project, a total sum of membership fees and equivalent compensation for upon-success return, over her initial signaling investment to the head, should outweigh the potential loss, provided some percentage of the total pledged loan by the head. Here, the likelihood of failure of the project is assumed known by the head with an insider's view assumption, while it is unrevealed to the other investors. A potential investor incurs loss by investing in an unsuccessful project with probability of failure if the net return in a simplified form is negative. This is a sufficient condition for a project that fails to reward the investors for sure. In other words, for any project with negative return, the head systematically signals only if the potential gain upon her initial investment level and signaling service fees is greater than the loss incurred.

That is, a rational head maximizing her net gain takes the risk and signals to the project if the potential net gain from signaling is greater than the net loss she might incur by signaling this project. Given the probability of failure for the project, a profit-maximizing head signals to the project if and only if the required signaling amount she is supposed to lend is less than her upper optimal boundary of share.

For example, when the head knows that the project is not promising, heads signaling investment should at least help issue the protection note. The head should also gain from the service charge for both the stimulation and service charge to the mass investor in her team. Suppose the membership fee is 1% (i.e., a proportion of the potential investment capacity of the individual, allowing for proportional contribution by each member). In addition to the membership fee, the entrepreneur rewards the head with a stimulation fee of 2% of the expected amount of total crowdfunds for the project. Suppose the protection note issued to this specific project costs the head 0.5% of the total protection note issued in the group. The entrepreneur offers interest rate of 12%, including the risk premium. Consider a project with a probability of failure 0.5 upon the public rating and let the head's overall expected gain on her loan (including the interest and ex post stimulation fee) be 10% of her total transaction during the process. Then, given this set of information, funding by the head will be less than 0.1875. That is, the upper bound to her possible signaling investment of this project should be less than 18.75% of the total funds requested by the entrepreneur for the project in which an ordinary investor would incur loss with the stated probability of failure and an insider's view.

Hence, given the provided rate of return by the entrepreneur and a conversion discount of the convertible note into a shared stock relative to the next fixed priced round, there will be a higher probability of loss to a regular investor. This is with the signaling effect of the head with less than 18.75% of investment participation out of the total amount requested for the startup financing. Therefore, based on this criterion, potential investors can filter reasonable signals on investment projects they are interested to invest in. Hence, the filtering is applicable regardless of the unrevealed type of the other parties involved.

This solution concept is ideal for most crowdfunding projects where self-financing capacity is rare and thus proposing a second-party (head of team) signaling.

Implications for Crowdfunding Practices

As discussed previously, the applicability of crowd-based financing is limited by the market inefficiency arising from the effects of fear and mistrust, as well as the access to asymmetric information. The model presented for crowdfunding implies that, under the return-based investment decision, collaboration in the market takes place as long as the optimal net return$_i^*$ is not less than the required net return. However, with the mistrust and fear effects in the market, co-utile collaboration takes place at the Pareto-optimal point at which the optimal level of no fear and trust is attained, and this point lies above the threshold level at which the return-based investment decision takes place. Hence, such market inefficiencies do also reduce investment at a given interest rate, and they are among the most important factors affecting the broader applicability of this business model. Studies show that there exists a significant variation in the success rate of projects being financed across different crowdfunding platforms (Jeffries, 2013, and Lau, 2013). These success rate variations across project types and platforms are also related to the *fear* and *mistrust effect* issues raised earlier in this chapter.

Along the variation within and across the platforms, we can draw repercussions for the behaviors of investors and entrepreneurs in the crowdfunding ecosystem. For instance, a significantly visible difference between Kickstarter and Indiegogo is that the former is focused on specific project categories and geographical settings and has more restrictions on the types of projects and incentive schemes offered by individual projects. As of January 2016, Kickstarter is open for worldwide backers, while it is limited to the projects from the United States, the United Kingdom, Canada, Australia, New Zealand, the Netherlands, Denmark, Ireland, Norway, Sweden, Spain, France, Germany, Austria, Italy, Belgium, Luxembourg, and Switzerland (see Table 2-1 for a sample of successful projects listed on Kickstarter). Moreover, the funding model that it follows is the "all-or-nothing" method, which has the effect of increasing the donors' willingness to donate and leads them to donating according to their preferences (*self-capacity signaling of projects*) and hence builds trust. However, this method disincentivizes coordination (Wash and Solomon, 2014); the community-based reputation mechanism under the proposed crowdfunding mechanism section of this chapter can be used to handle such a coordination problem. Hence, in addition to the project qualities and other platform-related marketing packages, the relative credibility (the higher trust to the entrepreneurs on this platform coming from the platform's setup itself) and the focus group targeting of the platform have contributed for a relatively higher success rate of projects' running campaigns through this platform. This credibility also has something to do with the reduction in the fear of failure effect; hence, more projects come upfront for soliciting finance from the crowd.

Table 2-1. Most successfully fully funded Kickstarter projects as of January 2019[25]

Crowdfunding Project	Total Funds Raised (in Million USD)	Year of Campaign
Pebble Time	20.34	2015
Coolest Cooler	13.29	2014
Pebble 2, Time 2 + All-New Pebble Core	12.78	2016
Kingdom Death: Monster 1.5	12.39	2017
Travel Tripod by Peak Design	12.14	2019
Critical Role: The Legend of Vox Machina Animated Special	11.39	2019
Pebble: E-Paper Watch for iPhone and Android	10.27	2012

(continued)

[25] Based on the data from the Kickstarter; available at www.statista.com/statistics/222489/ most-successful-completed-kickstarter-projects-by-total-funds-raised/

Table 2-1. (continued)

Crowdfunding Project	Total Funds Raised (in Million USD)	Year of Campaign
The World's Best Travel Jacket	9.19	2015
Exploding Kittens	8.78	2015
OUYA: A New Kind of Video Game Console	8.6	2012
Snapmaker 2.0: Modular 3-in-1 3D Printers	7.85	2019
THE 7th CONTINENT – What Goes Up, Must Come Down	7.07	2017
The Everyday Backpack, Tote, and Sling	6.57	2016
Fidget Cube: A Vinyl Desk Toy	6.47	2016
Shenmue 3	6.33	2015

On the other hand, Indiegogo encompasses more types of projects and a relatively wider geographical coverage.[26] Furthermore, the funding model it follows is more flexible and also encompasses the "keep-it-all" method (in addition to the "all-or-nothing" method), which encourages coordination with a less efficient outcome than the "all-or-nothing" method (Wash and Solomon, 2014). A study conducted by Cumming et al. (2014) on the mixed funding model used by Indiegogo since 2011 provides sample evidence that projects using the "all-or-nothing" method have more average completion rate and more attraction to investors than projects using the "keep-it-all" method. Here again, this has implications for the *mistrust effect* underlying the "keep-it-all" mechanism.

Despite the traditional investment (see Romer, 2011) for analysis of the imperfections of financial markets), crowd-based project financing most commonly does not rely on the entrepreneur's wealth, in which we have also assumed that the entrepreneur's wealth invested in a project is zero. Hence, whether a project on a crowdfunding platform is funded depends only on the potential output, but not on the financial base of the entrepreneur. Additional catalysts could be the product type and novelty, the ability to run a successful campaign, incentive schemes including the risk premium and product offer, and the like. This implies that the effect of shocks that may occur outside the financial system is low: any outside shock affecting the entrepreneur's wealth will not have any implied effect on the project's output. Crowdfunding also

---

[26]See sample popular Indiegogo crowdfunding projects including Ethan Van Sciver's CYBERFROG 2: REKT PLANET (the biggest crowdfunded comic), Sculptor (Auto-Rotating 4K Touchscreen Monitor), Pollution & Viral Filtration Mask With Botanicals, and so on at www.indiegogo.com/

allows for any individual entrepreneur to get financing from the crowd regardless of the individuals' wealth. In this regard, even though the efficiency of this business model has not been tested over the long run, its potential survival rate in any business cycle will be relatively high, unlike the traditional funding model.

Besides, the funding success rate of new projects owned by previously successful entrepreneurs is high, which implies a *reputation effect*. For example, this rate is reported to nearly double that of the overall site average in Kickstarter[27] (Table 2-2). Based on the analysis offered in this chapter, if the reputation of the entrepreneur is high (e.g., because he has a long record of successful projects), then even low returns can be co-utile for the investors. An additional factor here can also be the experience acquired in the previously run campaigns (this builds the trust on the side of investors and somehow tackles the fear effect on the side of entrepreneur).

Table 2-2. Success rate of entrepreneurs' first projects compared to that of subsequent ones by category in Kickstarter, March 24, 2015[28]

Category	First Projects	Second or Later Projects	Increase in Success Rate
Games	26%	56%	116%
Technology	21%	36%	75%
Crafts	23%	40%	73%
Design	31%	50%	60%
Publishing	29%	41%	41%
Comics	45%	62%	39%
Fashion	24%	33%	35%
Food	28%	35%	26%
Photography	30%	36%	21%
Journalism	25%	30%	20%
Art	42%	50%	18%
Dance	64%	75%	16%
Theater	61%	67%	9%
Music	53%	57%	9%
Film and video	39%	41%	6%

---

[27]See　www.kickstarter.com/blog/by-the-numbers-when-creators-return-to-kick-starter website, accessed on May 22, 2020.
[28]www.kickstarter.com/help/stats

Further, we can specify an intermediate playing field of cases in which some types of projects guarantee a safer transaction either to the entrepreneur or the investor or both. Concretely, if the type of the entrepreneur involves fear of disclosure, there is co-utility for the entrepreneur only if the investment by the investor is higher than a threshold representing the expected loss when the investor leaks the idea. This means that receiving small contributions can be co-utile only if the fear of disclosure is very low, say, if the entrepreneur feels no one other than himself can successfully carry out the project. For example, projects that are more artistic/skill-oriented suffer less from fear of disclosure than projects consisting of developing a mass produced/digital item (that can be copied). Likewise, projects with better potential expertise suffer less from fear of failure and therefore are more trusted by potential investors (especially if the entrepreneur offers defined reward guarantees, like perceptible prototypes presented during campaigns). In addition, those projects with a focus group targeting (i.e., where the investor targets and defines interest groups like the ones we see in Kickstarter) tend to have a better success rate. Moreover, projects owned by previously successful entrepreneurs will have a higher success rate, which implies a *reputation effect*: if the entrepreneur's reputation is high (see the discussion about Kickstarter earlier), even low returns can be co-utile. Projects with timely issues and special orientation to a focus group also tend to enjoy higher trust, attracting sympathetic investors; in this category, we can mention green startups, medical solutions or projects with a social dimension (say, assistive technologies for the elderly), and so on.

Crowdsourcing

Crowdsourcing means outsourcing a task to a group of self-interested individuals by means of an open call to expertise or individuals with a given skill set offering rewards (financial or non-financial) for work. It is one of the outcomes of the collaborative economy made possible by the catalyst role of information technology. The crowdsourced tasks can be as diverse as image annotation, data labeling for machine learning systems, English proofreading, language translation, consumer surveys, rating search engine results, spam detection, product reviews, article review, and so on. Typical examples of crowdsourcing are the Wikipedia (which is open source by nature),[29] proof-read on Project Gutenberg (open source),[30] or Amazon Mechanical Turk listings like business process outsourcing or machine learning development and more![31] The millennial generation is

---

[29]www.wikipedia.org/
[30]www.gutenberg.org/
[31]www.mturk.com/

crowdsourcing itself in many of such digital micro jobs listed across major crowdsourcing platforms and companies' social media pages.[32]

Like in crowdfunding, players in crowdsourcing also have heterogeneous motives for participation. Note that some authors consider crowdfunding as a special case of the "parent notion" crowdsourcing (e.g., Schwienbacher and Larralde, 2012). However, there is a clear-cut distinction between the two business models, even though they have general public sourcing in common. According to Brabham (2013), "crowdfunding describes a *funding model* for financing projects and ideas through general public participation in soliciting funds, while crowdsourcing is a distributed *problem-solving and production model* to leverage the collective intelligence of online communities to serve specific organizational goals."

Slivkins and Vaughan (2014) identified heterogeneity underlying the crowdsourcing market as individual task performance levels, relative difficulty in the task, attitude of workers, and satisfaction. Consequently, incentive schemes in such markets have a significant effect on the functioning of the peer-to-peer interactions, especially with an anonymous large crowd. Huang et al. (2012) found an adverse effect of increasing rewards on the quality of the solutions produced by the crowd: higher rewards do not guarantee higher quality, because participants may exert more effort in the competition itself than in cooperating to achieve quality. The authors proposed a policy that can induce more participation and higher effort with higher expected payoff.

Earlier work by Terwiesch and Xu (2008) presented an analysis of the type of innovative tasks that can be executed through crowdsourcing contests and the associated optimal reward structure. A larger crowd size encompasses diversity and in effect benefits the requester, whereas performance-contingent reward in the market induces more effort. A related work by Anari et al. (2014) states that the requester derives some utility by hiring the crowd and there is a minimum level of wage each worker wants to get paid for getting hired. Yet, there is information asymmetry between the requester and the worker, because the information on the minimum wage the worker wants to get paid is private to the workers. With this underlying asymmetric information and the budget constraint of the requester, they designed a budget-feasible mechanism with a given effort level in order to choose the right set of workers that maximize the requester's utility.

According to Ghosh and McAfee (2012), quality and participation (with an associated cost of effort) are the key issues that arise in crowdsourcing analysis. They argue that the level of effort an agent chooses to exert depends on the underlying incentives offered. In this regard, they analyzed mechanisms

---

[32]Are Millennials Crowdsourcing Themselves Out of Jobs? Forbes, October 22, 2012, available at www.forbes.com/sites/larissafaw/2012/10/22/are-millennials-crowdsourcing-themselves-out-of-jobs/#721d0b2c2813

that can incentivize high effort in case entry (i.e., joining the effort) is an endogenous strategic choice by the participating crowd. Their analysis for crowdsourcing based on attention rewards shows that when the cost of producing the lowest possible quality content is low, the optimal mechanism displays all but the poorest contribution. And in the cases where there is a fixed total reward randomly distributed to the participating crowd, subsidizing entry may improve the expected quality of the average contribution, but not the expected quality of the best contribution.

The crowdsourcing activity may be launched through an offline campaign with self-interested part-time workers or most commonly through online platforms. The accompanying rewards for the participant may take the form of monetary rewards by the task generator (pay-on-task or contest/prize) or in the form of attention rewards for the so-called user-generated content (UGC)-based sites. Here, we should take into account that in this model, the transaction takes place directly between the two market players (the crowd and requester/task assigner) on a two-sided marketplace platform. CrowdFlower, Mechanical Turk, InnoCentive (open innovation problem-solving), Presans (connect and solve R&D problems), Ideake (collaborative crowdsourcing), Innovation-community.de (community of innovators, creators, designers, and thinkers), and Challenge.gov (crowdsourcing for government problems) are some examples of crowdsourcing platforms.

Zhang et al. (2012) argued that there are intrinsic incentive problems underlying the crowdsourcing market, where all the players (the crowd and requester) are selfish, that is, they strategically optimize their selfish interest. They propose incentive mechanisms based on social norms by integrating reputation mechanisms that can induce high effort.

On the other hand, according to Slivkins and Vaughan (2014), there exists information asymmetry in the crowdsourcing market and workers and requesters can behave strategically. Accordingly, persistent reputation scores for both workers and requesters will limit spam and induce worker effort while encouraging requesters to be more considerate. They further argue that the basic models for reputation systems have limitations when applied to crowdsourcing markets (e.g., limitations in the domain-specific design goals, reputation designed separately from task assignments, limited information about the players, etc.), and they pointed out that there is a need for defining an optimal reputation mechanism specifically designed for the crowdsourcing market.

Here, it is worth noting that in this market there is usually a platform/two-sided marketplace that acts as a catalyst third party in return for reasonable service fees (see Figure 2-3). Therefore, the basic transaction takes place directly between the two players as in a peer-to-peer system, though strictly speaking, it is not a peer-to-peer system.

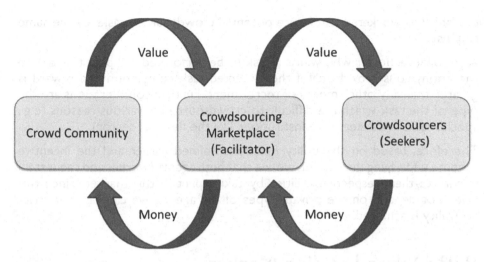

Figure 2-3. The crowdsourcing value chain

Given a crowdsourcing platform and agent's utility functions, there exists a co-utile protocol which is mutually beneficial for workers and requesters irrespective of their individual interest. Co-utility in this market is viable provided that the goals of the requester and worker are complementary and the qualification type of the worker matches the task.

Given the level of effort to perform the task, expected reward, and the task-specific cost of effort to worker (it can take the form of time devoted to reading, understanding, and performing the task, expenses incurred to perform the task, etc.), worker will not exert effort to perform a task, a given type task, however he values the reward associated with the task. Yet, in the case of a work type match, the working decision depends on the accompanying reward and time. The participation decision of an individual entails a trade-off between labor-leisure choices (neoclassical model of labor supply). Hence, there should be a reasonable incentive scheme influencing the worker's participation.

On the other hand, consider the monetary reward-based crowdsourcing. The goal of the requester is to maximize her expected utility from crowdsourcing a task. That is, she wants to maximize the value she receives from the completed work minus the payments made. Usually, the cost and amount of effort exerted by the crowd workers are unknown to the requester. A requester who wants a task to be performed faces the choice between sending an online request to the anonymous crowd and relying on an offline traditional employee. Note that when a worker who exerts low effort (shirks) is hired, the requester considers the cost to be both wage and disutility from hiring a shirking individual. Yet posteriorly disclosed behavior of the individual (reflected by the quality or quantity of the output produced) can help filter out shirking workers from future potential crowdsourced tasks by the same requester.

A rational requester who wants a task to be performed will post the task to the anonymous crowd only if the expected task completion and reward is greater than any other means of recruitment. Further considerations are the type of the task which are difficult to crowdsource for various reasons (e.g., special tasks in conservative institutions like the financial sector).

Therefore, based on the utility functions defined earlier and the incentive scheme underlying the market, we see that both agents (worker and requester) maximize their respective utilities by taking part in this market. Since this does not depend on the private types of the agents, we can say that strict co-utility is achieved.

P2P Online Lending Market

Peer-to-peer (P2P) lending is the practice of lending money between peers (individuals or businesses) through online marketplaces by a direct transaction between the borrowers and the lenders. The platforms that facilitate this practice operate, in return for a service charge they receive from the customers, by rendering services of match-making and credit checking. Some examples of such online marketplaces include LendingClub (currently the world's largest P2P online lending platform), Prosper Marketplace, Funding Circle, Zopa, SoFi, Comunitae, RateSetter, and ThinCats. There also are some non-profit global person-to-person microlending platforms such as Kiva and Zidisha (unlike Kiva, Zidisha involves no local intermediaries in its global operations).

Peer-to-peer lending has the potential to disintermediate the traditional retail banking with a lower cost structure and access to micro-level loans directly originated from individual peers. P2P lending commonly follows the installment loan type, in which loans are repaid in periodic installments (usually monthly ones) that include the principal and the interest. These loans can be unsecured or secured and, normally, do not have government insurance protection, being operated based on a private deal. Some platforms (e.g., Zopa and RateSetter in the United Kingdom) offer protection funds. Risk perceptions are commonly reflected in terms of the interest rate following the platforms' individual loan rating (see individual platforms' loan grade/rating[33] and also Collier and Hampshire, 2010). See Table 2-3.

---

[33]See, for instance, LendingClub loan grades at www.lendingclub.com/foliofn/rate-Detail.action

Table 2-3. Originator returns[34]

Originator	1-Year Net Return	3-Year Net Return	As of Date
DK			
Flexfunding	7.7	25.5	July 31, 2019
EU			
Creat.sa	5.4	17.7	December 31, 2019
October	2.6	13.8	December 31, 2019
United Kingdom			
LendingCrowd	8.6		February 29, 2020
CrowdProperty	8	27.7	January 31, 2020
CapitalRise	9.7	34.4	November 30, 2019
Landbay	3.5	11.4	July 31, 2019
Assetz Capital	3.9	17.2	June 30, 2019
United States			
Prosper	4.6	14.6	December 31, 2019
LendingClub	3.9	13.7	December 31, 2019

Individual agents engage in a P2P lending market for diverse reasons. For instance, borrowers post loan requests in the online P2P marketplaces to finance various aspects in their lives such as travel, medical, or even wedding expenses. Lenders in this market view loans as investments to obtain some returns. Also, lenders may have motivations beyond returns, such as to do social good and help the community (Krumme and Herrero, 2009). See Table 2-4.

Table 2-4. Regional volume of P2P online lending in million USD as of December 2019[35]

Region	Last 3 Months	Last 12 Months	Cumulative
Asia	241	828	1449
Australia and New Zealand	142	810	2871
Europe	1811	6727	14,918
Latin America	11	42	126
United Kingdom	654	4814	23,027
United States and Canada	4699	22,474	124,086

---

[34]https://brismo.com/market-data/
[35]https://brismo.com/market-data/

The regulatory frameworks for the P2P lending market vary depending on the country to which they are operating at. For instance, in some countries like the United States, there is a quota restriction requirement for the maximum amount a lender can invest in a given P2P lending marketplace (Serrano et al., 2015). Other regulatory and policy frameworks in the P2P online lending deal with the minimization of operational risk and customer protection (Milne and Parboteeah, 2016) through segregation of the platform user money, well-ordered platform cessation, default and debt management, and transparent and informative lending process. For Funk et al. (2015), one of the regulatory requirements to operate a P2P lending market in some countries is partnership operation with the traditional banks in facilitating the lending process. They stress that external stakeholders like banks and credit agencies are vital in P2P lending marketplaces. On the internal aspect of the P2P lending platforms, they suggest a restructuring of the internal form of the P2P platform itself with a focus on the business models, organizational design, and those factors that generate success of P2P platforms. Furthermore, other regulatory policies focus on enhancing competition and ensuring efficiency through a fair access to credit.

Zeng (2013) has presented a detailed analysis of the United States' and Europe's legal frameworks concerning the P2P lending. Following the 2008 regulations in the United States, P2P lending market is made more transparent with the Securities and Exchange Commission (SEC) making updated reports of the P2P companies through its Electronic Data Gathering, Analysis, and Retrieval (EDGAR) system. Further, a secondary market operation for the notes following the regulation enabled the liquidity of the P2P loans. According to Zeng (2013), the major regulatory issues regarding the P2P lending market in the United States and Europe are the same. Some of these include the following:

- Securities laws require the SEC registration of P2P platforms, P2P offerings, platform notes, of any P2P transaction broker and investment advisers, and platforms' report the record of P2P notes to the SEC and comply with federal securities laws (see the 1933 Securities Act that requires investors to be informed about public offerings of securities). Prosper and LendingClub, for example, are registered with the SEC.

- Lending laws/lender licensing, usury laws, state licensing requirements, and bank secrecy act regulations (i.e., requirement of the P2P platforms to verify the true identities of both the lenders and borrowers, e.g., criminals or members of terrorist organizations based on information from federal agencies), which involve reporting any suspicious account activities and information sharing and anti-money laundering programs, and third-party usage of bank charters.

- *Consumer protection laws*: Lenders/funding bank and P2P lending operator are required to provide sufficient information to the borrowers and investors in a given transaction regarding the loan terms, and any form of consumer discrimination is illegal (securing a fair access to credit). Furthermore, the debt collection process should be complying with the law (e.g., collecting a debt in a harassing or abusive way is illegal).

Note that the preceding regulation list is in the context of the US law and the SEC considered as the authority here, while the European system has its own regulatory body. One of these bodies of the P2P financing in the United Kingdom is the Financial Conduct Authority (FCA).

The form of P2P lending Rotating Credit Association (RCA), commonly practiced in many countries including the United States, the United Kingdom, Asia, and Africa, has been controversial due to the usury issues associated with this form of lending. This is because RCAs are commonly formed between members with regular contributions to a common pool, which is sequentially distributed to each member. In most cases, this form of lending relies on a social trust, and high interest rates are set (about 30%) to offset potential default. As a result, countries like the United States and Canada have usury laws that prevent excessive interest rates on loans (e.g., Revised Code of Washington (RCW) 19.52). This law does not exist in the United Kingdom, which has served a tax haven for the US payday lenders. This also is an indication for some of the problems associated with the global regulatory framework disparities in the P2P lending market.

Marot (2014) analyzed the expected returns in the P2P online lending market in connection with the probability of default underlying each loan. Accordingly, he predicted that the risk of default varies with time during the loan period and that there is an increasing risk of default with time, which will start to decline when the loan is close to maturity. According to Emekter et al. (2015), loan grade, debt-to-income ratio, credit score (FICO), and revolving line utilization have a significant effect on the probability of default. In the same line, Funk et al. (2015) have presented a detailed review on the factors that define borrower's probability of successful loan origination (liquidity) and those that determine the probability of successful return to the lender. Here, they identified a generalized category of borrower characteristics as financial, demographic, and social like friends and group affiliation (see also Lin (2009) for the categorization of borrower characteristics into hard and soft credit information).

Main Problems in P2P Online Lending Markets

The P2P online lending market is prone to the following key problems: liquidity risks, fraud, security and operational risks (dangers of fraud, cybercrime, and operational outages), platform failure, risk of default, usury and systemic financial risks due to liquidity, and credit risks in the business cycle. In order to tackle some of the problems stated here, government regulations, systematic agreements, and feedback mechanisms are recommended (Zeng, 2013, and Yang and Lee, 2016). Milne and Parboteeah (2016), on the other hand, believe in developing a reliable business process model that can tackle the underlying problems and industry-wide standardization that help achieve the legal requirements set by the monitoring authority.

> *In the UK the related initiative (HM Treasury, 2014) to develop standardized APIs (application programming interfaces) for SME data so that transaction information can be shared by all potential lenders, and not only the bank providing a business with payment and bank account services. This standardization could be a further support for the growth of P2P lending.*

> —Milne and Parboteeah (2016)

The market is prone to a mistrust problem between the borrowers and the potential lenders. In practice, the platforms make loan grading/rating to identify loans based on their level of risk. This factor displays the inefficiency of the market, which has room for improvement both for lenders and borrowers. As Krumme and Herrero (2009) argued, the long-term sustainability of the P2P online lending network depends on the reconciliation of risk and expected rewards. Moreover, there are formation of third-party platforms (platforms with an automated investing tool: LendingRobot and BlueVestment (for LendingClub), LendingMemo, etc.) that thicken the P2P lending market layer with the addition of middle-ground players. Such platforms cause the market to deviate from its original peer-to-peer nature. These third parties use automated algorithms that can filter out the credibility of the loans in the platform in return for the service charge they receive, hence replacing the basic individual-level manual filtering mechanism. By doing so, they indirectly signal those loans with higher potential return, and hence, they discard the potentially defaulting loans.

Information asymmetry risks underlying the market creates difficulties in the online P2P lending markets' day-to-day transactions (see, e.g., Funk et al., 2015; Lin, 2009; McIntosh, 2010; and Serrano et al., 2015). Accordingly, identifying credible borrower's identity is one of the key factors for the lenders' profitability from this kind of investment. Some scholars in the field, like Serrano et al. (2015), argue that P2P lending platforms are responsible to provide accurate information on the borrower characteristics in order to foster the efficiency of the lending process. Numerous P2P lending platforms are flourishing in this sector of the financial industry. Hence, increasing the participation rate in these platforms depends on the credibility of the platform itself in addition to the borrowers' characteristics and lenders' herding behaviors. Yang and Lee (2016) identified the following three categories of trust for the credibility of a P2P lending platform:

- System-based trust through service quality (efficient and flexible transactions), information accuracy, security, and systematized contractual terms and conditions, which will also help reduce adverse behaviors arising from the information asymmetry.

- Cognitive-based trust by creating first impressions through awareness, reputation, and addressing perceived risk.

- Affective-based trust (confidence developed from affection between individuals), for instance, the utilization of social networking which helps for a long-term strategic alliance, which builds trust and mutuality.

Associated with the information asymmetry in this market and mistrust effect, several types of filtering and reputation methods are at play in the market, including third-party algorithmic investing, basic filtering, and community-based reputation. In this regard, Collier and Hampshire (2010) analyzed how structural and behavioral community signals interact with a borrower's signals to the mistrust effect in P2P lending. As a result, they developed a model and theoretical application to community reputation systems, by considering a person's social reputation together with an outcome-based reputation, which produces an implied market-related reputation. Hence, social capital risks, that is, the social network and connections between members that help incorporate the soft credit information about the borrower, is considered as one of the tools to bridge the information gap between borrowers and lenders in this market (Lin, 2009, and Greiner and Wang, 2009). Yet, the effect of social capital in filtering credible borrowers depends on the participants' creditworthiness where an agent can strategically mask itself under the social capital shield whenever a group effect is considered.

Sabater and Sierra (2002), on the other hand, analyzed a reputation system from the individual dimension (i.e., based on direct interaction of individuals in the light of outcome-based reputation), social dimension (i.e., extended social interaction: witness, neighborhood, and system reputation based on the role played by a target agent), and ontological dimension (i.e., a complex reputation mechanism based on a combination of other related behavioral structures of an individual agent). In addition to these three dimensions, the reputation system they recommend also takes into account an outcome reputation deviation, where greater variability in rating values implies volatility of the target agent in fulfilling her promises.

Since the operations managed by humans are carried out through an online interface, the P2P lending ecosystem encompasses both technical and human factors. The underlying rational human behaviors (both on the side of borrowers and lenders), which autonomously interact through the facilitation of the technical ebusiness system, define the efficiency of the market. The problems arising from the human and technical factors can easily make the system a complex and hard one to control. It is also worth noting that the human factors play a prominent role, and the way a technical algorithm responds to manage such factors accordingly is one of the key indices of the efficiency of the system.

Furthermore, individual investors in the conventional P2P lending markets today face stiff competition from the institutional investors that can relatively better sink the potential risks with the economies of scale at an institutional level. Moreover, unlike the private investors who are not commonly financial experts, the institutional investors have their own credit algorithms that help them evaluate loan pricings (e.g., TruSight by the Ranger Capital Group). For instance, in the United States, like the New York-based investment firm Eaglewood Capital,[36] there are many financial institutions that invest in the P2P lending marketplaces risks. In 2016, banks invested in more than 25% of the loans in LendingClub;[37] institutional investors bought more than 50% of the P2P loans in LendingClub and Prosper.[38] Such a scramble over the P2P lending by institutional investors can draw us back to the legacy centralized financial market, rather than the genesis collaborative economic system built in the P2P sectors. In this like setting, it is clear that the forerunning P2P lending marketplaces will through time be monopolized or taken over by institutional investors and a vicious circle of capitalist system persists, not the collaborative economic setting.

Value Co-creation in P2P Online Lending Market

Peer-to-peer lending marketplaces provide services matching potential investors with borrowers on online platforms, thereby serving borrowers' and lenders' interests. Unlike the classical setting risks in which lenders determine the loan rate through bidding for prices, nowadays rates are

---

[36]www.ft.com/content/b0696414-3f3f-11e3-9657-00144feabdc0
[37]https://bankinnovation.net/allposts/operations/sales-mark/lending-club-talks-transforming-banking-but-banks-fund-25-of-its-loans/
[38]www.ft.com/content/28247fe4-6597-11e2-a17b-00144feab49a

assigned centrally by the platforms based on the credit score of borrowers (see Prosper Rating[39]). Non-qualifying borrowers are filtered out from the market, and loan notes that satisfy the credit grade standard of the platforms are approved for credit listing. In most cases, about 90% of loan applications are filtered out of the market (e.g., LendingClub and Prosper). These platforms use loan approval credit and pricing models for assigning rates to the applications based on their level of risk. Yet, some of the models applied by LendingClub and Prosper had raised legal issues, because their current loan ratings were claimed to violate the state interest rate caps in the United States.[40] By the fourth quarter of 2019, LendingClub issued about $56.8 billion loans.[41]

Another form of the P2P lending is the non-profit lending market (e.g., Kiva and Zidisha). The interaction in this form of global level P2P lending networks is co-utile, in which a chain of interaction between the P2P microfinance website, local microfinance institutions (MFIs), borrowers, and the non-profit humanitarian lenders is formed in a mutually beneficial way. Here, the MFIs get capital at a near-zero cost, the MFI borrowers are linked to the potential lenders through the global lending website, and the non-profit global lending site links lenders to the MFI borrowers. Note also that the probability of default and the level of information asymmetry are larger in the non-profit lending markets.

Kiva uses a multi-tiered system of credit scoring for rating the local microfinance institution (MFIs). By overviewing the Kiva's internal monitoring system and considering the strategic incentives created by MFIs, McIntosh (2010) showed that, if a borrower on Kiva listing defaults, it's highly probable that the MFI (who gets capital from Kiva at a 0% interest rate) will cover the repayment in order to keep its Kiva score high, and consequently, Kiva's reputation scheme doesn't directly ensure the underlying reliability of the end users. Hence, unlike successfully rating the institutions, the rating mechanism employed in this platform is far from being directed to the individual borrowers. Hence, this and other related factors make the non-profit P2P lending different from the individual peers' level analysis of the profit-oriented P2P lending market.

---

[39]www.prosper.com/plp/invest/prosper-ratings/
[40]See an article by Matt Scully of Bloomberg Business on August 31, 2015, for the details on this: www.bloomberg.com/news/articles/2016-02-25/microsoft-says-it-will-file-an-amicus-brief-to-support-apple
[41]See LendingClub total loan issuance from 2012 to 2019 at www.lendingclub.com/info/statistics.action

Investment Decision in P2P Online Lending

The following key points are vital in characterizing and understanding P2P online lending markets:

- There is asymmetric information.

- The P2P online lending market is perfectly competitive with a large number of borrowers and lenders.

- Lenders are risk-averse and borrowers are risk-neutral. Hence, a borrower's utility function is weakly concave in that they can be risk-neutral (or risk-averse in some exceptional cases with lower impatience to borrow). On the other hand, lenders who invest in the loan notes of anonymous borrowers have strictly concave utility function (strictly risk-averse).

- Lenders and borrowers are expected to be utility maximizers, with strictly increasing preferences.

- The income of the borrower and the loan amount originated are exogenously defined, and strategic default is an endogenous factor depending on the loan type.

- There is a visible deterministic functional relationship between the loan type (based on the level of risk) and the interest rate assigned to it, which is trivial from the intrinsic quality of the loan.

In the discussions that follow, I will take two different cases to analyze the market depending on re-investment possibilities.

Case 1: Lender Cannot Borrow

This is a unidirectional investment scenario in which loans are originated only by potential lenders. In this case, lending and borrowing tasks are performed by two disjoint groups (borrowers and lenders).

Borrower

We assume that there are no constraints on the payment profile and, as stated previously, borrowers are risk-neutral. This means that they will only be concerned by the origination of the loan at any cost given the level of urgency of the need for loan financing. Based on the formula for calculation of present value of annuities, the present value of a loan amount I_0 with future

annuity payments, P, is given by $a_{n|i} = \dfrac{1 - (1+i)^{-n}}{i}$, where n is the number of terms of the loan (commonly 3–5 years' terms in online P2P lending market) and i is the per period random interest rate, accounting for risk premium. This accounts for the time value of money (interest rate), and the future value and present value are linear in the amount of payments of the loan. The present value of monthly payments of P is $PV(i, n) = P. \, a_{n \mid i}$. From this follows that the payoff to the borrower after the origination of the loan is the net gain over the loan term discounted to present value. Hence, borrower's net gain from

the loan origination, Π_b, is $\Pi_b = I_0 - P.\dfrac{1-(1+i)^{-n}}{i}$. The utility of the borrower

depends on the borrower's residual income after the loan repayment is discounted to its present value over the term of the loan at a presumed level of impatience: the more patient the borrower is over her current financial need, the more she can wait before borrowing.

Lender

Risk diversification through an investment portfolio is common in P2P online lending. For lending as an investment, preferences on loan notes depend on the respective expected return from each loan. Hence, a rational investor composes her portfolio of investment with loan notes that can guarantee optimal expected return. From the portfolio of investment, our focus is on the individual interaction of a lender with each individual borrower, provided that there is a diverse probability of default across the borrowers. Investment on an individual note depends on the expected return for that note.

The market interaction between a large number of borrowers and lenders defines the optimal interest rate for different loan type categories. Edelstein et al. (2003) argue that the volatility in the interest rate, the covariation among market interest rates, the borrower collateral and income, the loan term, and the risk preference of borrowers and lenders determine the optimal loan interest rate contracts. The lender's profit is the difference between the cost of funds and loan repayments by the borrower. Krumme and Herrero (2009) predicted that lenders in the P2P market fail to maximize the expected payoff, where there is suboptimal behavior by lenders because of the investment preference for riskier and highly defaulting loans. They argued that a lender investing in a higher credit grade scoring has greater expected payoff than one investing in a lower grade, as there is a high rate of default associated with a low loan grade.

With a large number of lenders, the loan market is competitive and there is a minimum non-zero spread between the contract and market interest rate below which no lending occurs. Lenders identify a potential probability of default based on the observable borrower attributes that generally depict the borrower's creditworthiness based on past record of a given borrower characteristics (McIntosh, 2010). Note that a lender aims at profit maximization which is the sum of profits from the loan origination to all potential borrowers from her portfolio of investment across the notes.

The lending rate across the notes can differ depending on the level of riskiness of the target borrower. Provided this, a lender's profitability depends on probability of repayment of each borrower, interest rates, and the size of each note in the portfolio composition. Lenders choose to invest in the notes of a P2P lending market if the return rates are high enough to compensate for the loss, which implies that the higher the interest rates are, the more likely the lender will be willing to invest in the risky notes. However, the valuation of the loans in the conventional P2P lending markets is questionable. In this regard, Emekter et al. (2015) argue that the higher interest rate charged on riskier loans at the LendingClub is not enough to offset the associated incremental risk due to default by comparing the theoretical interest rate with the actual one set for the loans at the LendingClub.

In line with this, Iyer et al. (2009) contend borrower's creditworthiness depends on factors other than the platforms' rating and argue that about 28% of the interest spread between the highest credit grade (AA) and that of the lowest grade (HR) in the Prosper Marketplace is due to the other borrower characteristic variables. Likewise, the loan grades in the LendingClub accurately predicted about 60% to 80% of the loans' probability of default (Serrano et al., 2015). Yet the remaining inaccuracy with the predictive power of the loan grades calls for a more robust technique that could handle the potential credit risks underlying the market and hence keep the accuracy of lenders' expected profit.

Case 2: Lending with Re-investable Borrowing

Another scenario to be considered is one in which re-investment is possible. That is, lenders can also borrow from others to re-invest in the same market. Here, the lender is assumed to rely on short-term loans for extending long-term loans to her borrowers. In this case, individual lenders mimic banks in that they rely on borrowing in addition to their own capital to make loans for profit. Thus, investors make profit through arbitrage opportunities in the market, P2P loan carry trade. *P2P loan carry trade* refers to an investment technique seeking profit from the spread in interest rates in re-investable borrowing of the online P2P lending market.

Lenders maximize profit by choosing how much they would like to lend and the loan type, based on their risk preference by taking the lending rates as given. Rational players engage in the market to maximize their respective financial goals. As long as their respective goals are met, there is a self-enforcing mutually beneficial interaction between the borrowers and lenders in the market.

Proposed Mechanism for P2P Online Lending

As previously stated, mistrust is identified as one of the main problems underlying the P2P online lending market. In this section, I will briefly discuss the solution concept we proposed in our prior study of this market. This solution concept is the *decentralized co-utile reputation mechanism* (Turi et al., 2017, and Domingo-Ferrer et al., 2016b). The mechanism outputs a global reputation for each target agent that is computed by a set of anonymous score managers, who take as input local reputation scores derived from interactions of the target agent with other agents.

Thanks to its fully decentralized nature, the mechanism does not rely on a central authority to compute reputations. A central authority is problematic for at least two reasons:

1. Possible biases in the reputation calculation introduced by the authority for its own benefit (which would break co-utility)

2. Privacy issues caused by the systematic compilation of agents' opinions and reputations by a sole central entity

Beyond avoiding a central authority, the protocol also presents several other features that make it interesting for P2P lending, such as

- *Anonymity*: Being fully distributed, the protocol relies on agents' collaboration in order to compute reputations. However, agents remain anonymous to each other during the calculation process, which prevents them from colluding in order to distort a target agent's reputation for their own benefit.

- *Low overhead*: Even though a distributed protocol usually requires more information exchanges than a centralized one, the protocol limits the number of messages and communication iterations needed to compute reputations. Moreover, the reputation calculation can be done in parallel and without interfering with the main purpose of the P2P network.

- *Proper management of new agents*: Newcomers do not gain any reputation benefit, and hence agents cannot expect to neutralize a bad reputation by taking a new identity (which in turn disincentivizes bad behaviors).

- *Attack tolerance*: The protocol is also robust against a number of tampering attacks, both targeted at increasing the agents' own reputation and at decreasing the reputation of others. In fact, agents trying to tamper with reputations can be easily detected by others (and punished by lowering their reputations).

The protocol calculates reputations based on the well-known EigenTrust model (Kamvar et al., 2003), which distinguishes between local and global agent reputations. Local reputation refers to the reputation score (trust) of an individual target agent, computed by another agent, who had a direct transaction with her. The global reputation of an agent is the aggregation of each local reputation value computed by the agents who directly interacted with her. The global reputation in a P2P lending is the overall reputation score of a borrower based on the local reputations obtained from a set of transactions she undertook with a set of lenders in the market. This score, if available, is the one used as an immediate reference for the future credible potential transaction.

A simplified computation of a lending transaction is presented in Figure 2-4, in which a score manager i computes the global reputation score of a single borrower k. The figure depicts a graph with local-trust-value weighted nodes of a network of interaction of peer k. The computation of k's global reputation, $\hat{g}_k$, by a single score manager, SM_k, is based on their network of interaction.

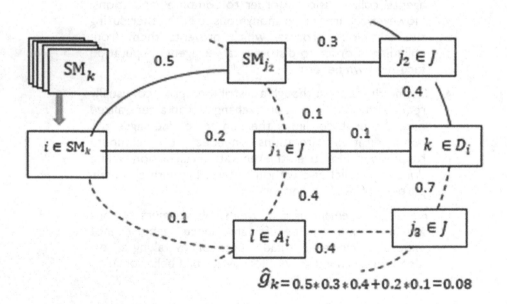

Figure 2-4. Co-utile reputation calculation (*SMk* and SM_{j_2} are the score managers of k and j_2, respectively)

A decentralized co-utile reputation system for the P2P online lending market is defined as an electronic system using a distributed chain of computation that signals the creditworthiness of a given borrower for a potential transaction to be handled by a specific platform. This is done by formally embedding the actual performance or reputation effects into the information system of the P2P marketplace. Based on the calculation of local and global reputation values, we can build a trust-oriented and *strictly peer-to-peer* lending market, in contrast to the current P2P lending market, which needs a middle layer and hence is not strictly P2P. The system is set in such a way to encompass the type of loans and underlying behaviors of the participating agents.

The co-utile nature of the aforementioned reputation protocol applied to P2P lending lies in the mutual benefit of agents computing the reputation, that is, the lenders: if borrowers can also lend, then all agents are interested in the availability of a reliable reputation to assess the loan risk; if borrowers cannot lend, then only lenders are interested in computing reliable reputations, and mutual benefit holds between lenders. Co-utility, and in particular the self-enforcing nature of the protocol, ensures correct computation of reputations by lenders, with no incentive to deviate.

Furthermore, the key characterizing features of the co-utile reputation system depicted earlier have a significant potential for improving the efficiency of the P2P online lending market. For instance, the decentralized nature of the protocol assures the operation of the market without central authorities. This has a very important advantage in extending the operation of P2P lending practices beyond geographic boundaries where there is no common legal framework that binds individuals across the globe to specific rules. In addition, decentralization eliminates third-party platforms acting as intermediaries and hence reduces operational costs. Furthermore, the self-enforcing property of this protocol ensures correct computation of reputations, without incentive to deviate.

Moreover, the proper management of new agents embodied in this protocol can be useful in guaranteeing differentiation of existing players from new entrants, which also will resolve one of the underlying problems in the community-based lending. In this regard, one of the prominent examples can be the problem underlying the community-based reputation mechanism (Hildebrand et al., 2014, and Collier and Hampshire, 2010) in which communities signal the creditworthiness of an individual member agent. A finding by Krumme and Herrero (2009) shows one of the drawbacks underlying the community-based reputation, where the lenders' preference pattern with regard to credit grade remains unchanged across community groups with different reputation and, hence, there is no identification effect of the community-based reputation when combined with the credit grading effect. Such a reputation mechanism has a problem with the management of new entrants because if a previously existing community has poor loans, it would be easier to start all over with a new community of no history. A specific case is a seller with a poor rating in eBay: he will be rationally interested in whitewashing his reputation by mutating into a new seller with a new pseudonym. New entrants can be filtered out with the underlying zero reputation score, and loans with higher risk are already priced at a higher interest rate. This implies that in order for a borrower to obtain a trusted loan (in favorable conditions), she should have a positive normalized reputation value from her local transaction score. The adaptation of the aforementioned decentralized co-utile reputation protocol to the P2P online lending market promises to deter whitewashing and improve the efficiency of the system.

The decentralized computation of the reputation is done by score managers, who are defined for each borrower using a distributed hash table (DHT) (Domingo-Ferrer et al., 2016b). A score manager computes the borrower's global reputation based on the local reputation fetched from the set of direct transactions by the borrower. The electronic system must publicly maintain the computed reputation score of each agent within the market, and it is continually updated with upcoming transactions (reputation scores can be updated on a daily or a weekly basis). Once the global reputation for each agent in the market is computed in a decentralized way, transactions are more predictable to a rational investor. Before deciding to lend money to a borrower, a potential lender asks the reputation system for the global reputation of the borrower or directly refers to the local reputation she gave to the borrower if a transaction took place between the two in the past. In some cases, where there is a direct transaction record between the borrower and lender, the lender might realize a variation between the global reputation score and that of the local reputation record she has about the borrower. In this case, she compares the two and takes the one with a lower value for further investment decisions regarding k. The normalized local reputation score identifies if the borrower is credible (positive reputation values) or if she is a defaulting type or just a borrower with a first-time loan request in this market (zero reputation value). In addition, the global reputation score reveals the borrower's creditworthiness based on her weighted local reputation scores.

Since P2P loans have no collateral, reputation capital (reputation of the borrower) is intangible collateral of this transaction. A borrower defaults if the value of default is greater than the value of paying back. Her gain from the default is the loan amount originated, given an initial presumed small positive reputation of the system. Yet, with the current transaction's default, she will also lose her reputation. Thus, reputation gain punishes an intention to default.

Figure 2-5 depicts the workflow of the decentralized reputation protocol when applied to the online P2P lending market. In the figure, consider that a potential lender, A, in an online lending market wants to invest in the loan requests of borrower, B. The various steps of Figure 2-5 are as follows:

1. *B* is a registered borrower in a platform.

2. A set of lenders, *J*, who had past transactions with borrower *B* give local reputation scores to *B*.

3. The reputation system in the platform assigns a global reputation score for each member based on a decentralized co-utile reputation protocol. Hence, the score manager of *B* queries the set *J* and computes the global reputation of *B* based on the transitive trust assumption.

4. A potential lender *A* queries the global reputation system for the reputation scores of his target notes, in order to make investment decisions on her preferred loan note out of the entire return rate category based on her risk preference.

5. In addition to checking the global reputation score of *B*, according to the implementation rules of the protocol, if investor *A* has already interacted with borrower *B* and, thus, has calculated a local reputation value, then *A* can make her investment decision by directly referring to *B*'s local reputation. Here, self-experience is considered a good reference point. However, local and global reputation values may not always be the same, since global reputation is a weighted sum of all the local reputations that borrower *B* has. In that case, it is better for *A* to take both valuations into account and make the investment decision based on the comparison of these values (with a negative bias, taking the one with the lower reputation value).

6. The potential transaction between lender *A* and borrower *B* is realized based on *B*'s reputation.

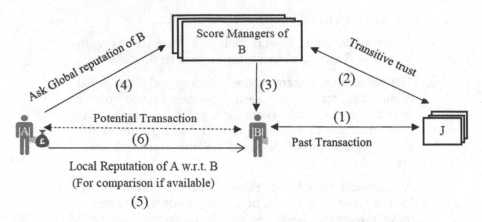

Figure 2-5. Workflow of the decentralized co-utile reputation system for P2P lending

Note that Figure 2-5 is drawn under the assumption of non-diversified investment (for simplicity of presentation), whereas investors can have a portfolio of diversified investment.

The application of the reputation protocol to the P2P lending market helps neutralize the negative utilities arising in the market. With a perfect trust and exact valuation of notes in the market, participation in the P2P online lending market offers the highest possible reward. The reason is that investment in a P2P online lending market generates better rewards than traditional banking market, because

1. Many loans that would not have been approved by traditional banks are listed for financing in these marketplaces with a relatively higher rates of return.

2. The reputation protocol can help identify the creditworthiness of the individual borrower (which helps exploit all potential loan listings) so that investing in that borrower's note is better for a rational utility-maximizing lender.

Moreover, there is no way for the lender to get a better payoff without getting the borrower worse off (maybe through increased rate of return or refusal to finance). In the same way, it is not possible for the borrower to get a better payoff without a decrease in the lender's payoff (maybe through defaulting or imposition of a lower rate of return).

A limitation of this reputation approach is that it is outcome-based and it does not take into account the individual behaviors other than the specific transactions, based on past records of the transaction. Also, it fails to leverage any previous reputations available for newcomers (who are assigned zero reputation with the aim of thwarting whitewashing).

Summary

Crowdfunding platforms facilitate the match between the entrepreneurs, investors, and backers and hence should be designed in such a way that all the players communicate the transactional information and maximize their respective utilities. Even if crowdfunding has been a very relevant funding source of the collaborative economy in the recent few years, it has not yet reached maturity and access to the greater share of the global population. Hence, there is still a potential for this industry to increase its current trend of growth to its fullest potential. In addition, redefining the crowd-based business model to fit a variety of project types, as well as flexible applicability under various conditions (mainly in developing countries as an alternative to the existing microfinance models), can be avenues for further research. There is a need to understand and examine the dynamics of the crowdfunding industry and its potential to be applicable to any type of project financing and attract the largest number of backers/investors. Here, considerations in the design of incentive schemes should be the dynamics of the market with time, factors that affect the success of a given crowdfunding campaign, networking effect, self-enforcing reputation scheme, crowdfunding type, project type, methods of reward, and so on. Note also that incentive design is at the core of the collaborative economy.

As discussed earlier, reputation is the backbone of the collaborative economy, which is in general prone to the information asymmetry risk. A direction for future work is to take a stride toward merging the outcome-based reputation with the social reputation (using state-of-the-art social media, like Facebook, Twitter, Instagram posts, or LinkedIn connections in which a bunch of personal data are available) and with the market-related reputation (such as Amazon or eBay purchases and credit card expenses or length of phone calls). This will help consider the initial reputation of the target agent's behavior in these social networks and markets other than in the platform under review. As a result, a richer and multi-dimensional understanding of the borrower's foreseeable behavior will be reached. Extending global reputation in this way will also pave the way to new risk assessment methods, not merely reliant on outcome-based reputation (which only considers credit history, credit scores, and such like). Hence, the next question will be how to best use the data from the social media, other marketplaces, and all other information sources for the reputation purpose in P2P lending markets.

A promising avenue is to seek an aggregated reputation. This can be done by integrating outcome-based, social, and market-related reputations for P2P online lending. Here, proper weights for each reputation type, including the target peer's economic, commercial, and social records beyond the lending market, should be set while properly punishing malicious peers. Such a compounded reputation can clarify the expected behavior of an agent much more accurately. For example, an individual can be reputed loyal if she has a good reputation of not defaulting on previous loans, being loyal in social interactions, having a stable income base, having a stable credit card record, not being bankrupt or in a devastated economic condition that would prevent paying back, being careful, and so on. Thus, it would be highly interesting to develop such an integrated reputation.

This chapter also covered another form of crowd-based digital business model, crowdsourcing. This model has proved efficiency in outsourcing a task to a large number of people via the Web. Tasks listed in centralized marketplaces or open source platforms can be paid or unpaid. The non-financial rewards underlying some of the crowdsourced tasks have redefined the classical theories of labor allocation and wage determination.

Web 3.0: The Distributed Information Network Economy

This chapter presents the Web 3.0 economy with a primary focus on the network economies of blockchain technology and distributed ledger technologies (DLTs). It is designed to present a general overview of the Web 3.0 distributed network economy in light of some business, finance, and economic theories and practices. The chapter thus lends the analyses to aid understanding the applications of economic thinking and design to the newly evolving digital economic system. The chapter provides a conceptual review of blockchain tech economics by organizing dispersed thoughts in the field.

© Abeba N. Turi 2020
A. N. Turi, *Technologies for Modern Digital Entrepreneurship*,
https://doi.org/10.1007/978-1-4842-6005-0_3

The technology is one of the forefront developments in the digital economy, and it facilitates efficient utilization of scarce resources by disintermediating the traditional business models. Besides cryptographic techniques and algorithmic consensus mechanisms, the value co-creation process and the consensus on an update of a state for blockchain-powered distributed networks relies on the economic theories of mechanism design and cryptoeconomics. Such networks are composed of rational economic units, and their economic characterization will help better understand the system and its dynamics in light of the existing economic and business models. Decentralized platforms under this economic system have opened the potential for new ways of exchange over the Internet and broader financial inclusion. Here, I will cover the panorama of the distributed ledger technologies with further discussions on blockchain-powered nano-economies and tokenization, asset valuation, cryptocurrency markets, and some foundation on cryptoeconomics and consensus mechanisms. I will also present a discussion on the governance of decentralized Web 3.0 economies and open source projects by taking the case of the QuadrigaCX.[1]

Distributed Ledger Technologies

Blockchain (broadly speaking, distributed ledger technologies) refers to a type of distributed digital ledger that facilitates the transfer of an item of value in a distributed way. Every block contains a group of valid transaction records and attributes of the transacted item in a given period. Token sales (commonly, secure token offering (STO) or initial coin offering (ICO)) for mining (issuing) digital coins or mining transactions are the most common funding models employed under this system. The technology deemed to allow decentralization of the notion of trust using cryptography and peer-to-peer verification mechanisms that enables issuance of cryptocurrencies such as Bitcoin and other nano-economy tokens. Some scholars argue that blockchains operate as trust machines (see, e.g., Vigna and Casey, 2019) and some question the tech as a trust machine (see, e.g., Hileman and Rauchs, 2017).

Key features of the distributed ledger and blockchain technologies make it attractive to financial institutions and other transactional networks. These key features are

- *Security of the transaction*: The tech is distributed, secured with cryptographic validation of transactions, and efficient, and transaction records are transparent.

---

[1]One of Canada's largest cryptocurrency exchanges which was issued a Termination and Bankruptcy Assignment Order by the Supreme Court of Nova Scotia early April 2019, www.quadrigacxtrustee.com/

- *Efficient in transaction processing time and cost*: A one-time data entry in a distributed way without a double and separate record of events resulting in a significant reduction in costs of data reconciliation, checks, and transfers.

- *Support of smart contracts*: A smart contract (a.k.a. chaincode of business rules in the Hyperledger Fabric language) refers to a computer program for a digital agreement built on top of a given protocol.

- *Transparent and distributed records of transactions*: Building an enterprise business on top of blockchain platforms helps for a secure transparent traceability and audit of the business process transparently, hence increasing the business efficiency by reducing transaction costs. For instance, a well-built banking blockchain network can improve the monitoring of payments and immutable audits as they go across different banks and helps in speeding up payments and lowering costs. In the banking sector, where security is at the forefront, a permissioned blockchain technology is viable for a faster, more accurate, secure, and transparent banking operation like processing of payments and reconciliation of transaction records.

Panorama of the Distributed Ledger Technologies

Blockchain technology is known for its versatile features in which it can be adapted to a broader set of functions beyond the hard-core cryptocurrencies.[2] It can be utilized for any transfer of an item of value in peer-to-peer (P2P)-based networks. Some applications of blockchain technology to transactional record systems and financial services, other than the cryptocurrencies, include securities settlement, currency exchange, supply chain management, green energy trading, P2P transfers, asset registration, correspondent banking, regulatory reporting and anti-money laundering (AML) rules, provenance, property rights, finance (payments, record of business transaction agreements like bonds, invoice financing, letter of credit, transaction settlement in international trades, etc.), healthcare, environmental protection,[3] and so on.

---

[2]See Swan, M. (2015). Blockchain: Blueprint for a new economy. O'Reilly Media, Inc.

[3]See World Economic Forum's report "Building Block(chain)s for a Better Planet," September 18, 2018, for a list of potential blockchain application for environmental protection (a total of 65 cases including valuation of natural capital, natural resource P2P trading or permits, supply chain, etc.), https://cointelegraph.com/news/world-economic-forum-outlines-over-65-block-chain-use-cases-for-environmental-protection/amp, accessed on April 2, 2020.

Lately, several institutions are developing blockchain platforms with some as open source. IDC Market Glance depicts Blockchain segments of the growing blockchain industry and vendors that are offering solutions worldwide as of the year 2019.[4] These platforms can generally be categorized as Bitcoin-based platforms, FinTech Blockchain platforms, smart contract platforms, institutional Blockchain platforms (commonly consortium or private blockchains), and sidechain platforms. In its current form, it is hard to tell whether the technology is a bubble or a sustainable solution toward enhancing the efficiency of the digital economic system. However, the technology has a considerable potential to meet its expectations or at least be a base for the forerunning new technological solutions that rely on its fundamentals as a stepping-stone.

Some of the companies and vendors offering blockchain solutions worldwide include Ripple Labs Inc., Genpact Ltd., MaidSafe.net Ltd., Bitmark Inc., TIBCO Software Inc., IOTA Foundation, Chronicled, Inc., MultiPlan, Inc., Virtusa Corporation, Google Inc., Beijing Dajie Zhiyuan Information Technology Co., Ltd., The Boston Consulting Group Inc, OpenBazaar, Bank of England, US Securities and Exchange Commission, AlphaPoint Corp., BlockCypher, Inc., Microsoft Corporation, and so on.[5]

The technology is in the early stages of adoption in the banking sector mainly in the intra-bank cross-border payments (e.g., Royal Bank of Canada is exploring the potential of the tech for its payments of Canadian and US banks). In its current form, it is hard to tell whether the technology is a bubble or a sustainable solution toward enhancing the efficiency of the digital economic system. The Gartner Hype Cycle for blockchain business 2019 shows that the tech is in a trough of disillusionment and about 5 to 10 years away from transformational impact.[6] However, the technology has a considerable potential to meet its expectations or at least be a base for the forerunning new technological solutions that rely on its fundamentals as a stepping-stone.

---

[4]Some of the companies covered in the IDC Market Glance include Ripple Labs Inc., Genpact Ltd., MaidSafe.net Ltd., Bitmark Inc., TIBCO Software Inc., IOTA Foundation, Chronicled, Inc., MultiPlan, Inc., Virtusa Corporation, Google Inc., Beijing Dajie Zhiyuan Information Technology Co., Ltd., The Boston Consulting Group Inc, OpenBazaar.org, Bank of England, US Securities and Exchange Commission, AlphaPoint Corp., BlockCypher, Inc., Microsoft Corporation, and so on; see IDC Market Glance: Blockchain 1Q19 at www.idc.com/getdoc.jsp?containerId=US44837919

[5]See IDC Market Glance: Blockchain 1Q19 at www.idc.com/getdoc.jsp?containerId=US44837919

[6]Gartner.com available at www.gartner.com/en/newsroom/press-releases/2019-10-08-gartner-2019-hype-cycle-shows-most-blockchain-technologies-are-still-five-to-10-years-away-from-transformational-impact, accessed on April 2, 2020.

Enterprise solution Blockchain applications are also worth highlighting here. Distributed ledger technologies utilized for enterprise solutions, for example, Hyperledger Blockchains platform from the Linux Foundation, are one of the promising outcomes from the developments in the field of blockchain tech. Some examples of the enterprise solution blockchain include Hyperledger Sawtooth (mainly for the supply chain management helping traceability of produce using the Internet of Things), Hyperledger Fabric (permissioned enterprise blockchain), and Hyperledger Indy (for a distributed identity recording).[7] These forms of enterprise blockchain platforms are mostly permissioned ones in which authorization and task identifications are centrally assigned. The technology facilitates the business process within a defined business network while guaranteeing the immutability of data.

Provided that such ledger platforms are permissioned by nature, a legal compliance check can also be done through read-only access to the external stakeholder. Still, scalability issues are yet to be addressed to reach the full potential of this technology in most business process applications. In this regard, the possibility for keeping track of and linking data off-chain to related on-chain data for a specific transaction, known as the archival bond, is a crucial feature (Lemieux and Sporny, 2017). For example, in a land registry application of the blockchain, the land transaction record (i.e., the state change) is recorded on the main chain, while the other issues like the purpose of the transaction and other related information for the state change go to the off-chain record. The archival bond ensures the reconciliation and readability of both the off-chain and on-chain data to each other.

Tokenization

Tokenization, in the context of the digital economy, refers to the modeling of value as a digital token. In simple words, tokenization is the process of converting an item of value into digital tokens. This implies a tangible representation of a digital asset through a pledge that helps for valuation and transfer of a digital asset. The idea of a tokenized economy is not new. Tokenization enables the creation of new assets (e.g., cryptocurrencies, property tokens). The English merchant tokens are one example of these like tokens in the physical world, outside the cryptocurrencies' space.

Historically, coins had intrinsic value being mint out of precious metals like gold. Like elsewhere, during those days in England, the minting of gold and silver coins was a royal privilege. However, with the intrinsic value underlying these coins, the smaller size of coins/changes that can reduce in value with the amount of the precious metal used was infeasible in production and usability.

---

[7]See Hyperledger frameworks at www.hyperledger.org/projects

Moreover, a shift to other inferior metals like bronze or copper would require a larger size in order to keep the intrinsic value. Hence, small change coins, namely, metal tokens with lesser intrinsic value than their face value, were used for local exchange purposes.

During the reign of Queen Elizabeth I, Bristol issued its tokens for circulation within the city and ten miles around it. Local merchants during that time used to privately produce small change (leather, lead, and tin) tokens and used them in their local daily exchanges. These tokens were accepted at their face value only within that boundary. BerkShares are the other tokens accepted at retail stores in the region of Massachusetts. Adams Community Bank, Lee Bank, Salisbury Bank, and Trust Company and Pittsfield Cooperative Bank provided the exchange of BerkShares for USD at a rate of 95 cents per BerkShares.[8] Ethiopia's primitive money of salt block token called "amole tchew" is another similar example. During the mid-20th century, local daily exchanges in the country took place with these locally accepted salt block tokens, while gold was used for large-scale transactions. Likewise, cryptocurrency refers to programmable token money which is deployed on a distributed network.

Blockchain-Powered Token Nano-economies

The rise of information networks and the advances in information technology have led to a dramatic shift in the traditional forms of economic systems and organizations. The logic is that blockchain is a technology that facilitates a consensus on the state of the world. Hence, once the consensus can be reached, it is all about to build an entirely new economic system on top of it. The blockchain network operating with native tokens (cryptocurrencies) as a unit of value can be represented as an economy with an initial endowment. The cryptocurrencies injected into the market through the mining process are the monetary base of that token economy.

A token refers to a quantified unit of value and a native token within this like economy facilitates the exchanges of value through the built-in protocol. Tokens can have asset, payment (transfer of value), security, equity, utility functions, or a hybrid function within the ecosystem they operate. Even if the market coverage for a token-based economy can be global, the setting in these like markets is confined to its own network and is bound to the holders of the token. Such platforms are commonly built on three layers: social layer, data layer, and technical layer (Lemieux et al., 2019). In general, economic agents in such a nano-economy obtain cryptocurrencies for (1) utility purposes or (2) as a currency for a store of value or (3) payment purpose or as an asset depending on the type of the cryptocurrency.[1]

---

[8]www.berkshares.org/berkshares_banks, accessed on April 2, 2020.

Members of a blockchain network are economic units that participate in the token economy for a specific transaction purpose. Such networks commonly are composed of three principal economic units:

- *The general blockchain network*: The community which utilizes the native token for their consumption and production decisions (the token users).

- *Developers*: Developers mimic the social planner/policymaker role in the traditional economic setting, thus drafting the rules of the game in which a decentralized coordination between participants is achieved.

- *Validators*: Validators verify if the transactions in the token economy run according to the rules of the game. This role of the validator in the blockchain network is like the notary public witnessing signatures on documents in the traditional economy.

Economic units in the conventional cryptocurrency markets can generate value through either a crypto investment or as miners/transaction validators for the creation of coin and validation of other investors' transactions.

This economic set has its business model in which it injects helicopter[9] money in the form of initial coin offerings or other forms of operating tokens which I will discuss in Chapter 4 of this book. These native tokens are then used to exchange items of value (goods and services) in that specific token economy and also for an exchange to other crypto- or fiat currencies. Further, as the nano-economy grows in network, new tokens are minted and circulated within the system. The blockchain technology handles the exchange record and transaction verification in a distributed setting. Some of the functionalities on which the token economies are based are in line with the principles of a free market economic system. In these markets, the price of the tokens and transaction fees adjust with the market, while the amount of coin creation over time is algorithmically defined. The blockchain tech facilitates transparency in the transfer of values created by self-interested economic units. Thus, a token economic system built on a blockchain tech with an efficient distributed consensus mechanism is automatic, in that it regulates itself to generate value.

Blockchain-powered platforms have structural similarities with the models of a closed economy, in that there is market clearing in the token economy. The value created is consumed by the economic units in the nano-economy. Besides, labor inputs into production (extraction of the native coins and

---

[9]Helicopter money is a term in monetary economics referring to central banks making direct payments to individuals, mainly in times of liquidity trap.

transaction validation) are supplied by the consumers/blockchain network's community. For example, Ethereum-based cryptocurrencies with utility value are spent on services or are earned for performing a task within that specific platform. In order to see the fixed supply conditions under the cryptocurrencies, consider the liquidity preference-money supply analysis of Keynesian macroeconomic theory (represented by the liquidity preference-money supply, LM, curve). As in the closed economy's model, the interest rate for the cryptocurrency depends on the equilibrium of supply and demand for the cryptocurrency. Given the amount of cryptocurrency supplied in the blockchain network, real income, and real interest rate, the demand for a cryptocurrency depends on the real income of the blockchain community and interest rate of the cryptocurrency. The equilibrium of a cryptocurrency market implies that, given the total amount of cryptocurrency supplied in the network, the interest rate is an increasing function of the output level. Hence, assuming a fixed supply of a cryptocurrency, with higher income, the demand for the cryptocurrency rises and decreases with the increase in the interest rate (the rate at which the cryptocurrency is borrowed and lent in the cryptocurrency exchange market).[1]

Value in Token Economies

The valuation of things that cannot be traded is a complex scenario. Untradeable things like true friendship are valued by the proxies like the time we give for the friendship, inviting dinner, or giving presents. Another example, respect or honor that can be won or reflected (which is exchanged in human interactions) is one of the human elements that have a value but cannot be monetized per se. Likewise, reputation commonly referred to as social capital is some other human element that can be built but not monetized.

The developments in trade, exchange, and coinage have resulted in the monetary valuation of economic resources. The price valuation of goods and services within the economy works only for monetized things. However, in reality, the world is full of many other human interactions that are priceless and hence not accurately captured through the conventional economic models. One example of this phenomenon is the practice of gifting, which is one of the nonmonetary social systems.

Gift economies are a much discussed and controversial topic among economists. The question of "why people give gifts?" is a topic that goes under behavioral economics. One of the key features of a gift is that it is priceless. For example, redacting price stickers from presents implies that the value of the gift, which is the willingness to give (the value of the item in the eyes of the bearer), is more important than willingness to pay (price) for that item. A gift in this sense has a value, but not a price.

When a market fails to function well (e.g., a monopolistic market, speculative market bubbles, or promotional gift for a competitive advantage), prices fail to capture value. In this case, the willingness to pay correspondence of utility (willingness to pay as a measure of consumers' satisfaction) fails. Hence, the notion of tokenization can also have enormous implications for the theoretical analysis of the gift economy, which has remained a gray field of study and the value theory in general.

Paying a monetary unit for an exchange of goods and services of value is one of the characteristics underlying currency as a store of value. There is nothing without value, but not everything can be directly monetized in the traditional form of monetary units. Thus, tokenization allows the valuation and transfer of value of any kind through a fungible unit of currency that is accepted within that specific token economy. Hence, in a token economy, we have a broader set of values that are accounted for using tokenization than solely a monetary value. The word "token" implies a sign or a symbol. In the language of a currency unit, tokens signify a currency (digital or physical) that does not have intrinsic value. For the fiat currencies, this feature of a currency is backed by a legal tender. On the other hand, digital tokens are quantified units of value built through a defined protocol. Tokens are fungible (unique) in that they can be used to indicate any form of value which cannot be quantified using the traditional form of monetary unit (e.g., we can tokenize the social capital of an individual through reputation token which is hard to capture through a traditional monetary unit). This introduces a new form of valuation for goods and services that have previously been undervalued or not measured in terms of a unit of currency. Tokenization makes it simple to value other forms of value that cannot be quantified through the traditional monetary units.

For example, a crowdsourcing platform can reward participants for every task they perform based on the reward model of the marketplace. However, how about a user liking or commenting on content from a social media or a user's social capital in a given network? How will that be monetized through a unit of currency? In this regard, tokenization brings a monetary unit measurement to the next level. Unlike the fiat currency, which is indivisible and unique, tokens are fungible, in that it is possible to exchange tokens with different specific forms of value. A token allows accounting for all values (social, natural, cultural, etc. capital). Digital currencies of this form are unique to their ecosystem and are programmable currency units in that terms and conditions for the exchange and use of the token are programmed, often on a smart contract to run the protocol.

Asset Valuations in the Token Economy

Agents' expectation affects the usability of a platform and thus the increase in the value of the token. Most token and cryptocurrency-based platforms feature an endogenous response of platform productivity depending on the size of the network. This is because increased usage of a token results in an appreciation of the token accompanied by an increase in its value. Thus, such nano-economies experience endogenous growth.[10] According to Cong et al. (2018), intermediate transactions on decentralized networks and their trading create an inter-temporal complementarity among users, generating a feedback loop between token valuation and platform adoption. In this nano-economic setting, agents' expectations about the native blockchain application on which the token is powered and the resulting network effect from the broader usability of the platform are significant contributors to the growth of the token-based nano-economies. In fact, late 2017 and beginning of 2018 has been the time where the price exploded, after which the decline in the interest of users resulted in a significant decline of the recent price of bitcoin.[11] The fluctuation in the price during this period has further financial explanations beyond this; however, here we are interested in the network effect that draws the interest down. Besides, the value of the token underlying the platform and thus the growth of the nano-economy are enhanced by positive network externalities and spillover effects. Network externality refers to the concept that a change in the product's value changes as the number of users of the product changes. Network externality is common in other forms of social media platforms like LinkedIn, Facebook, Twitter, YouTube, and so on in which the user base is significant in the early stages of their adoption.

Keeping all other factors constant and ignoring the current price of a token, let us see the demand and supply curves for a token with a network externality. The willingness to buy the token with the network externality depends on how many people use the platform. As stated earlier, the private benefit of each network participant (token user) increases as the number of participants

---

[10]In macroeconomic theory, Paul Romer (1990) developed a theory of economic growth with "endogenous" technological change. The theory explains how to construct an economy of profit-maximizing agents that endogenize technological progress. Economic growth, according to this theory, depends on population growth and capital accumulation. The robust prediction of the variant of this model is that an increase in population or an increase in the share of people working in the knowledge sector will increase economic growth.

[11]CNBC on June 4, 2018, ran a story, according to which "Google searches for 'bitcoin' nosedive 75% this year as interest in struggling cryptocurrency wanes." Quoting the significant price increase of about $20,000 in December 2017 and the following fluctuations in the price of bitcoin, they reported that the prices dropped in 2018 by roughly 50%, www.cnbc.com/2018/06/04/google-searches-for-bitcoin-nosedive-75-percent-this-year.html

increases. For the ease of presentation, we assume that network participants are homogenous (Liebowitz and Margolis, 1995). Figure 3-1 depicts the relationship between average network benefit (ANB) and the size of the network (measured in the number of users of the token). The average network benefit of a token user within the platform is an index for the willingness to pay for one unit of network participation, which is positively related to the number of the token users. Without the network effect, the average benefit of all the participants is fixed and thus is a horizontal ANB curve. Here, the marginal network benefit (MNB) is the change in total benefits to users of the token when an additional token user joins the network. Note that, with the network eternality, an additional user of the network results in an increase in the valuation of the token and the rise in the benefits for all users of the network.

Thus, the ANB curve lies below the MNB curve. There are arguments on whether the marginal cost of a token is near zero.[12] Here, by the marginal cost of a token, we mean the cost of hashing the added block containing this token, assuming a fixed cost of building the blockchain system running this application. The associated costs with the creation of a token and mining a new block depend on the consensus mechanism in play. For instance, in the proof-of-work (PoW) consensus mechanism, this cost of mining a new block (creating a new token) is the cost of electricity and hardware used for this purpose. Mining decisions are made if the expected return is higher than the cost of mining a new block. If the token's value increases, the profit of mining at the current difficulty increases. As a result, the number of miners increases, and the protocol increases the difficulty level. The marginal cost of bitcoin production is positively related to the computational power, electricity prices, and energy efficiency of the hardware and is directly associated with the price of bitcoin (Hayes, 2019). During periods of excess demand (e.g., the bitcoin price bubble of the late 2017 and early 2018), two main forces will be at play either individually or combined. These are the decline in the market price and/or the increase in the mining difficulty (in the case of a proof-of-work mechanism) to resolve the discrepancy. During the bitcoin bubble, the price fell and the mining difficulty rose simultaneously.

Thus, from the idea that marginal costs are associated with the price of the token, we can argue that the marginal network cost of a token increases with the number of tokens used by the network. At the equilibrium, the marginal benefit should equal marginal cost. Under a perfectly competitive market structure (which is the case in the decentralized networks of this kind), it holds that the marginal benefit is also equal to price. The optimal price, p^*, is the threshold below which a miner would not participate in the network.

---

[12]Especially, in the collaborative economic settings of the zero marginal cost society; see Rifkin (2014).

Thus, p* < MBN. The optimal network size under the given cost condition and optimal price of the token is q*. Even if there are a large number of miners (suppliers), a unit of token added is only by one of the winning blocks, thus keeping the equilibrium at q*, unlike other forms of decentralized networks which contain many suppliers of the network commodity (Liebowitz and Margolis, 1995). However, this discussion followed from the PoW mechanism; the general conclusion applies to most of the other token cases where the exchange/indirect usability of digital currencies like bitcoin and mainly ethereum are the typical cases in most token economies. Moreover, despite the different types of cryptoassets, generally speaking, a token of any kind is a means of exchange, store of value, and unit of account functions in its blockchain network.

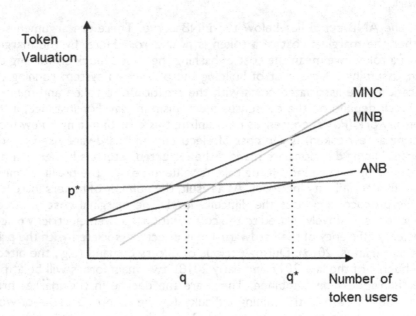

Figure 3-1. Demand and supply for a token with a network externality

Look at Table 3-1 on positive network externalities in cryptocurrencies and their respective prices (token valuation).

Table 3-1. Top 15 cryptocurrencies by market capitalization in USD as of March 19, 2020[13]

Name	Market Cap	Price	Volume (24h)	Circulating Supply
Bitcoin	$113,193,719,218	$6,192.97	$49,882,929,515	18,277,762 BTC
Ethereum	$15,003,539,578	$136.19	$15,830,871,054	110,164,022 ETH
XRP	$7,148,358,270	$0.163046	$2,427,087,345	43,842,625,397 XRP *
Tether	$4,658,625,726	$1.00	$62,045,605,131	4,642,367,414 USDT *
Bitcoin Cash	$4,092,496,762	$223.15	$4,975,368,443	18,339,625 BCH
Bitcoin SV	$2,870,477,716	$156.54	$2,907,288,042	18,336,740 BSV
Litecoin	$2,521,655,104	$39.21	$4,011,582,714	64,319,331 LTC
EOS	$2,098,479,412	$2.28	$3,486,829,871	921,041,644 EOS *
Binance Coin	$1,874,519,818	$12.05	$382,317,138	155,536,713 BNB *
Tezos	$1,152,356,758	$1.64	$175,951,633	704,220,499 XTZ *
UNUS SED LEO	$989,875,888	$0.990372	$9,930,413	999,498,893 LEO *
Stellar	$835,634,003	$0.041232	$444,658,405	20,266,506,673 XLM *
Cardano	$796,042,197	$0.030703	$115,256,676	25,927,070,538 ADA
Chainlink	$792,786,462	$2.27	$443,840,759	350,000,000 LINK *
TRON	$781,752,707	$0.011724	$1,241,341,891	66,682,072,191 TRX

A token being a currency unit facilitating the transaction within its nano-economy, we can augment the equation of exchange for its valuation.[14] This model can help for the abstraction of a token valuation. The equation of exchange[15] for a token is given as MV = PY, where M is the token supply (a token base, similar to the monetary base concept of fiat currency, the number of tokens in the nano-economy); V is the velocity of the token, measuring the number of times a token changed hands in a given time period; P is the price index measuring the average price of goods and services provided by the blockchain platform utilizing the native token (e.g., in the Plastic Bank,[16] a Vancouver-based blockchain platform, it means the average price of plastic waste); and Y is the total expenditure (total number of transactions within the nano-economy, a similar case for the plastic bank will be the aggregate volume of plastic waste sold in the Plastic Bank over a given time). Thus, the

---

[13]The asterisk (*) in the circulating supply column refers to "Not Mineable" cryptocurrencies. Data available at Coinmarketcap.com.

[14]Burniske, C. (2017). "Cryptoasset Valuation." Medium, September 24, 2017.

[15]Spindt, P. A. (1985). Money is what money does: Monetary aggregation and the equation of exchange. *Journal of Political Economy*, 93(1), 175–204

[16]www.plasticbank.com/

term PY represents the total exchange value of the Plastic Bank over a given time in terms of the native tokens (the gross domestic product of the nano-economy in the conventional macroeconomic terms).

Another essential factor to take into account in the valuation process is the discount rate,[17] coefficient of risk aversion, and the network externality. The preceding model is limited in that it does not account for the latter two factors.

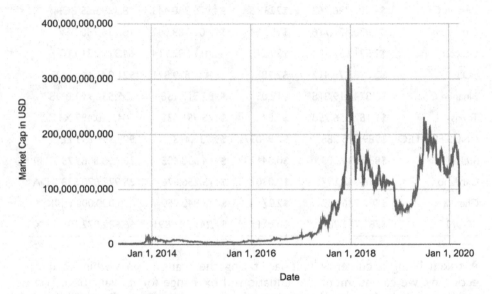

Figure 3-2. Market capitalization: the total USD value of bitcoin supply in circulation, as of March 19, 2020.[18] The figure implies the monetary base, M, of Bitcoin

---

[17]Burniske (2017) rethinks the conventional asset pricing discounted cash flow (DCF) model mixed with equations of exchange for the cryptoasset valuations, "…using a discounted cash flow (DCF) analysis is not suitable. Instead, valuing cryptoassets requires setting up models structurally similar to what a DCF would look like, with a projection for each year, but instead of revenues, margins and profits, the equation of exchange is used to derive each year's current utility value (CUV). Then, since markets price assets based on future expectations, one must discount a future utility value back to the present to derive a rational market price for any given year."

[18]Data available at https://coinmarketcap.com/currencies/bitcoin/historical-data/?start=20120320&end=20200320

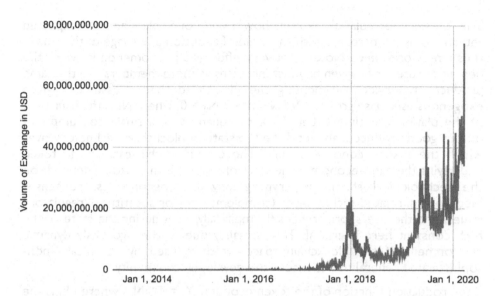

Figure 3-3. Bitcoin USD exchange trade volume as of March 19, 2020, approximating the PY term of the exchange equation for the Bitcoin's native blockchain protocol[19]

From our discussion of asset valuations in this section, we have observed the network externality a token economy exhibits and its implied effect in the token valuations. In this regard, the endogenous growth model is ideal for capturing the user base effect in the growth of the token nano-economy. Following the nonrivalrous idea-based theory of increasing returns[20] (which is a variant of Romer's endogenous growth model), the blockchain platform can be used at any scale of production after being developed. Given a fixed cost of building the blockchain system that runs the tokenized application, the standard replication argument implies that subsequent value generation occurs with constant returns to scale. Including the blockchain system development, production is characterized by increasing returns.

There are two key factors that drive per capita growth in the token nano-economy: network size and increasing returns to scale (growth in the network size results in growth of the scale of the token economy, where the increasing returns to scale of the value of the nano-economy translates the growth in scale into growth in per capita income) (Jones, 1997).

---

[19]https://coinmarketcap.com/currencies/bitcoin/historical-data/?start=20 120320&end=20200320

[20]Jones, C. I. (1997). *Population and ideas: A theory of endogenous growth* (No. w6285). National Bureau of Economic Research

The following formulation explains how a value of a token and the expected returns to users increases with the scale of adoption and usage of the token, thus a network effect. Note: a network effect is a phenomenon in which the benefit for users of a given product increases as more members use the same product or service. Augmenting the idea-based theory, assume a given exogenous user base growth, $\dot{N}/N = n > 0, N_0 > 0$, where Nt is the user base of the platform at time t. Let Y_t be the quantity of a single consumption/output good produced, and let T_t be the state of blockchain technology over which the token economy is built. The output in this case is the token underlying the nano-economy. The state of a blockchain protocol depends on the technological shocks in cryptography, cryptoeconomics, consensus mechanisms, related technologies (complementary or substitute), regulatory issues, and the users' preferences.[21] Empirically, considering the state of the tech constant here is crucial. This is mainly due to the rigorously dynamic environment of the blockchain space which is used by technically non-sophisticated general users, except the developer community.

The production function of the token economy $Y_t = T^{\sigma}_t N_{ut}$, where N_{ut} is the user base of the platform (including the investors/token holders and those working for the validation of the transaction taking place in the blockchain platform) and $\sigma > 0$ imposes the assumption of increasing returns to scale. Holding the state of blockchain protocol constant, there are constant returns to scale: doubling the quantity of the user base (here only N_{ut}) will double output (the value of the platform). Thus, as the number of the token users in a blockchain-based platform increases, the value of the token underlying the nano-economy increases. Because the protocol over which the token economy runs is nonrivalrous, the existing technology T can be used at any scale of token production, leading to increasing returns in T and N together. Production function for ideas—the model for the blockchain protocol development and improvement in the consensus mechanisms—$\dot{T} = \delta N_{dt}$, $T_0 > 0$, where $\dot{T}$ represents the rate of changes (advances) in the blockchain technology and DLTs over time, N_{dt} is the number of developer community working to improve the blockchain protocol and the underlying consensus mechanism, and $\delta > 0$ is a parameter quantifying the number of new protocol designs and improvements in the consensus mechanism the developer community adds to the nano-economy. The total nano-economy network size at a given time, t, is the summation of the developer community (N_{dt}) and users of the platform (N_{ut}): $N_t = N_{ut} + N_{dt}$. Consider that a fraction of the nano-economy network, w, also work as developers: $N_{dt} = wN_t$ and $N_{ut} = (1 - w)N_t$, where $w \in (0, 1)$. Thus, the per capita nano-economy income, $y_t \equiv Y_t / N_t = T^{\sigma}_t (1 - w)$. Therefore, the growth of per capita income of the nano-economy, $\dot{y}/y$: $g_y = \sigma g_T$. Note: $\dot{T}/T = \delta wN_t /T$. From this, in order for the

---

[21]Cong, L. W., Li, Y., and Wang, N. (2018). Tokenomics: Dynamic Adoption and Valuation

blockchain technology protocol over which the nano-economy application runs to be stable (constant), the term N_t/T should be constant implying g_T is constant k. Therefore, the long-run per capita income growth rate of the nano-economy is given by $g_y = \sigma k$. For network size growth and increasing returns, per capita income growth is proportional to the rate of network size growth and the increasing returns to scale is indicated by the factor of proportionality, σ. This implies the expected return to the token users is proportional to the network size growth, that is, innovation diffusion and adoption of the token at a scale.

This implies that long-run per capita growth in the value of the nano-economy is the result of a growth in the network size and increasing returns. The nonrivalry nature of the distributed blockchain protocol and developments around the technology's consensus mechanism implies that the token nano-economy exhibits increasing returns to scale. As the size of the network increases, the size of the developer community increases, thus resulting in more advancements of the blockchain protocol over which the nano-economy runs. Moreover, some of the robustness of the consensus mechanisms over which such distributed systems run depends on the size of the network (e.g., the proof-of-stake consensus mechanism). To conclude, as Cong et al. (2018) stated, in under any consensus mechanism, a network effect plays a crucial role. For example, in proof-of-stake consensus mechanism, it is vital that the stake is not concentrated in the hands of a single user for the majority rule to apply. Thus, the user base needs to be large and dispersed in order to hold a majority of stake and have an efficient consensus. Likewise, in the proof-of-work consensus mechanism like the one underlying bitcoin, more miners potentially deliver faster and more reliable confirmation of transactions, and miners' participation in turn depends on the size of the user base. The user base and scale of adoption reflect the general usefulness of the platform. As more people participate in a given blockchain platform, more transactions take place including token exchange, mining, or any other forms of transaction validation which increases the value of the underlying token. Moreover, as Cong et al. (2018) noted, a greater user base lures greater resources and research and development into the blockchain community, accelerating the technological progress.

Cryptocurrency Market Depth and Efficiency

Do cryptocurrency markets' pricing satisfy the efficient market hypothesis? The cryptocurrency market is inefficient where recent bubbles and volatility have been experienced in these programmable currencies (especially, Bitcoin). Moreover, investments in ICOs are commonly based on speculation. There are controversies on whether the price of cryptocurrencies fully reflects the available information, thus satisfying the efficient market hypothesis (see, e.g., Brauneis and Mestel, 2018, and Caporale et al., 2018, who found that these markets are inefficient and Jakub, 2015, who argues the other way around).[22]

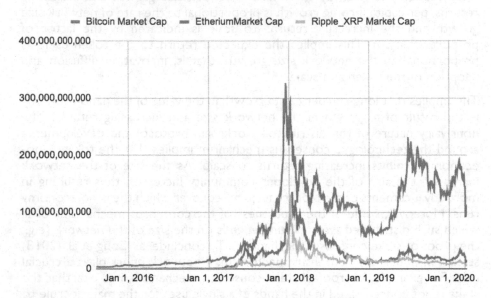

Figure 3-4. Cryptocurrency market capitalization for Bitcoin, Ethereum, and Ripple, respectively, as of March 20, 2020[23]

Cryptocurrency market depth shows how easy it is to get in or get out from a security market (e.g., in relation to liquidity and volume of bitcoin market, if the market is deep, then a large volume of pending bid and ask orders keep prices unchanged for a large order). However, a high volume of a cryptocurrency exchange does not necessarily mean a deep market where a potential mismatch of orders can create high volatility in a cryptocurrency valuation. Cryptocurrency market is a shallow market because many people are willing to trade with high frequency. Market depth for the cryptocurrency is affected by the velocity of cryptocurrencies as a medium of exchange. Moreover, the underlying cryptocurrency protocols affect the depth of these markets. In the ethereum network, GHOST (Greedy Heaviest Observed Subtree) protocol of financing blocks that are simultaneously created and are off the main chain

---

[22]CNBC on December 22, 2017, reported "Bitcoin-mania stock volatility shows the fallacy of 'efficient markets'" following the Bitcoin bubble that their emotion beyond rational decision-making drives investors, www.cnbc.com/2017/12/22/bitcoin-mania-stock-volatility-shows-the-fallacy-of-efficient-markets.html, accessed on April 2, 2020.

[23]Data available at Coinmarketcap.com.

(orphan blocks) can inefficiently inflate prices. Besides, there are more gray fields in the cryptocurrency market. For example, in the "zero address accounts" (Ethereum's 0x0 accounts),[24] a large number of transactions are sent to these unknown either externally owned account (EOA) or contract addresses where millions of dollars are locked.

Cryptoeconomics

In this section, we will cover the state of Blockchain-powered networks from the economic point of view. The newly growing field of cryptoeconomics that deals with the incentive analysis of the distributed ledger technologies mainly focuses on the core economic concept of cost minimization (cryptoeconomic security margin optimization) and profit maximization (social welfare of the network in general). In this regard, the economic characterization of such distributed networks will help analyze such networks using the economic models which are employed in the analysis of economic units.

Distributed ledger technologies, from the perspective of cryptoeconomics, have two main components: consensus algorithms and smart contracts. Besides the cryptographic tools, the theoretical underpinnings in the currently emerging field of the cryptoeconomics are one of the key engines driving the developments in blockchain technology (Davidson et al., 2016; Pilkington, 2016; and Catalini and Gans, 2016). Cryptoeconomics refers to the field of study that utilizes reward models and cryptography for well-functioning coordination of a distributed network. More specifically, it is a line of study for the incentive analysis of distributed networks like the blockchain-powered platforms. A closely related field of study in this regard is the reverse game theory, mechanism design, social choice theory with smart contract technology, and behavioral economics.

This has a more significant implication for the governance mechanisms of the distributed networks based on the blockchain technologies in general. The conventional blockchain technology protocols revolve around the mechanisms to sustain a consensus for the distributed networks. Distributed networks like the blockchain depend on a self-governance principle. Such defines the coordination of the agents according to the protocol. Block authorization or verification in the transaction record process of the conventional blockchain networks is accompanied by incentives. These incentive schemes are designed in a way that thwarts anarchy using different consensus mechanisms, some of which include proof of work, proof of stake, proof of value, and so on.

---

[24]See etherscan at https://etherscan.io/address/0x0000000000000000000000000000000 0000000000000

Conventional Consensus Mechanisms

The Byzantine Generals Problem (an agreement problem) is a term used for inconsistent failure detection by the actors in a distributed computer network system. It describes a situation where a system failure in a distributed network leads to imperfect information. The problem is related to a story about the Byzantine army surrounding a city with a mission to attack the city. The decision to mount an effective unilateral attack or retreat is made through a distributed consensus.

Variation in the individual decisions may have the risk of failure, or it is costly. Thus, either a coordinated attack or coordinated retreat is the best strategy to follow. Hence, the coordination protocol design in this particular situation should take into account the best strategy that will result in consensus. However, the presence of malicious generals complicates potential coordination. The generals might be divided into a position to either attack or retreat. Malicious generals, who are part of the Byzantine army, can use the diversity signaling two different commands of a retreat and attack to the two groups of generals which results in uncoordinated war and weakening of the Byzantine army. Another challenge for potential coordination results from the geographical disparities. The messages sent through messengers that cross through the city may fail to be delivered (say, if the messenger is caught or the message is tampered with). In this case, the Byzantine fault tolerance consensus can be reached only if the honest generals achieve the majority vote (retreat or attack signal). If the message delivery failure is the majority, then a pre-set strategy is followed, say, attack.

Computer system analysts use this story to illustrate the problem of reaching a consensus in a distributed network of computers. The analysis is further used for the protocol development and mechanism design in a distributed setting of digital information exchanges.

Similarly, cryptoeconomics has a lot to fetch from the history and story of human interactions of this form. Tomas Sedlacek, in his book *Economics of Good and Evil: The Quest for Economic Meaning from Gilgamesh to Wall Street,* argues that economic discipline is beyond the abstract mathematical modeling; it is instead a discipline that is framed based on human philosophy, art, culture, history, myth, religion, and values. The book provides an insight into the history of economic thought starting from the "the epic of Gilgamesh," set in ancient Mesopotamia, to the modern mainstream economics describing the economic taught beyond mathematical inquiry and abstraction.

There are some insights that the cryptoeconomic principle can borrow from historical event records and myths. For instance, an interesting consensus mechanism is presented in the old testament story of the book of Judges 7, where a consensus was reached for a coordinated unilateral attack by "God's army." The story presents Gideon's 300 chosen mighty Israelites crew and the defeat of the Midianites, the Nation of Graspers. In this story, Gideon started by filtering out unwanted warriors for this purpose and reduced the numbers of thousands of warriors who showed up into only 300 through a repeated filtering mechanism. Then, he followed the attack strategy provided to him by God, dividing the warriors into groups of three. Accordingly, during the night of the attack, the 300 Israelites' warriors encircle the Midianite camp, and following Gideon's signal, they created a simultaneous noise by blowing their trumpets, breaking their pots with loud noises, and waving their torches. The coordinated noise created the impression of a huge army surrounding the Midianites, which resulted in their defeat. The association of this consensus mechanism with cryptoeconomics can show us how the filtering and the incentive mechanism imposed within this protocol led to a victory of the Israelites.

Any mechanism design that aims to create a self-enforcing mechanism with a consideration for a cryptographic algorithm implementation should answer the following key questions:

- What are the key incentives to verify a transaction?

- How to incentivize honest behavior of adding a valid block on the main consensus chain?

- What are the constraints to consider when analyzing the incentive dynamics in the network: reward and cost of a malicious actor (balancing incentives)?

- What is the optimal reward or penalty that guarantees self-governance within the network?

Once these questions are addressed, the incentive mechanism can be analyzed based on the behavior of the actors in the network. The security of a protocol designed based on the cryptoeconomic principle is measured by the cryptoeconomic security margin (CESM). CESM is an economic measure of security of a network which estimates the cost/economic loss of malicious behavior for violating a protocol's guarantee. The higher the CESM, the more secure the network is; this is guaranteed through a robust penalty assignment mechanism. A distributed network using blockchain technology mainly relies on the consensus algorithms for a value co-creation purpose. The consensus mechanism in this setting stands for the agreement of the distributed nodes in the network for an update of a given state. Hence, the main work in the design of a business model for a blockchain technology lies on how a consensus can be reached inclusively. In the case of the Israelites' army, deviation from the Gideon's command could result in loss of their harvest and their life; thus, every warrior agrees on a unilateral attack after the filter. An additional incentive scheme in this scenario was the belief that God (a superpower) had full trust in the system. Thus, cryptoeconomics, by definition, refers to the mechanism design that helps guarantee the consensus in such a distributed setting.

Some of the conventional consensus mechanisms employed in these systems include

1. *Byzantine fault tolerance:* Consensus is reached based on the information signed by all validators whose network membership is centrally approved.

2. *Federated Byzantine Agreement:* Consensus depends on the collective knowledge of a set of trusted validators whose individual agreement matters for the consensus.

3. *Deposit-based consensus:* Relies on a skin in the game principle where validation of a transaction that is not in line with the chain, whether the main chain or off the main chain, is approved by the GHOST arbitrator (Greedy Heaviest Observed Subtree) costs a security deposit.

4. *Proof of work (PoW):* Demands hashing power for verification of a transaction that ends in the main consensus chain.

5. *Proof of stake (PoS):* Verification of a transaction (mining a block) requires initial consumption of validator's coin (kernel) in that same block to be validated according to the hash function, and the signature of the block by the bonded validator is rewarded if it ends in the chain with the highest total coin consumed.

6. *Proof of value (PoV):* A social operating system that relies on reputation mechanism and reward of native coins.

7. *Proof-of-elapsed time (PoET):* Requires time and capital investment like that of the PoW, except that instead of puzzle-based authorization like in the PoW, it relies on a central trust execution and authentication; it is a distributed model that relies on a centralized leadership.

8. *Proof of burn:* Is a non-reimbursable coin sent to an address that gives the privilege to authorize a block on a random basis. The probability of mining the next block increases with the amount of coin in which a miner burn and continuation of the mining process require continual coin burning like an investment in hashing power for the PoW.

There are two general theories which cryptoeconomics borrow to achieve coordination in distributed networks like the Blockchain:

1. *Cooperative game theory:* A category of games that involve competition between groups/coalitions in which cooperation is achieved through external enforcement. In the first stage of a coordinated choice model, a player decides whether to join the coalition or not. The second stage is to maximize the total welfare of the coalition and individual utilities.

2. *Non-cooperative game theory:* A category of games that involve competition between players and in which cooperation is achieved through self-enforcing mechanisms. The uncoordinated choice model assumes that all players have individual incentives. We can consider two main self-enforcing solution concepts to achieve cooperation under this category of games. The bribing attacker model also works under the assumption of the uncoordinated choice model with a potential bribing attacker (with a nil cost) that thwarts the system. Hence, in the case of bribing attacker, a cryptoeconomic mechanism starts by considering the cost and budget constraints of the potential briber.

    - *Coordination protocol:* A self-enforcing protocol with a coordination mechanism that is designed based on the players' preference, for example, a Vickrey auction.

    - *Co-utile protocol:* A self-enforcing protocol without a coordination mechanism in which cooperation is achieved only through a self-enforcing and mutually beneficial interaction between the players.

Developing a reward model in a cryptoeconomic analysis starts with the abstraction of the expected level of coordination and assumptions about the cost constraint and budget plan of a potential attack. A coordination protocol can be achieved through adjustment of utilities of the game using rewards, punishments, or utility transfer such that individuals are fairly treated and that optimal network value is derived. The goal is to maximize the social welfare function of the platform on which a cryptocurrency is based using a robust consensus mechanism. This is a constrained optimization subject to incentive compatibility, cost of an attack, rationality, feasibility constraint, and resource constraint. The utility function of each economic unit in the platform defines the platform's social welfare function, which indicates the general well-being of the economic state in the network. A given mechanism over a platform maximizes the social welfare of the network if it is Pareto efficient. Otherwise, there exists another mechanism of resource allocation that generates a strictly greater utility for at least one economic unit in the network.

The voting process to agree about a given state in the blockchain network is as follows:

1. A total of K unconfirmed transactions in the network arise.

2. Given a set of validators, N, in the network, there are $M \subseteq N$ successful miners mining block B containing transactions $k \in K$.

3. *Miner* $J \in M$ who mines block B first gets a reward and block B is recorded in the main chain with a total of M number of votes (consensus over the state of block B).

4. All N/J get no reward from this transaction, that is, a total of all other mined block except B goes to the unconfirmed transactions pool and the process continues in this fashion for all transaction validation.

See Figure 3-5 for a simplified presentation of a single transaction verification process without a loss of generality. In the figure, the transition verification passes through a hashing and encryption process in order for it to be recorded in the chain of the existing blocks of transactions. The transaction fee is paid to miner J, who adds a valid block to the main chain first from the set of successful miners M. The consensus about a given state in the network can be represented as a market in which the state over which consensus is drawn is a commodity, and the number of votes validating the state can be considered as the price for that state. Accordingly, as in the invisible hand principle, a robust consensus mechanism can lead the distributed free market system to equilibrium.

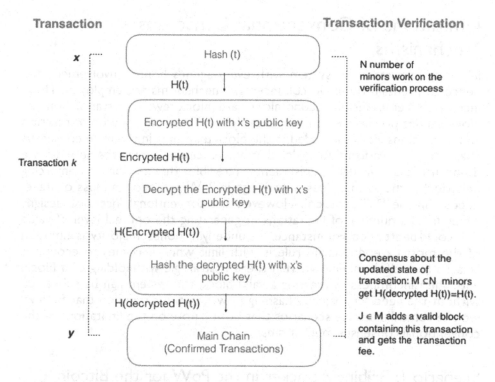

Figure 3-5. A simplified abstraction of the consensus process on a blockchain for the verification of a transaction t between x and y

A reward model in a mechanism design minimizes attack by making potential attacks expensive (through punishment that raises the cost of potential attack). For example, in the PoW, the cost of a 51% attack or cost of any deviation to any miner chains other than the main chain is made expensive through a hash power requirement. Likewise, in the PoS, the cost of deviation to the miner chain is equated to the amount of coin burned in the block, skin in the game. One comparison between the consensus mechanisms can be made by comparing the utility functions of each economic unit which is a function of their respective profit functions. For example, the profit function of a miner in the PoS mechanism is a function of the hash rate defined by the miner's relative computational power, difficulty factor, block mining time, block reward, and the transaction fees. On the other hand, the profit function of a miner in the PoS mechanism is a function of the stake (security deposit), block mining time, and the transaction fee.

Limitations of Conventional Consensus Mechanisms

In order to sustain the system with every agent's honest involvement and hence to maintain the protocol, incentive mechanisms are employed. These incentive schemes include economic reward (block reward or transaction fee/ block renting privilege which, respectively, is for the coin creation transaction and other transactions included in the block that ends in the main consensus chain) and app/platform utility. In addition, malicious peers in the network are disincentivized through punishments (credible threats for self-enforcing behavior) in the form of loss of privilege in PoW protocol and loss of stake/ deposit in the PoS protocol. However, the conventional incentive designs suffer from a number of limitations in generating the optimal level of value that could be attained. For instance, the underlying honest majority assumption of the most extended chain rule is with limit when it comes to economic attacks like selfish mining wherein there is strategic withholding of a block; with the randomness of creating a valid block, the system can be subverted without the need for majority hashing power. In the discussion that follows, we see some illustrative scenarios that posit a note on the limitations of the conventional consensus mechanisms.

Scenario 1: Bribing Attacker in the PoW for the Bitcoin Mining

According to the PoW reward scheme, a block is valid if it ends in the main consensus chain, and verification of this valid block is accompanied by a block reward in BTC. Under both coordinated and uncoordinated choice models, one has the incentive to add a valid block (on the main chain where the majority adds) because she gets the block reward of 12.5 BTC (at time of writing) only if she is in line with the others (panel a). All other miners have the same incentive to verify a valid block transaction for the same reason, and hence the main chain consensus is guaranteed. Note that, under the PoW scheme, the cryptoeconomic security margin (the cost of adding invalid block) is the hashing power consumed with no any other accompanied punishment. The mechanism is computationally expensive. See Figure 3-6 for an example of mining game.

Transaction Verification	J adds a block to chain A	J adds a block to chain B	Transaction Verification	J adds a block to chain A	J adds a block to chain B
Others add a block to chain A	12.5BTC	0BTC	Others add a block to chain A	12.5BTC	0BTC
Others add a block to chain B	0BTC	12.5BTC	Others add a block to chain B	12.5BTC + β	12.5BTC

| (a) | (b) |

Figure 3-6. Mining game

Under a bribing attacker model (panel b), with a bribing attack budget of β units (e.g., subsidized mining pools), the payoff of the validator for adding a block is presented in the following table. Note that there is no cost to the attacker to extend her chain.

Scenario 2: The Soft Fork Penalty Assignment

In distributed networks, a hard fork refers to a change in either the consensus rules or protocol and building a different history of records. A typical example of a hard fork is the case for the decentralized autonomous organization (DAO) which deployed a different smart contract in the ethereum history. This virtual blockchain-based company (a global distributed crowdfunding business model with autonomous governance for blockchain projects) raised about $150 million in less than a month of operation before it was hacked resulting in a loss of about 40% of the funds. For DAO contract's reentrancy attack, a hard fork was the last resort solution which the ethereum foundation took in order to recover the stolen funds to the native account.[25]

On the other hand, a soft fork builds over the same history of records under a given protocol. Consider the soft forking scenario in the longest chain rule. Block reward is assigned for the block that follows the longest consensus chain. Only those transactions on the longest consensus chain are valid. Now, consider a soft fork where two blocks B and C appeared making two different branches of the chain (subtree) due to strategic actions of the miners or network faults (latency or failure). Given the immediate predecessor block A (with an existing reward +1), the conventional mechanism blindly assigns a penalty of 0 in PoW and −1 in PoS mechanisms making the transactions in both the soft fork blocks invalid regardless.[26]

---

[25]See a blog post by Vitalik Buterin, the co-founder of Ethereum, on the completion of the hard fork (July 20, 2016), https://blog.ethereum.org/2016/07/20/hard-fork-completed/, accessed on April 2, 2020.

[26]Bentov et al. (2016)

Then, the protocol continues by rewarding (+1) to the next block D that makes one of the two branches longer. Here, we see that there is a possible unfair penalty assignment to either B or C. Hence, is there any other penalty assignment mechanism (other than the blind punishment) that identifies and penalizes the malicious one in case it appears that the soft fork happened only due to either B or C, but not both? Avoiding such unfair penalty assignments requires to preselect validators before any possible fork. This in turn depends on whether all the nodes are simultaneously online, allowing for a secure selection of validator in the same way for each block on both chains. Besides, even if the online availability issue is manageable, the system could still suffer from other vicious circle problems, specifically successive validators' collusion risk in a chain for a 51% attack.[27]

Scenario 3: Market Concentration Hashing Power

The cryptocurrency market is a competitive market with newly growing coins being continually introduced to the market. Unlike the early ages of the bitcoin, the market share for the bitcoin has significantly reduced with a shift of investment in the newer cryptocurrencies (Iwamura et al., 2014). In addition to other market powers and security issues, the hard fork in the bitcoin is one of the reasons for its reduced market share. On the other hand, the consensus mechanism within the bitcoin market itself bears some market concentration in the hands of a few mining pools with more substantial hashing power, mainly in areas with relatively cheaper electricity. This is similar to the principle of higher odds of winning with buying a greater share of tickets in a lottery game. The same thing happens for the stake pools in the PoS consensus mechanism. This diverts the truly distributed nature of the network on which this cryptocurrency is based. For example, see Figure 3-7.

---

[27]https://github.com/ethereum/wiki/wiki/Proof-of-Stake-FAQ

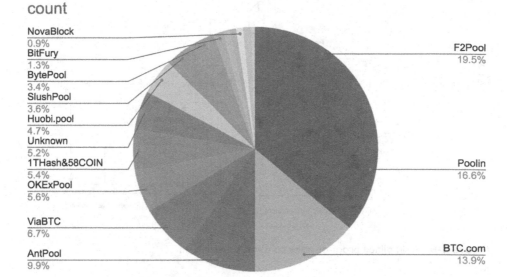

Figure 3-7. Hash rate distribution among largest Bitcoin mining pools as of March 20, 2020[28]

Scenario 4: Nothing at Stake vs. Sufficient Skin in the Game for the PoS Consensus Mechanism

A proof of stake is a consensus mechanism that uses stakes of native tokens by potential validators (see Figure 3-8 to understand a simplified workflow in a PoS). A fork for a double-spend of a digital good (rewriting of a transaction history) does not cost if a malicious agent has nothing at stake in that block. Still, even if there is some stake in the block and the return from the fork is higher than the coinage burned in the stake, there will be an incentive to subvert the system. Hence, what is the threshold stake that can guarantee sufficient skin in the game? The burned stake (money) within the proof of stake does not go to anyone (wasted money). Hence, issues can arise on the ways to transfer the burned money at stake to some other party within the network. Similarly, there is a concern on the length of time the money under this consensus mechanism has to be at stake.

[28]www.blockchain.com/en/pools

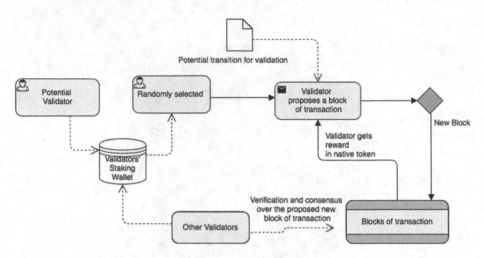

Figure 3-8. A simplified proof-of-stake consensus mechanism

Scenario 5: Tragedy of the Commons and Market Failure in Distributed Networks

As opposed to the centralized monetary policy, the cryptocurrency economy is governed by the algorithmic setting of open source code that defines the money supply and its value in circulation. Unlike the unlimited supply of fiat currencies, the supply for some of the cryptocurrencies like bitcoin and Litcoin is limited. The total number of bitcoin in circulation as of the writing of this book is about 16,898,563 BTC out of the total expected supply of 21 million. As a result, the block reward scheme (halving every four years) for transaction verification will shift to transaction fees as the total number of bitcoins get exhaustively mined through time. As compared to the transaction fees, the block reward generates a higher return to the miners. The shift in the incentive dynamics through time can result in the tragedy of the commons for a shared resource. In the context of the digital economy, such decentralized networks of the unregulated digital assets with open source code are prone to the commons, that is, contrary to the common good of the network; individual miners act selfishly with a motive to maximize their profits in the transaction verification process. For instance, the incentive for mining might reduce and hence subvert the efficiency of the network. With lesser miners in the network, there will be higher market concentration, censorship of transactions, and an increase in transaction fees (a similar scenario for a different reason arises with the block ceiling issue will be further discussed in Chapter 4).

Governance of Decentralized Web 3.0 Economies and Open Source Projects: The Case of the QuadrigaCX

The transition from the traditional economic system to the digital economic system has created a new age in the history of economic thought. For instance, the developments in the digital currencies, unlike fiat currencies, have challenged the traditional thoughts about the issuing of a currency by a central trusted party, the central bank. On the other hand, governance and regulation are one of the most critical issues arising in relation to the decentralized platforms of the Web 3.0 economies in light of the institutional economics and public choice theories (Brown, 2019; Guo and Liang, 2016; Atzori, 2015; and Yeoh, 2017). In this section, by taking a specific case of the Quadriga hack (a typical example of the unregulated world of cryptocurrencies), I will highlight key challenges in the regulation of the decentralized Web 3.0 economies.

Quadriga was one of the largest Canadian cryptocurrency exchange startups with a platform for storing and exchanging of various digital tokens and coins (including Bitcoin, Litecoin, Bitcoin Cash, Bitcoin SV, and Ether). The exchange, according to the 2019 Ernst and Young's report,[29] is affiliated with three main legal entities (Quadriga Fintech Solutions Corp., Whiteside Capital Corporation, and 0984750 B.C. LTD.) doing business as QuadrigaCX and Quadriga Coin Exchange. Following the controversial death of its founder and CEO Gerald Cotten in December 2018, QuadrigaCX collapsed. This resulted in a central point of failure wherein customers being unable to access their digital wallets with the loss of passwords and the underlying protocol, which were solely handled by Cotten. As a result, the online startup was insolvent with a liquidity problem. Following this, tens of thousands of clients who were online users of this cryptocurrency exchange platform came forward with a claim for the loss of investments in millions of dollars.

Moreover, with the artificially created user accounts and multiple aliases, the CEO mixed personal and corporate finance. The controversial death incident resulted in the freezing of about $180 million CAD in cryptocurrency exchanges. Early April 2019, the three affiliate entities were issued a Termination and Bankruptcy Assignment Order under the Bankruptcy and Insolvency Act.

---

[29]Available at https://documentcentre.eycan.com/eycm_library/Quadriga%20 Fintech%20Solutions%20Corp/English/CCAA/1.%20Monitor's%20Reports/6.%20 Fifth%20Report%20of%20the%20Monitor/Fifth%20Report%20of%20the%20 Monitor%20dated%20June%2019,%202019.PDF

As there was no physical presence for the company other than Cotton's home office, jurisdiction was one of the issues in dealing with this case at the court that later relied on Nova Scotia as a base jurisdiction in consideration of the location of Cotton's home office. The other major issue in open source projects (including the cryptocurrency industry) is that there is no defined set of regulations specific to these industries. Moreover, cryptocurrency exchange markets rely on third-party payment channels for liquidation without any traditional bank accounts, which creates a limit in their physical presence and traceability. In the traditional financial market regulations, one of the means of customer protection is setting of capital requirements which implies that the owners of financial institutions hold substantially more assets than the value of the investment in the financial market (like the value of a bank deposit). In contrast to this, as of April 12, 2019, Quadriga owned about $28.6 million CAD in assets as compared to about $215.7 million CAD it held from investors.[30] Further, with the limited physical traceability, some argue that the business was a scam that with cold wallets (deemed to be created by the founder for "offline security reasons") lacked records on the blockchain, thus making it suspicious.[31] There also are several disputes surrounding the veracity of the death of the CEO—who held the key to millions of dollars in his brain—the Quadriga conspiracy.[32]

The immediate challenge for cryptocurrency users is the lack of a clearly defined customer protection framework that takes into account the developments toward investment in such open source projects and exchange markets. A more profound challenge in this regard is the limited physical presence of such digital platforms and further geolocation issues for legal jurisdictions. An interesting issue to be taken into account by regulatory frameworks in relation to such open source projects is about the sophistication level of investors in such platforms. Usually, in such projects, most investors are not that sophisticated in understanding the underlying smart contracts and the dynamics of assets of the platform as are such open source projects. Thus, depending on their geographic jurisdiction, a strict disclosure duty and

---

[30]See Ernst and Young's report (a trustee overseeing bankruptcy proceedings for the Quadriga cryptocurrency exchange) on the bankruptcy of Quadriga Fintech Solutions Corp., Whiteside Capital Corporation, and 0984750 B.C. LTD. of the city of Halifax in the Province of Nova Scotia, www.scribd.com/document/409470435/Trustee-Report-FINAL, accessed on April 2, 2020.

[31]On February 9, 2019, CBC reported the incident with a running head "Quadriga mystery deepens with little evidence of cold wallets containing $250M," www.cbc.ca/news/canada/nova-scotia/quadriga-mystery-deepens-with-little-evidence-of-cold-wallets-containing-250m-1.5011573, accessed on April 2, 2020.

[32]On February 4, 2019, Bloomberg reported the news with a heading "Crypto CEO Dies Holding Only Passwords That Can Unlock Millions in Customer Coins," www.bloomberg.com/news/articles/2019-02-04/crypto-exchange-founder-dies-leaves-behind-200-million-problem, accessed on April 2, 2020.

collateralized debt obligations need to be imposed on such open source projects and exchange markets. An important thing to consider is also to answer the question of how such open source projects like the crypto exchange markets get backed when there are no bank accounts to which they link. A similar issue is highlighted for the stable coins (see the discussion under Facebook's stable coin initiative, Libra, in Chapter 5).

Moreover, there are ethical challenges in the decentralized Web 3.0 economies. The most interesting ethics issue is what duty such open source digital platforms have to their variety of stakeholders and investors. This depends on the platforms' specific roles (e.g., cryptocurrency platforms like that of Libra, identifying whether the platform is acting as an issuer, a trader, or an agent working for investors is vital).

The Quadriga hack is a typical example of the regulatory challenges and loopholes around the decentralized Web 3.0 economies and open source projects. Equal with the challenges in regulating digital platforms is the countervailing effects of vague regulatory frameworks on the potential developments and advancements of the Web 3.0 economy. The regulatory concerns connected with such digital platforms are still controversial with some playing a countervailing effect on the advancements in the area. Brown (2019), in his cryptocurrency and financial regulations analysis, presents the tension in the regulations of the cryptocurrency market, highlighting the rejection of many cryptocurrency-based projects by the SEC. See, for example, the shutdown of a stable coin startup, Basis, due to regulatory constraints faced from the US Securities and Exchange Commission (SEC).[33] Recommendations are for the regulatory bodies to understand the tech under consideration in order to achieve salient regulatory goals and also follow tech neutral approaches not to limit advancements in the digital space.

On the other hand, new business models give rise to new challenges and uncertainties. Thus, in keeping a healthy digital economy space, such marketplaces and open source projects operating in the dynamically evolving technological business environment need to cope with new regulatory and legal codes.

In conclusion, many other questions arise as far as the regulation of the decentralized platforms is concerned. For instance, even if the underlying principles of decentralization of platforms is the notion under the Web 3.0 economies, with new developments in the digital economic system are the creation of big players in the industry space. Thus, another concern is to manage regulation where such big players can still lobby to their best interests.

---

[33]See the interview with the Intangible Labs CEO, Nader Al-Naji, to Forbes on December 13, 2018, www.forbes.com/sites/michaeldelcastillo/2018/12/13/sec-rules-kill-cryptos-top-funded-startup/#5e1fc8b2918c, accessed on April 2, 2020.

Moreover, with the potential global level operation of these like networks and existence of arbitrage opportunities, standardization and harmonization of international regulations are vital, thus bridging the gap that might arise when malicious open source projects can exploit regulatory havens. However, as it is common in most of the global regulatory frameworks, proposed regulations are prone to fail politically across regions.

Summary

This chapter has presented in-depth coverage on the state of the art and developments in distributed ledger and blockchain technologies covering concepts from introduction to the underlying tech, economics of blockchain-powered networks, cryptoeconomics, governance, and consensus mechanisms. Moreover, the chapter has pointed out directions for future work to stir further study efforts into this area.

At the core of distributed ledger and blockchain tech is the access to data in a more transparent and distributed fashion. In today's knowledge-based economy, facilitating access to aggregated data is needed for business sustainability. This will enable leveraging of business intelligence system in an integrated and more efficient way which is prominently vital. Data-driven decision-making has continued to be a growing field in the current era of the digital economic system. For example, with the growing trends of rapidly increasing quantity and variety of data from customers, integrating and exploiting the benefits of such information in inductive reasoning surrounding strategic business decisions has proven to be successful (Caulkins et al., 2018; Erevelles et al., 2016; and Fan et al., 2015).

Lately, the hype of decentralization through distributive technologies seems to nearly breaking, unlike the vibe around the tech during the past few years. This is mainly due to the immature and volatile applications (like the cryptocurrency bubbles) and that they are not the only game in town with advances in Fintech. In this regard, identifying the major bottlenecks for innovation diffusion and maturity of distributed ledger technologies is vital. One question to ask is whether the Internet and centralized marketplaces shadowed this tech not to reach the critical mass. The future is data science, doing this at a scale and hitting the critical mass calls for more technological advancements and developments in the digital economy space. Expectations are that blockchain and distributed ledger technologies are stepping-stone for a newer form of data management in the information society, just like the developments from Web 1.0 to Web 2.0.

Further work in transitioning the technology to its full potential calls for

1. In-depth cryptoeconomic analysis and programmable incentives that sustain distributed networks

2. Analysis of the dynamics of the token economy under various business cycles

3. Governance of distributed networks and the associated financial systemic risk assessment

4. Design of robust consensus mechanisms for blockchain and DLT-powered platforms and identifying the optimal properties of such consensus mechanisms

5. Understanding market structure of the cryptocurrencies, price volatility, and monetary policies with a decentralized settings of the cryptocurrency

6. Viability of global wallets and digital currencies issued by central banks and their implied effects

Lastly, considering the technology as a disruption to the trust management models is questionable. As we have discussed under the governance of decentralized Web 3.0 economies, with major hacks that the distributed ledger technologies' space has faced, considering the tech as a trust machine of the digital economy is misleading.

Blockchain and Distributed Ledger Technology Applications

In about a decade of its existence, blockchain technology has seen some level of innovation diffusion to many sectors other than its genesis application of cryptocurrencies (see Figure 4-1). This chapter presents an objective view of the developments of blockchain and distributed ledger technologies beyond the cryptocurrencies. By drawing from the current states of the tech, I will present a detailed analysis of existing and potential use cases including ecommerce, Vickrey auction, self-sovereign digital identity management, and

A. N. Turi, *Technologies for Modern Digital Entrepreneurship*,
https://doi.org/10.1007/978-1-4842-6005-0_4

vital statistics recording. The chapter further lends key points to consider for applying blockchain and distributed ledger technologies in businesses. Here, starting from justifying why blockchain is a potential solution concept for a business, I will cover points such as asset digitization, participants identification and the degrees of permission, tokenization, decentralized applications, smart contracts and robust consensus algorithm, scalability of data throughput, payment channels, as well as a business model development for token sales.

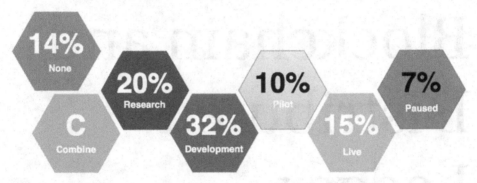

Figure 4-1. Phases of Blockchain adoption across companies, based on 2018 PwC Survey[1]

How You Can Think About Using Blockchain in Your Endeavors

There are standard procedures, methods, and approaches that blockchain analysts follow in blockchain protocol design. By focusing on blockchain, distributed ledger technologies (DLTs), and smart contract applications, in this section, I will provide recommendations for designing and deploying distributed ledgers and smart contracts. This helps make strategic decisions for businesses considering adoption of blockchain and DLT solution concepts, thus adding to the evaluation, development, and selection process of this technology. Figure 4-2 depicts five key challenges businesses face in adopting blockchain technology and tips to overcome these challenges.

---

[1]Data Source: PwC Global Blockchain Survey 2018, available at www.pwc.com/gx/en/issues/blockchain/blockchain-in-business.html

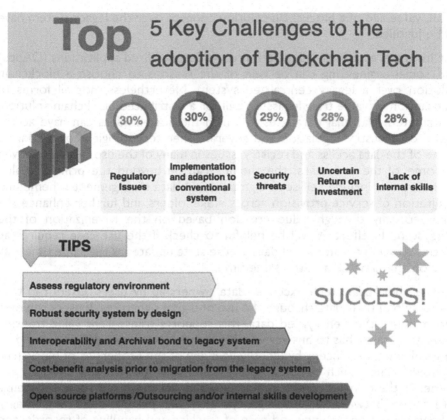

Figure 4-2. Five key challenges for adoption of Blockchain into businesses and tips for success[2]

Generally speaking, in the design of a blockchain platform, a blockchain analyst should take into account the following key points.

Justify Why Blockchain Is a Potential Solution Concept for the Problem Under Consideration

Behind any blockchain solution is the need for immutable preservation and recording of relevant information and ease of retrieval whenever lost. Here, feasibility, efficiency, usability through best practices or a pilot platform (together with innovation diffusion to the end users), functionality, and, most

---

[2]Source: Author's analysis based on data from Deloitte's 2019 Global Blockchain Survey

of all, value-add of a blockchain solution concept over the legacy system have to be justified.

For instance, economic value-add through decentralized applications (DApps) and social engineering can be one of the reasons to choose a blockchain solution over a legacy centralized system. Nevertheless, not all forms of transaction or value transfer issues call for a distributed blockchain solution. Distributed relational databases in which the stakeholders can have access based on industry regulation and several other technologies could address some of the data access and registry issues in many of the use cases. However, in some of the use cases, the themes can be beyond the principal value exchange and include self-sovereign personal data management scheme and facilitation of service provision across stakeholders and further enhance the mini-economy through value creation based on the tokenization of the ecosystem. In effect, it will be helpful to check if the use case requires all parties to see the same set of data on the state updates at the same time—all eyes on the same data at the same time.

Besides, blockchain tech excels at data ownership by users. Users can take ownership of their data through the use of digital signatures. If users can own and maintain their encrypted data, this supports transparent value transfer. Thus, the analyst has to answer why blockchain (or any other DLT) would be an ideal solution concept by identifying if any of the properties of blockchain tech add value, which can be of interest and solve the issue in the use case. Some of these include safe, immutable, and decentralized record systems, interaction between different groups (for the permissioned blockchain), tokenization, transparency and ease of tracking and handling of records, and preservation of the archival bond (and data mapping across participants and reconciliation) with a chain of records across different clusters and groups, facilitating the empowerment of service provision (blockchain enables value generation through a distributed network). Therefore, blockchain tech or DLT-based solutions are useful in the following circumstances:

- *Business network*: A business network must exist, with multiple organizations that are willing/interested/incented *to work together.*

- *Need to share data*: There is a need for shared visibility of data or transactions between participants in the business network.

- *Multiple "writers"*: The information to be shared must originate from more than one participant. Multiple organizations must provide data/execute transactions. Together with this, attention should be given to the compliance of the requirement for regulations and audits in choosing between a public and permissioned blockchain solution.

- *Trust issue*: There is a need for a single source of truth within the network; participants do not inherently trust any one party to hold that data.

- *Business value analysis (BVA)*: There must be sufficient business justification for the project. That is, the blockchain solution must provide tangible, material business benefits.

Digitization of Assets

The digitization of assets defines the assets (representations of tangible or intangible goods, or information) that are used within the business network and represented on the blockchain ledger. For example, this would be designing a blockchain application for a vehicle auction on Hyperledger that articulates who are the participants and models the asset and access control rules. Creating Hyperledger Composer applications on the Fabric Testnet includes the following process starting with the creation of the asset to running the transaction:

1. Create participants (e.g., buyer and seller for the vehicle).

2. Create vehicle owned by one of the participants.

3. Create vehicle listing to put it up on blockchain.

4. Run a new transaction to make an offer.

5. Close the bidding by running that transaction.

6. Check that the vehicle has changed hands.

Further, integration with other technologies such as AI, biometrics, and IoT can be taken into account for the digital presence of the asset.[3] The advances in the information networks and specifically the blockchain technology enabled traceability and a transfer of digitally identified things in more secure cryptographic hashes (digital signature or fingerprint of data) and transparent way. The supply chain management, distributed ride-sharing of the autonomous car, and land registry on the blockchain are some examples of the digital migration of the physical world assets to the blockchain-based platforms. In this vein, blockchain technology has facilitated and organized information networks that let the digital transformation of the real-world assets through the means of tokenization. For example, in the real estate market, the asset

---

[3]In the supply chain blockchain solutions, traceability of products is ensured through the Internet of Things sensors which are attached to the product. See, for example, Fishcoin: Blockchain-based Seafood Traceability & Data Ecosystem, https://fishcoin.co/, accessed on April 6, 2020.

representing a property (the deed) is digitized, allowing it to be represented in a divisible form (like any form of a digital token).[4] This will allow partial/full selling or renting of the property ownership by just sending an equivalent token representing the portion of the property to the transacting agent. Migrating real-world assets to the blockchain through tokens requires a secure and accurate mapping with the underlying physical assets.

Identify the Participants and the Degrees of Permission

Identifying the participants and the degrees of permission defines economic units based on their stakes in the ecosystem and ability to maximize the social welfare within the system through added values. It is vital to have a defined set of internal stakeholders and clearly set blockchain business network through abstraction of the business, privacy, data access policy, and compliance requirements of any external stakeholders.

For a permissioned blockchain, participants are the business networks that are collections of known and identifiable organizations that work together. The type and relationship between the target network members have to clearly be identified in framing the business network. Start by identifying if the subjects are competing or complementing. For example, in the case of an auction, buyers placing a bid over a listing are competing with each other, and thus, transparency of the actual bids might be a challenge for Vickrey auction-like settings (I will discuss this in connection with the potential applications later in this chapter).

Because with the transparent traceability of transactions on the blockchain registry, it is not feasible to have two or more competing companies/subjects to co-create value over a common blockchain platform. Hence, effective strategies (e.g., masking or reduction) for operating competing companies in a common platform should be framed if there is a potential for value co-creation through a blockchain solution concept.

For a permissioned blockchain, businesses have to decide whether to be within the blockchain business network based on a business value analysis (BVA).

---

[4]See blockchain platforms Bankex and Polymath for the Proof-of-Asset Protocols and LINQ, a project by Nasdaq for the digital representation of physical assets, available at `https://bankex.com/` and `https://polymath.network/`, respectively.

Tokenization and Decentralized Applications (DApps)

The analyst can create an application[5] on top of the blockchain platform that can foster a value creation process (mostly for use cases with the goals of social engineering beyond the economic derive, e.g., see the Plastic Bank blockchain solution—a Vancouver-based startup aimed at tackling ocean plastic to alleviate global poverty through blockchain-based token rewards[6]) within the mini-economy and incentivizes the participants. Hence, on top of the distributed solution, we can build a DApp that can generate additional values (like a monetary reward) for the participants. This can be achieved through the tokenization of the system beyond the core value transfer, that is, to design the incentive scheme over which value transfers on the platform take place. In the analytical phase of token engineering, consider utilizing the tools from game theory and mechanism design concepts (mostly referred to as cryptoeconomics in DLT designs) for analyzing the incentive schemes and dynamic optimization for maximizing the nano-economy's welfare.

Develop the Smart Contract and Use a Robust Consensus Algorithm

A smart contract contains a set of business logic that is enforced by an underlying code that verifies, facilitates, and executes the "if-then" statements of the agreement, thus auditing and reconciling the business process as the application runs. It defines "what can be done" within the business network resulting in queries and updates to assets represented on the ledger. For example, if a payment for a given asset transaction is not fulfilled, the defaulting buyer is locked out of the asset. Note that the user initiates a smart contract. In the Ethereum platform, to initiate a contract for a given application, you start by making a transaction that sends ether to an externally owned account (EOA) and then go for an initial coin offering (ICO—a prepaid funding model) that builds the users of the network for that specific application. Such contracts help confirm a transaction and the associated obligations of a given asset transfer in an indisputable fashion. Further, the endorsement policies or consensus on which transaction is to be put on the chain and who runs the smart contract has to be defined, that is, models of the business network: *founder-led* (relying on other participants to validate) or *consortium* (everybody is responsible for each stamp validating transaction, and the tech sets the compliance).

---

[5]To learn more about the decentralized applications, see State of the DApps at www.stateofthedapps.com/, accessed on April 6, 2020.
[6]Available at IBM case studies: www.ibm.com/case-studies/plastic-bank

Evaluation and implementation of this technology to any form of business solution should also take into account archival bond and interoperability which were discussed in Chapter 3 of this book and scalability of data throughput and possible payment channels. Let us now have an in-depth look at scalability of data throughput and payment channels.

Scalability of Data Throughput

As it has repetitively been mentioned, scalability issues are one of the key problems in the conventional blockchain protocols. At time of this writing, Bitcoin and Ethereum's speed of transaction processing is 4 and 13 transactions per second, respectively, unlike the Visa transactions of 2000 per second.[7] The most common issue with the scalability of the existing blockchain protocols is the block ceiling (a limit on the number of transactions per block). Removing the block ceiling comes with an increase in the bandwidth requirement. In the PoW consensus mechanism, this implies a concentration of mining power in the hands of a few big miners, which induces higher transaction fees and lesser security of the system. The block ceiling also results in censorship of transactions based on transaction fees. As a result, some solutions to address the scalability issue have been proposed (Decker and Wattenhofer, 2015; Croman et al., 2016; and Luu et al., 2016).[8] The first solution is the micropayment channels (to record the final transaction out of a series of transactions between nodes). The second is the SegWit (segregated witness), which proposes for the storage of signature data into extended blocks. The third solution in this regard is the off-chain oracles in which external entities take part in the computation process outside the chain. The other solution concept proposed is the sharding of transactions into groups (segregation of transactions).

Payment Channels

Payment channels, also known as micropayment channels, are a class of techniques to allow users to make multiple Bitcoin transactions without committing all of the transactions to the bitcoin blockchain. In a typical payment channel, only two transactions are added to the blockchain, but an unlimited number of payments can be made between the participants (two transactions: to open the channel and to close validation of refunds to the respective parties according to the balance sheet and storing of BTC), that is,

---

[7]https://towardsdatascience.com/the-blockchain-scalability-problem-the-race-for-visa-like-transaction-speed-5cce48f9d44

[8]See also www.bloomberg.com/news/articles/2019-01-17/mit-stanford-academics-design-cryptocurrency-to-better-bitcoin

the Lightning Networks. A similar enabling scale channel for Ethereum is known as Raiden Network. The scalability of the Bitcoin blockchain lightning network is considering the off-chain approach. Also, only two transactions could be taken into account in the case of multiple transactions and opening a payment channel (multiple signature address). For instance, multiple transactions and balance transfer between a customer and restaurant can be set through a payment channel with the restaurant where both deposit a given amount of BTC in a common address.

Considering the larger blockchain network as a single economic unit, the network can attain economies of scale by efficiently utilizing the underutilized blocks to include a greater number of transaction records. In this context, the economies of scale (increasing returns to scale) implies the cost advantage which the network experiences with an increase in its transaction throughput and increase in the value created by the network (number of confirmed transactions in a given time). More specifically, scalability as economies of scale to a blockchain protocol is a declining unit cost of transaction processing (bandwidth cost and individual transaction fee) as a function of the number of the total transaction being processed.

The scalability of a blockchain protocol implies a constant/decreasing unit cost of a block capacity with an increase in the number of processed transactions in that block. The increasing returns to scale is the distributed economies of scale, indicating cost saving in a value co-creation process. As more transactions are being processed in a given time, more tokens are being consumed, and the number of users increases with the number of transactions. Accordingly, the value of the underlying cryptocurrency increases, and there will be faster circulation of the token within the network, unlike the common cryptocurrency hoarding issues. This results in an increased velocity of money.

As discussed earlier, the economies of scale for the PoW consensus mechanisms can come from monopolization of the mining power by fewer miners at the cost of decentralization of the network.[2] However, according to Catalini and Gans (2016), PoW mechanism results in economies of scale due to a network effect that guarantees security. That is, with an increase in the number of users, the value of the underlying cryptocurrency increases, which attracts miners with higher expected reward from transaction fees and increases the security of the system. Despite its promising features, the scalability issue underlying blockchain technology is one of the main challenges in adopting the technology to various sectors of the economy.

Once the economies of scale with the scalability of blockchain protocols are achieved, a large amount of data in the real-life transactions can be processed faster and secure on blockchain platforms. Hence, identifying the potential distributed economies of scale that can be attained by the network will help in determining optimal mechanism design that maximizes the social welfare function of the blockchain network. Network effects with increased usage of a cryptocurrency result in the appreciation of the cryptocurrency accompanied by an increase in its value. Hence, network effects are the demand-side economies of scale in a cryptoeconomy. This increasing returns to scale is the competitive advantage the incumbent network enjoys in the cryptoeconomy over new hard forks. The more the protocol is scalable, the more the blockchain community enjoys the economies of scale from the enhanced speed of transaction (total value/output) at a lower/fixed cost of a transaction.

Develop a Business Model for the Token Sales

Depending on the classes of token for securities regulation, the crowdsale business models for a token sale can follow an initial coin offerings (ICO) or security token offering (STO), similar to initial public offering of legacy financial model. The initial coin (token) offering a business model is a decentralized investment crowdfunding model for raising the inceptive capital of a blockchain network. It enables monetization of the underlying tokens by selling initially issued tokens to early adopters, thus allowing access to the goods and services the network provides. Note that in a tokenized system, the value of the underlying token depends on the size of the network. Thus, the ICO has an impact on the token valuation. In the scarce token economic system of capped token supply, ICO pitches mostly focus on the fixed supply of the token, justifying the law of demand for the token market. Bitcoin and Litecoin supply, for example, are fixed to 21 million.

On the other hand, there are some cases to opt for the uncapped supply (for instance, the increase in price for assets with a high velocity of money does not sustain over the long run). The creation of digital currency, like cryptocurrencies, has opened a new window in the financial industry. In this regard, it is crucial to identify the differences between coins, utility tokens, and tokenized securities. The utility tokens (e.g., Filecoin for a file storage network or a voting coin in governance that identifies voting eligibility) are used to access services within a given network.

Utility coins, in general, are consigned to be a privilege of membership in these ecosystems. In these networks, the value of the token depends on the utility of the service within the network. The value increases with the size of the network. An initial coin offering grants access to the network's expected services and goods' provision in a similar way to the coupons that organizations give to their members. Tokens can also take the form of assets, that is, cryptoassets, categorized as security tokens in which investors invest in a token sale or an ICO with the expectation of future profit (through dividends, shares, interest, or investment in other tokens or assets). A good example of security tokens is tZERO, a blockchain-powered capital market platform. Provided the aforementioned classes of crowdsale, the blockchain analyst has to make an appropriate decision of which model of ICOs to follow and ways to comply with the legal requirements underlying the fuel token. In the United

States, token sales are subject to the *Howey Test*, which identifies if a given token is subject to abide by the securities law.[9] Utility tokens are commonly locked under some terms and conditions through smart contracts like the ones in the Ethereum platform.

Financing projects through ICOs (unregulated) funding model is found to be risky as a result of growing scams. Consequently, the STO (regulated) business model has come into place as an alternative to the ICO crowdfunding business model.[10] STO is one of the distributed networks' crowdfunding or venture capital financing business models. It represents tokenized securities powered by DLTs and is regulated by the laws and agencies in the relevant federal and state authorities. Unlike the traditional securities trading (like IPOs or equity crowdfunding), STO tradings are more transparent and instant in clearing without the need for intermediaries and are easily exchanged in the secondary markets. The Money Morning reported that the STO crowdfunding model is estimated to generate about global funding of $10 trillion by 2020.[11]

In coping with the security, token valuation, and incentive-compatibility issues, other variations of venture capital funding for open source projects have also been proposed. One of these is the interactive coin offerings mechanism proposed by Teutsch et al. (2017) in guaranteeing a fair valuation equilibrium in the token sale dilemma of certainty of valuation and participation through token quantity specification at each point of token valuation.

Fabric Ventures and TokenData report (2018) reported that more than $5.6 billion had been raised in ICO by the startups in the year 2017, accounting for about 48% of the total listings across different blockchain platforms (see also Table 4-1). Key factors identified for successful ICOs and STOs include trust (which can be built through an efficient reputation scheme), transparent information disclosure, smart contract and governance of self-regulated blockchain community, tradability of the underlying token or coin, venture-specific related qualities (identified through the accompanying whitepapers, web hosting like GitHub repository, network effect, tokenized asset, project initiators' credibility, etc.), and the ICO/STO elapsed time (Amsden and Schweizer, 2018; de Jong et al., 2018; Fabric Ventures and TokenData report, 2018; Rhue, 2018; and Teutsch et al., 2017). Thus, most of the key factors underlying the crowd-based business models discussed under the equity crowdfunding determine the success rate of a project financing through the ICOs or STOs.[12]

---

[9]See Securities Act of 1933 and the Securities Exchange Act of 1934, which points out the transactions which are considered securities and the associated requirements.
[10]See Momtaz (2019) for the details on the token sales and the ICOs.
[11]https://moneymorning.com/2018/04/09/forget-icos-security-token-offer-ings-are-a-10-trillion-opportunity/, accessed on April 6, 2020.
[12]See Chapter 2 of this book which presents a detailed analysis of the crowd-based business models, especially the equity crowdfunding, for the key factors behind successful crowdfunding campaign.

Table 4-1. The ten largest token sales in 2018 by sector accounting for about 47% of the total capital raised in ICO[13]

Project	Sector	Raise
EOS	Infrastructure	$3,165,000,000
Telegram Open Network	Infrastructure	$1,700,000,000
Bankera	Finance	$150,000,000
tZERO	Trading	$134,000,000
Basis	Infrastructure	$125,000,000
Orbs	Infrastructure	$118,000,000
PumaPay	Finance	$117,019,041
Envion	Finance	$100,012,279
Hedera Hashgraph	Infrastructure	$100,000,000
Flashmoni	Finance	$72,000,000
Total raised		$5,781,031,320

In addition to the seven key points to how you can think about using blockchain in your endeavors, in the case of digital transformation of an existing business to DLT-powered platform, interoperability and integration (e.g., archival bond) with the prior data system have to be taken into account. Figure 4-3 depicts a visual summary of the stepladder of Blockchain tech application for a business.

---

[13]Fabric Ventures Report, 2018, available at https://static1.squarespace.com/static/5a19eca6c027d8615635f801/t/5bc72f94a4222f9ca0750b0e/1539780519641/State+of+the+Token+Market+2+FINAL.pdf

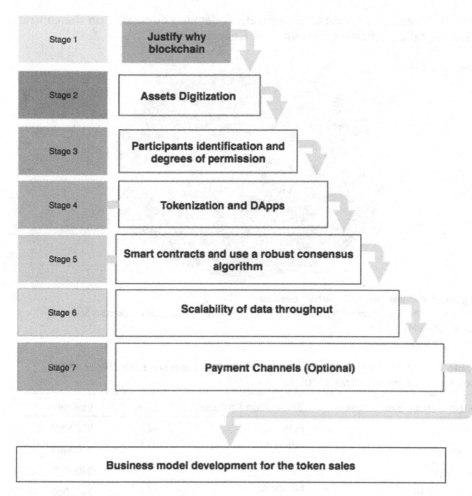

Figure 4-3. Stepladder of Blockchain tech application for business

Innovation Diffusion: Developments and Applications Beyond Cryptocurrencies

This section is designed to give a glimpse of some potential applications of the DLTs. Use cases ranging from identity solution, vital statistics records, ecommerce reputation scheme to auction are briefly discussed. Figure 4-4 shows the common use cases of the DLTs. Beyond the private sector, there is a growing demand for DLTs in the public sector. A global benchmarking study on the blockchain (Hileman and Rauchs, 2017) shows that about 63% and 69% of central banks and other public sector institutions are being involved in the DLT solution concepts, respectively. A detailed discussion on the central bank digital currencies is presented in Chapter 5.[14]

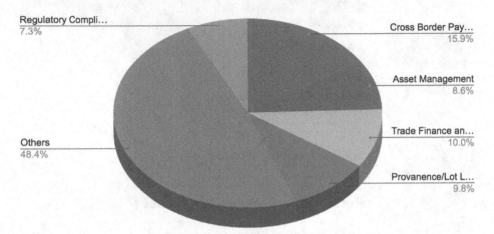

Figure 4-4. Best global blockchain use cases
Source: Author's extraction based on IDC's Worldwide Semiannual Blockchain Spending Guide, 2018H1

Table 4-2. Sample decentralized exchanges across Blockchain protocols DApps in the exchange category as of April 3, 2020[15]

Decentralized Exchanges	Blockchain Protocol	User	Volume
Newdex	EOS	667	9500000
Kyper	Ethereum	973	4400000
Uniswap	Ethereum	970	2400000
1inch.exchange	Ethereum	275	2400000
Tokenlon	Ethereum	364	1400000
ParaSwap.io	Ethereum	46	727400
Neutrino Protocol	Waves	247	512000
IDEX	Ethereum	326	401200
TronTrade	TRON	798	127400
Poloni DEX	TRON	677	50600

---

[14]Data Source: IDC's Worldwide Semiannual Blockchain Spending Guide, 2018H1
[15]Extracted from DappRadar available at https://dappradar.com/rankings/category/exchanges

Use Case 1: Blockchain-Based Co-utile Reputation Management for the Ecommerce

One of the key problems underlying electronic commerce is the lack of trust between transacting agents. This is due to the uncertainties and information asymmetry problems underlying these marketplaces. This section leverages a decentralized reputation mechanism powered by blockchain technology.[16]

The feedback system in the ecommerce marketplaces is important, especially with the information asymmetry and market-related risks underlying the market. This helps create a fair and efficient marketplace. Hence, an efficient reputation mechanism can allow us to sort out malicious buyers/bidders and sellers within the transactional network of this market. The reputation mechanism helps sort out malicious buyers/bidders by imposing buyer requirements in the marketplace to those with policy violations, retaliation feedback motive, unpaid items (after placing a winning bid or purchase order), or fraudulent payments. An incentive scheme for the buyers is that being positively reputed helps them to be identified and benefit from the loyal customers' benefits and rewards. A buyer with a negative reputation can encounter limits on account privileges (such privileges in the eBay, e.g., include eBay Money Back Guarantee and discount and reward offers, Gift Cards & Coupons, non-cash eBay Bucks customer rewards program (greater or equal to $5 in the form of an eBay Bucks Certificate to qualifying buyers), or the Amazon Prime (a paid service that gives buyers a few distinct advantages like free shipping).

In a Vickrey auction[17] of eBay, buyers compete and bid according to a private valuation of the product. Lack of trust implies that a deal between a winning buyer and seller collapses due to mistrust effects on both sides of the players. Apart from the payment failures, in eBay-like marketplaces, a seller with a default record commonly receives lower or no bids on its listings. The prominent assumption in this analysis is that the players' types are identified by their past record of the transaction. In a repeated stage game, in the long run with a sequence of transactions, no transaction deal will take place between rational utility and profit-maximizing players. In expectation of default by the seller in the initial stage game, all other buyers do not bid or do low valuations for a listing of this seller. As a result, with future reputation

---

[16]OpenBazaar, Monetha (Switzerland), Colu (Israel), Rate (Singapore), Retail. Global (Moscow), Ubcoin Market (East Europe), Purse (San Francisco), OB1, Shopin, AORA, Elementh, RAVELOUS, and so on are some of the ecommerce startups powered by the blockchain tech as of 2019.

[17]Vickrey auction is a type of sealed bid, which self-enforces second-price auction. That is, in a sealed bid, bidders privately submit true valuations of their bids and the winner pays the second-highest bid.

effects, a long-run player (seller) would prefer to be credible both in its product specification and delivery. In this case, the player is identified with the commitment types of players, commonly referred to as "irrational" players. One of the game-theoretic approaches, other than the Nash equilibrium,[18] to capture this like interaction is the Stackelberg action (an action in which a follower's strategy depends on a leader's action in a game). This method results in an outcome that commits the seller to be honest at any cost in fear of reputation loss. Therefore, when the reputation effect comes to play, the socially suboptimal equilibrium does not hold anymore, and that is what keeps the existing online marketplaces running. This way of analysis neither guarantees an optimal return to the seller with strategic behavior underlying the short-term buyers.

A reputation mechanism should be designed in such a way that it identifies loyal customers in the transactional network with these incentive schemes under consideration. Negative ratings result in a limit on these privileges or overall buying activity and account suspension in the extreme case. On the other side, selling performance measures can be used to rate the reputation scores of the sellers in the transactional network. These measures include defect rate (item description accuracy), late shipment rate (item delivery), shipping and handling charges, communication, and cases closed without seller resolution. Therefore, there is a need for a design of a reputation protocol which can be all-inclusive and distributed. This allows all involved agents in the network to rate each other in a rationally self-enforcing way. The science of building trust calls for varied insights from computer science, information systems, management science, and psychology, beyond the conventional microeconomic and game-theoretic human behavior modeling.

The subjective nature of feedback is commonly avoided by a scoring method based on a set of values for random variables representing the feedback (eBay feedback score and the detailed seller ratings). Another method suggested is clustering and filtering of the feedback scores according to their common features in order to capture the heterogeneities among individual raters (e.g., Amazon feedback and ratings). Collusive behavior, Sybil attacks, and biased ratings deviate online ratings. As a result, the reputation score aggregation

---

[18]A Nash equilibrium in game theory refers to an optimal state which leads to stability in interactions of different players. In this state, no player has the incentive to deviate since each payoff through the original strategy is optimally provided that other players' strategy remains unchanged. In games that operate suboptimally, we can achieve better results by changing the rules of the game (e.g., by applying self-enforcing protocols in order to attain mutually beneficial outcomes, co-utility). Selfish behavior can predict a Nash equilibrium. But this equilibrium may not encompass other forms of equilibrium that can arise in real life; the players can be not only selfish but also kind and may display kind intentions that lead to different types of equilibrium. Such equilibrium can be captured through different approaches such as reciprocal interaction through the notion of reciprocity equilibrium (Turi et al., 2017).

mechanism for online markets is an open research question. Moreover, cross-validating malicious reporting and whether enough feedback is solicited depends on the underlying incentive scheme under the feedback mechanism.

Incentive-Compatible Blockchain-Powered Reputation Mechanism

Given the strategic nature of feedback giving, in which users retaliate and reciprocate, a co-utile reputation mechanism powered by blockchain tech can enable to fill in the loopholes with online reputation systems. This mechanism helps compute individual user's reputations fairly based on a global reputation, which is derived from the normalized weighted local reputation scores. Turi et al. (2016) argue that reciprocity equilibrium can lead to a co-utile outcome for positive reciprocity, provided that the outcome is Pareto-optimal and results in a strictly higher payoff to the players. Therefore, reciprocal feedback can be co-utile feedback. Favoring one another in a reciprocal setting might lead to a biased reputation system at an aggregate level. Hence, the aggregation mechanism should be designed in such a way that it gives weight for each transaction in the network.

In the game-theoretic reputation models, feedback aggregation strategy depicts the behavior of the players in the equilibria selection (Aberer and Despotovic, 2004). Hence, the aim of a reputation system designer in a game-theoretic reputation modeling is then to draw feedback aggregation strategy that results in a single socially desirable equilibrium from the set of available equilibria. Some of the conventional aggregation strategies used by the existing online marketplaces include a summation of all the rating scores (all the negative, positive, and neutral scores) or an average of the total feedback score in a given period or percentage of positive reviews from the total reviews. With the co-utile reputation mechanism, as the designing mechanism is with the underlying assumption that the aggregated global reputation is derived from normalized local reputations computed in a self-enforcing way and aggregated in a distributed way with every player being the score manager making the computation fair enough, this aggregation mechanism performs better in depicting the true behavior of the players. Therefore, along with its other interesting features, this makes the co-utile reputation mechanism a viable complement to building a somewhat organized, efficient online marketplaces.

Like all other digital economy business models, ecommerce is far from perfection. Some of the major problems ecommerce markets face are depicted in Figure 4-5.

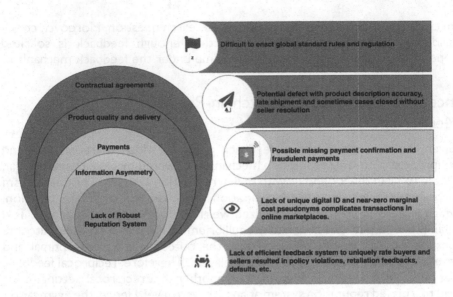

Figure 4-5. Common problems in online market

In a co-utile blockchain-powered reputation mechanism, incentive compatibility can be achieved through a co-utile reputation protocol. The co-utile reputation mechanism employs the first mechanism by setting zero reputation scores for all new and malicious players with an intention to disincentivize whitewashing. Setting zero reputation (the worst possible reputation) to new entrants in online marketplaces is proved to be the most reasonable mechanism to punish malicious players re-entering the market with a new pseudonym (see also Dellarocas, 2003a). For the second mechanism, blockchain tech can be utilized to record and track unique digital identities, thus verifying users. The aggregate of reputation data across the network is run on the blockchain tech using the smart contract that defines the business rules.[19] Thus, a blockchain platform offers a standardized way of accessing reputation data of users that have been accumulated.[20]

A decentralized co-utile reputation with a costly exit and re-entry can be applied to secure a transaction over such digital platforms (see Turi et al., 2017). The decentralized co-utile reputation mechanism is an extension to the well-known EigenTrust mechanism (Kamvar et al., 2003), with additional properties of being fully distributed and co-utile (Domingo-Ferrer et al., 2016b).

---

[19]See Dennis and Owen (2015), Brunie et al. (May 2016), Subramanian (2018), Carboni (2015), and Cai and Zhu (2016) for the details on the application of the blockchain tech in the online marketplace.

[20]On August 13, 2018, Forbes covered the potentials of the blockchain tech for building trust in the online marketplace, www.forbes.com/sites/shermanlee/2018/08/13/a-decentralized-reputation-system-how-blockchain-can-restore-trust-in-online-markets/#1f6b1e9f481a, accessed on April 6, 2020.

Being decentralized, it helps avoid interference by any central authority to compute reputations and hence reduce the problems of biased computation and privacy issues arising from computation by a sole central entity.

The protocol also has additional interesting features that make it relevant to the online market. Specifically, agents computing each other's reputation in a distributed way remain anonymous to each other during the calculation process. Besides, it is cost-effective with a limit on the number of messages and communication iterations needed to compute reputations, and, being an outcome-based computation, its computation can run parallel to the main transaction.

This protocol also manages new agents by assigning them zero reputation scores as if they were malicious agents, thereby disincentivizing the creation of new or multiple identities to "clean" malicious past behaviors. The protocol computes global reputation scores of agents based on local reputations resulting from individual transactions. The computation and aggregation mechanism of this reputation protocol makes it robust against several tampering attacks, both targeted at increasing the agents' own reputation and at decreasing the reputation of others. That is because the distributed nature of the protocol and weighted aggregation of the global reputation scores makes it hard for agents who try to tamper with reputations. Of course, these like malicious agents can easily be detected by others (and punished by lowering their reputations). Therefore, by adopting a proper weighted aggregation mechanism of the co-utile reputation protocol, it is possible to make the mechanism robust against tampering attacks. Furthermore, this mechanism is robust against common abuses of online rating systems of retaliation and reciprocal feedback systems like the ones on eBay (Bolton et al., 2013; Cabral, 2012; and Resnick and Zeckhauser, 2002).

Blockchain Solution Concept for Users' Verification and Reputation Data Tracking

In this case, a distributed identity solution preserving the record of relevant information and ease of retrieval whenever altered (for malicious acts of whitewashing and tampering) is important. Such a setting can be formulated with a blockchain platform that can create a token economy, helping to issue unique identifications to the users (buyers and sellers). Such a well-established record system enables easy verification and identification of the users. This setting can also help track and uniquely identify the users registered within the system, thus efficiently running the reputation system. In this network, blockchain is used to record users' unique identity and transactions and track and validate reputation scores and token transfers in the reputation network. The tokenization process follows a system in which the crowdsource of rating peers is monetized and circulated within the ecommerce platform. Here, the valuation of a reputation system can be achieved by tokenizing the users' reputations based on key characteristic variables.

For sellers, key factors that will help in the valuation of reputation scores include defect rate (item or service description accuracy), late shipment rate (item delivery), shipping and handling charges, communication, and cases closed without seller resolution. Likewise, for the buyers, factors like policy violations, retaliation feedback motive, unpaid items (after placing a winning bid or purchase order), or fraudulent payments are taken into account. The rating of a user in the system works like the voting system, but dichotomous voting scheme enabling upvoting and downvoting depending on the utility derived from the transaction. As the ID verification process builds up and the number of users for the platform increases, the demand and value of the reputation token increase, hence resulting in a co-utile system.

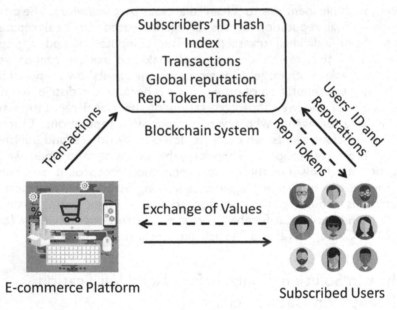

Figure 4-6. Ecommerce platform with a blockchain-powered reputation system

Use Case 2: Vickrey Auction

The well-known Vickrey auction, a.k.a. second-price auction, refers to a sealed bid where buyers place a coated bid on a listing.[21] This auction mechanism assigns the asset to the highest winning bid with a price of the second-highest bid. This form of bidding incentivizes bidders to place honest bids, thus revealing individual willingness to pay for an asset. The smart contract, distributed ledger, and other application developments on the blockchain space (like the Ethereum Name Service, ENS[22]) enable the execution of Vickrey auctions without the need of intermediaries. The technology enables the masking of bids until their reveal stage in order to preserve the underlying privacy principle of a sealed bid.

A typical example in this regard is the hypothetical Hyperledger Fabric car auction network which is supported by the IBM Blockchain cloud service for saving blocks of transactions and authentication and certification purposes.[23] In a Hyperledger Composer application, the participants of the network are defined by identifying members of the auction to populate the auction network, the asset to be auctioned, and the asset listing where members can place bids. The structures of such auctions run on a permissioned and public blockchain platform might pose a question on the authenticity and traceability of things in the physical world. Once a listing is made available with a unique name, the transaction is initiated where bidders place a coated bid on the listing. The smart contract applies the business rules by updating the ledger, ensuring the transfer of ownership of the asset to the highest bidder at the second bidding price.

The stages of auction execution on a blockchain platform are[24]

    1.   The auctioneer initiates the auction by registering an ethereum domain name for the auction.

---

[21]This use case is based on the existing recent developments of blockchain technology for auction purposes. Some examples of blockchain-based auction include the Auction 3.0 (www.eauction.idf.solutions/), a global decentralized auction for asset sale and lease, Christie's auction, a British auction house, and an Art Sale of $318 million on a Blockchain in partnership with the blockchain-based arts and collectibles platform called Artory (www.artory.com/). See Christie's press release on December 12, 2018, at www.christies.com/features/Barney-Ebsworth-Collection-results-9552-3.aspx?PID=en_hp_carousel_1 and the 16th-century Italian Renaissance Roman Mansion, Palazzetto, blockchain auction covered by the CNBC on June 19, 2018, at www.cnbc.com/2018/06/19/palazzetto-mansion-in-rome-italy-being-auctioned-for-bitcoin.html

[22]ENS is an Ethereum-based application built on smart contracts that allow users to register a unique domain name for their address, https://etherscan.io/enslookup

[23]See the car auction demo with Hyperledger Fabric at GitHub: https://github.com/IBM/car-auction-network-fabric-node-sdk, accessed on April 6, 2020.

[24]For the details on the cryptographic execution of the algorithm, refer to Galal and Youssef (2018) and GitHub Hyperledger Composer at https://link.springer.com/chapter/10.1007/978-3-662-58820-8_18, accessed on April 6, 2020.

2. The auctioneer deploys the smart contract with a bid opening and closing date for an asset listing based on the business rule under consideration.

3. Potential bidders place a deposit for participating in the auction based on a bid deposit requirement (this is a security deposit for revealing the bid at the reveal stage; a portion or all can be charged for not revealing the bid at the specified time).

4. Buyers place coated bids (bid mask, not the actual bid to preserve privacy) on the asset listing until the bid period closes. Bid mask can be generated with a privacy-preserving commitment to the actual bid, where bidders submit a hash of a nonce and their bid value which will be revealed at on successful closure of the bidding phase.

5. When the specified bidding period is over, all coated bids are revealed with actual bids.

6. After the reveal stage, the asset ownership is transferred to the highest winning bidder who pays the second-highest bid price, thus updating the ledger. The auctioned ETH is locked in a smart contract guaranteeing the ownership of the asset.

7. At the closing of the auction, those who placed and revealed lower bids than the highest bid amount withdraw their security deposit.

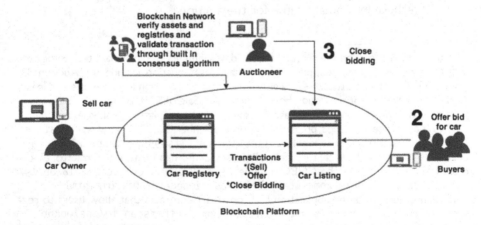

Figure 4-7. A simplified business network of a car auction on a blockchain platform

Use Case 3: Self-Sovereign Digital Identity Management

With the advent of the Internet and developments in social media networks over the past few years, digital presence has dramatically increased. This has led to the formation of digital identities that are directly or indirectly linked to the physical world. Most of the social media networks are used by a significant number of non-privacy-conscious users. Information asymmetry is one of the problems underlying the digital economic system. Thus, perfect identification of individuals through social media presence is hard with unstable pseudonyms and possible multiple accounts an individual can own. The ease of access and ownership of these digital IDs and the resulting zero marginal cost pseudonyms underlying these platforms complicate the identification of individuals through such platforms. In excelling over the digital presence of people, recent developments have emerged to tap the underutilized potential of digital IDs through distributed ID solutions.

A legally recognized identification is crucial for the socioeconomic and political inclusion of individuals. Identification is one means of social capital and trust for human interactions in modern society. Data breaches with centralized databases and fraudulent activities are some of the key challenges in the digital economic system. One of the major developments in the application of the blockchain and distributed ledger technologies includes the secure decentralized identification solution concept.[25] This contributes to a safe sharing of data through the Internet. These applications primarily focus on securing digital identities on DLTs[26] and further facilitate trust in identification-based service provisions. With its underlying features for digital identity management, the technology is referred to as a trust machine.[27]

ID2020

One of the developments in digital identity solutions is the ID2020, an alliance working toward identity provision. The alliance between Accenture, Microsoft, Mercy Corps, Hyperledger, and UNICC aims at providing digital identities for

---

[25]Decentralized digital identity management has gained significant attention following the advent of data sharing over the Internet. For example, the Canadian identity network, SecureKey, has been joined by two US credit agencies (Equifax and TransUnion), Bank of Montreal, Bank of Nova Scotia, Canadian Imperial Bank of Commerce, Royal Bank of Canada, Toronto-Dominion Bank (which poured about $20 million investment), and Desjardins in its early trial stage (Reuters, May 4, 2017), https://in.reuters.com/article/us-canada-blockchain-credit-idINKBN18020R, accessed on April 6, 2020.

[26]Evernym is an example of an open source self-sovereign identity solution on a permissioned distributed ledger: www.evernym.com/

[27]Vigna and Casey (2019)

undocumented people, thus facilitating the attainment of Target 16.9 of the UN Sustainable Development Goal: "By 2030, provide legal identity for all, including birth registration." ID2020 relies on blockchain tech to store and secure digital IDs. According to the Identification for Development (ID4D) global data, as of 2018, about 1 billion people in 151 different countries lack proof of legal identity.[28] As a result, ID2020 is designed to bridge this identification coverage gap. ID2020 is aimed at providing self-sovereign, unique, persistent, private (with encryption), and portable identity solution for the global undocumented population, thus providing them legal recognition. In decentralized identity solutions, for privacy reasons, private identifiable information including biometric data (fingerprints, retina scan, etc.) is encrypted and stored off the chain and is accessible upon permission by the subject.

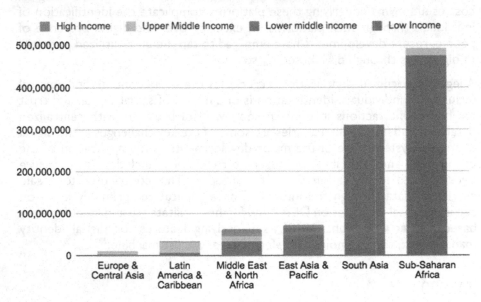

Figure 4-8. Regional identification coverage gap[29]

As it is indicated in Figure 4-8, the identification issue is a common problem all across the world. In developing countries, this mainly has to do with the poor record and governance system. In developed countries as well, there is a significant number of undocumented people, mainly in the urban areas of homeless communities. Homeless individuals, while living on the streets, face the risk of losing relevant documents, including government-issued ID, mainly due to the lack of personal storage and other personal conditions. Consequently, they face a challenge in accessing the needed government,

---

[28]https://datacatalog.worldbank.org/dataset/identification-development-global-dataset, accessed on April 6, 2020.
[29]Source: Identification for Development (ID4D) Global Dataset

health, social, legal, and financial services. Getting their ID back can prove difficult for them as they are unable to prove who they are. For example, in 2015, CBC News reported that in Vancouver BC, a homeless man Steve Borik won lotto worth $25,000 CAD, but could not claim the prize because he lacked ID.[30] Borik was trapped in a vicious circle problem that he could not get a photo ID without a birth certificate from his birth town of Montreal, Quebec, nor could he obtain a birth certificate without a photo ID. After five months of trial, CBC become involved and resolved the issue, helping him obtain a photo ID in about three weeks. In this situation, if there were a well-established record system and ID solution which does not require the subject to carry around the ID (especially for such vulnerable group of the society), the time and effort exerted to retrieve Borik's identity would have been minimized. Hence, creating a convenient identification mechanism for the undocumented people is an ideal solution. Hence, a distributed identity solution preserving the record of relevant information and ease of retrieval whenever lost is important. Such a setting can be formulated with a blockchain or DLT platform that issues unique IDs. The tech can provide legal recognition for undocumented people and also facilitates access to the service provisions.

Refugee Camp Food Distribution Blockchain Solution

Another example of self-sovereign digital identification is the ID solution for the undocumented/invisible refugees. The identification of a person has a significant value for the social capital of the individual subject. Refugee individuals often lose their vital documents like government ID and possessions because of the lack of personal storage or in the process of leaving their home country to escape war, persecution, or natural disaster vital documents, like identification, that reveal their background. This poses a challenge for building trust during their settlement process with the lack of trust. One of the international organizations that deal with the humanitarian act of settlement of the refugees has launched a pilot project that will facilitate its service provision addressing the issue of traceability with the lack of identity. The pilot project led by the World Food Program (WFP), Building Blocks (Blockchain for Zero Hunger),[31] is utilizing blockchain for its food distribution at the refugee camps in Jordan.

Initiated in 2016, the project aimed to facilitate the cash transfer without the need for intermediaries and an immutable record of beneficiaries' data. In 2018, WFP assisted 24.5 million people in 62 countries through cash transfers.[32] During this year, $1.74 billion in physical banknotes, e-money,

---

[30]CBC News: www.cbc.ca/news/canada/british-columbia/steve-borik-homeless-man-wins-lotto-1.3369155
[31]See the WFP Building Blocks at https://innovation.wfp.org/project/building-blocks, accessed on April 6, 2020.
[32]www1.wfp.org/cash-transfers, accessed on April 6, 2020.

mobile money, debit cards, or value vouchers have been transferred to the beneficiaries. Cash accounts for about 35% of WFP's food assistance portfolio.

The blockchain record system records biometric information of the beneficiaries through an iris scanner that uniquely identifies the food beneficiaries and further records the transactions with the WFP voucher. The technology is intended to save the transaction costs (of cash transfer through banks and financial institutions) and speed up services through a direct value transfer using the Ethereum platform. The eye scan payment system further helps resolve the risk of fraud and double-spending of the food vouchers through immutable records of transactions and unique identifications. The transparent record system also helps in reconciliation and tracking of the supply chain of food allocation services down up to the local units. This helps perform timely auditing without the cost of collecting and sharing information. Moreover, with the self-governance of secured data, the application is believed to empower the beneficiaries in the service provision. As of May 2018, about $9 million has been transferred to about half a million registered users through blockchain.

Civic

A similar blockchain-based identity solution is provided by the Civic[33] digital personal identity verification protocol which uses identity verification tokens called Civic utility tokens.[34] In 2017, with the aim to create an open source marketplace for identity verification, the platform raised about $33 million in a token sale. The civic distributed ledger protocol records attested identification data and civic token-based transactions and performs verification of users' encrypted biometric data. The DLT protocol facilitates identity verification between service providers. Encrypted biometric data are accessed by the subjects through mobile applications, and user's data can be accessed through QR codes scanning at the partner service provision center.[35]

Evernym

Evernym builds and operates Sovrin, a permissioned DLT-based global identity network that provides cryptographic digital credentials.[36] Sovrin is an open source digital identity platform that pledges a scalable self-sovereign and verifiable ID solution. The network operates on a permissioned blockchain,

---

[33]www.civic.com/, accessed on April 6, 2020.

[34]See also Tykn's identity and access management system at https://tykn.tech/, accessed on April 6, 2020. The platform provides common applications of identity authentication and proofing for organizations and facilitates digital transformations for governments.

[35]See Civic identity system provided in Civic white paper: Token Behavior Model May 16, 2018, https://tokensale.civic.com/CivicTokenSaleWhitePaper.pdf

[36]www.evernym.com/, accessed on April 6, 2020.

Hyperledger Indy of the Linux Foundation. The project is aimed at creating a self-governed personal identification system, unlike the centralized data storage system, which is deemed to be costly and mostly insecure being a honeypot for malicious agents. The Sovrin identity solution can ease and facilitate link contracts, escrow and payment systems, asset and document management, an online reputation system, and so on. A user's Sovrin identity on the distributed ledger is the collection of the user's Sovrin identifiers (verification key), claims, disclosures, and proofs.

In the same way as many other distributed ledger solution concepts, private identifier data of users are stored off the chain. The following diagram depicts the Sovrin ledger workflow. In the diagram, user Jane, with a sovereign digital ID, interacts with different participating institutions (banks, employer, government, school, retailer, and the chamber of commerce which has a claim over Jane's identity). Registered institutions share their respective public keys with Jane and vice versa for verification.[37]

Use Case 4: Vital Statistics Recording DLT Solution

Most of the developing countries have a poor record and event registration of vital statistics. For example, according to UNICEF Canada, only 7% of children under five have been registered at birth in Ethiopia.[38] Thus, this solution focuses on providing events recording mechanism for the undocumented perspective and future population in the developing countries.

An efficient birth record mechanism could help facilitate access services and prevent right violations (e.g., early marriage and child labor) and further helps the authorities in service planning like immunization delivery. In extension to the blockchain digital ID solution, vital statistics and events recording can be a handy and feasible solution concept mainly in developing countries like Ethiopia. Hence, a distributed event registration and birth record solution preserving the record of relevant information and ease of retrieval whenever lost is essential. Such a setting can be formulated with a blockchain platform that can create a nano-economy helping to issue unique certificates. Vital statistics recording using blockchain is being used or at least under pilot in the

---

[37]See the Sovrin ledger which is built on Evernym at the Sovrin Foundation; White Paper: "How Sovrin Works," available at www.evernym.com/wp-content/uploads/2017/07/How-Sovrin-Works.pdf
[38]www.unicef.ca/en/ethiopia-birth-registration

State of Illinois, the United Kingdom, and Brazil.[39] For example, the UK-based platform, Tykn, operates in recording data about life and death across borders. The platform is accessible to authorized agents who verify and record birth notification data.

Events and units can be recorded through various mechanisms. The relational databases which the stakeholders can have access based on the industry regulation and several existing technologies could address the problem of event recording. This is one of the issues that put the potentials of the blockchain tech under question. Regardless, there are some potentials of this tech in the vital statistics recording mainly in the developing countries where demographic data is poorly managed. Combined with other applications that incent the mini-economy, a blockchain-powered token system and events (birth, death, population statistics) recording solution built on top of it can be helpful. Here, one might raise the question of why blockchain would be an ideal solution concept. One potential answer for this is that most of the blockchain solutions embed a social engineering element, which makes it an ideal solution for vital statistics recording. For instance, beyond the data record system, self-sovereign personal data management scheme, facilitation of the service provision across the stakeholders, and further enhancement of the mini-economy through value creation based on the tokenization of the ecosystem are some of the features that make this solution ideal. This can also help track and uniquely identify registered members, thus efficiently addressing their demand (e.g., medical service provision).

---

[39]See Illinois Blockchain Initiative which was launched on November 16, 2016, with key participants of Illinois' Department of Commerce and Economic Opportunity (DCEO), Department of Financial and Professional Regulation (DFPR), Department of Insurance (DOI), Department of Innovation & Technology (DoIT), and Cook County's Recorder of Deeds at stake: https://blockchan.ge/blockchange-birth-registration.pdf, and Brazil's first birth record on blockchain at https://cointelegraph.com/news/first-blockchain-exclusive-birth-certificates-recorded-in-brazil

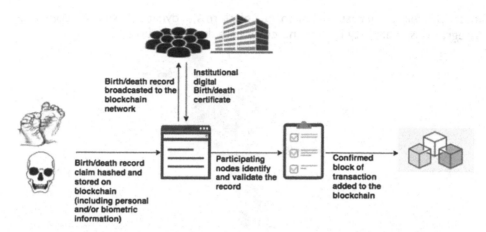

Figure 4-9. A diagrammatic presentation of birth and beyond record system on blockchain

On top of the event recording solution, a tokenized system that incents the participants and creates value can be designed. Such a solution concept has the potential to exploit the increased use and coverage of mobile technology in developing countries.

Summary

Despite slower pace adoption, Blockchain has remained to be an evolving technology with yet to be explored potentials for businesses and digital economy space in general. Gartner's recent study puts the technology as one of the top ten strategic tech trends for 2020.[40] In this chapter, we have covered strategic tools for adopting the tech to your businesses. However, it is important to bear in mind that applying the tech to businesses today calls for evaluation and prudent decision-making as the tech is not the only game in town. For example, with fintech waves in the financial industry, considering blockchain-powered payments depends on whether the tech outweighs any alternative fintech solution and/or if there is any possibility to combine the two. Moreover, applying the right strategy for the adoption of the tech to leapfrog the opportunities it offers to rewrite the economic power grid is pivotal. In addition, as the technology evolves in its path to maturity, businesses need to continually update their applications in order to be competitive. In association with this, in 2019, Gartner predicted that about 90% of blockchain-powered platforms will be obsolete in less than two years unless replaced mainly due to the issues of

---

[40]See Gartner Research at www.gartner.com/en/doc/432920-top-10-strategic-technology-trends-for-2020

interoperability across blockchain platforms, dynamic smart contract integrations, scalability issues, and corporate data structures.[41]

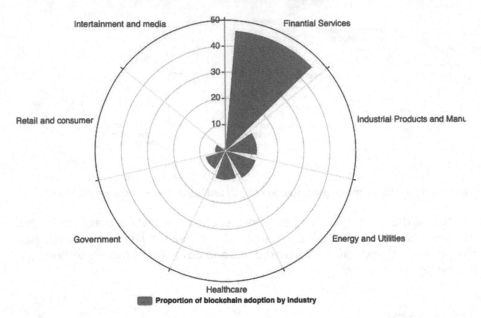

Figure 4-10. Blockchain adoption across industries, based on 2018 PwC Survey[42]

Coming to its potential applications, in digital identity, a self-declared data ownership by the identity owner is a key in guaranteeing rivalry and excludability of access to individual data. This allows users to grant or deny access to their data and for how long. It enables the individual to decide who should have access to what data and for how long. While the distributed ID protocol calls for a self-sovereign data management, there still is a need for institutional trust anchors that enforce and attest the validity and truthfulness of a claim over a digital ID. See Hileman and Rauchs (2017) for the key roles of gatekeepers in permissioned blockchain networks (listed as access control, terms and conditions, software maintenance and updates (optional), dispute resolution/arbitration, setting terms for asset issuance/tokenization, regular reporting, data mining, setting additional terms and conditions, assistance when there is a need for compromise, etc.). This will help in tackling the potential risks (e.g., fraud) and market failure resulting from a perfectly distributed system. Moreover, blockchain or other forms of the DLTs are not to replace the back-office systems, instead facilitate organization and access to the existing data. As Gerard (2017) noted:

[41]www.gartner.com/en/newsroom/press-releases/2019-07-03-gartner-predicts-90--of-current-enterprise-blockchain
[42]Data Source: PwC Global Blockchain Survey 2018

> *When blockchain schemes do promise some specific outcome, it is usually the magic of full availability of properly cleaned up and standardized data. The actual problem is cleaning up the data in the first place, or getting legacy systems talking to each other at all. For all the considerable effort at computerization, there is still too much paper and human effort. Settlements can still take days.*

Even if blockchain is considered to be a secure distributed system, the robustness of the security underlying this technology is questionable. Potential attacks and risks underlying this technology (mainly, cryptocurrencies and smart contracts) have been extensively discussed in different surveys about the blockchain system security and privacy (Hileman and Rauchs, 2017; Joshi et al., 2018; Möser et al., 2018; and Li et al., 2017). Self-generated and maintained keys face recovery attacks because the signature process lacks sufficient randomness in generating the keys. With the decentralized setting of these networks, in case of losses in private key, tracing tampering attacks with the lost ID can be hard.

Thus, this puts private security criteria of the self-sovereign ID solution under question. Also, depending on the consensus mechanism in play, double-spending (e.g., the usage of the same ID for more than one time in accessing a service provision) can be a problem in blockchain ID solutions. Thus, consensus mechanisms should be efficiently designed to tackle this issue. Transaction privacy leakage is one of the other issues raised. An empirical analysis on the Monero (a cryptocurrency platform) showed that transactions could be leaked with about 80% accuracy (Möser et al., 2018). Therefore, the algorithmic design of such networks calls further work (like replacing the mixing sampling distribution to near-real distribution sampling technique for the case in Monero).

As there are a significant group of non-privacy-conscious people (because of lack of knowledge or impatience in access), the privacy settings underlying such digital ID solutions should also be designed with greater care. More generally, regulatory issues, governance constraints, and bureaucracy are the other barriers in applying the DLT solution concepts. Hileman and Rauchs (2017) argued that critical challenges (mainly, privacy, confidentiality, regulatory environment, and legal risks) in the application of the DLTs persisted. Security issues are also detected around the smart contracts (a.k.a. chaincodes) mainly due to program flaws (Li et al., 2017). For further consideration in the business rule designs of the blockchain ID solutions (and beyond), see the summary of a taxonomy of vulnerabilities in smart contracts in Table 4-3.

Table 4-3. Taxonomy of vulnerabilities in smart contract sourced from Li et al. (2017)

Level	Vulnerability	Cause
Contract source code	Call to the unknown	The called function does not exist
	Out-of-gas send	Fallback of the callee is executed
	Exception disorder	Irregularity in exception handling
	Type casts	Type-check error in contract execution
	Reentrancy vulnerability	Function is re-entered before termination
	Field disclosure	Private value is published by the miner
EVM bytecode	Immutable bug	Alter a contract after deployment
	Ether lost	Send Ether to an orphan address
	Stack overflow	The number of values in stack exceeds 1024
Blockchain mechanism	Unpredictable state	State of the contract is changed before invoking
	Randomness bug	Seed is biased by malicious miner
	Timestamp dependence	Timestamp of block is changed by malicious miner

Using biometric data (e.g., like the one for the neural network facial recognition or iris scan for the WFP ID solution) in digital IDs may not persistently prove efficiency for all. Problem with a biometric data record like facial recognition is that it leads to social profiling of some vulnerable group of people (e.g., homeless). Immutability is a challenge in situations where reverting transaction records, like correcting errors, are needed (Hileman and Rauchs, 2017). In the long term, even if it is only the hash that is going to be stored on the chain, other background information stored in the integrated databases of the participating organizations can result in social profiling with an immutable record of biometric data. A digital ID can also pose a challenge for some people (e.g., those fleeing conflict and persecution without revealing their identity). In terms of cost, small-scale service providers (like private shelters) might find it expensive to use scanning machines.

Currency Under the Web 3.0 Economy

Digitalization, as a core development in the modern socioeconomic and political interactions, has called for sectoral digital transformations. In line with this, the digital economic system is evolving and so are currency and payment systems. Financial innovations through a development of new financial services and products to date have helped in reducing the costs of deposits and increasing the return from lending. Some of such developments have been discussed in Chapters 1 and 2 of this book.

This chapter starts with a discussion on the ongoing arguments and trends of central bank digital currencies (CBDCs). The discussion fleshes out the major issues arising in the adoption of this form of payment system by the conservative institutions, national banks. Further limitations and feasibility concerns about this form of payment system will be discussed in depth. The chapter starts with a brief introduction to the CBDCs, followed by the comparison with the conventional payment systems (including banknotes, bank deposits, other electronic currencies, etc.).

© Abeba N. Turi 2020
A. N. Turi, *Technologies for Modern Digital Entrepreneurship*,
https://doi.org/10.1007/978-1-4842-6005-0_5

The section on the purpose of the CBDCs answers the question of why CBDCs. Besides, CBDC distributed ledger technology solution concept will be presented in light of mechanism design for this form of currency. In addition, further consideration in the application of the CBDCs, including the cost-benefit analysis, monetary policy implications, regulatory issues, and the technical layer in the design of the CBDCs, will also be discussed. In relation to the effects of the introduction of CBDCs, the implication of CBDCs for the banks and non-bank financial institutions is also highlighted. Finally, the discussion on the CBDCs wraps up by pointing out concluding remarks on the prospects and controversies of its application of the CBDCs and directions for future work.

The chapter will further extend the discussion of the Web 3.0 monetary system to stablecoins. Stablecoins are price-stable cryptocurrencies pegged by other stable assets like gold, stable fiat currencies, or other cryptocurrencies. Here, I will review cryptocurrency volatility and its implied effects in cryptocurrency as a unit of account, medium of exchange, and store of value like any currency unit. Moreover, by taking a case-specific analysis on Facebook's cryptocurrency, Libra, I will assess its underlying stablecoin, dubbed GlobalCoin.

Central Bank Digital Currencies: Prospects and Controversies

Central banks (a.k.a. national banks, reserve banks, or monetary authorities) are institutions that oversee and regulate the banking system and control the monetary base. The world's oldest central bank is Sweden's Sveriges Riksbank, which awards the Nobel Prize in economics. The Federal Reserve is America's central bank, overseeing banking and making monetary policy. Others include the Bank of Canada, Bank of England, Bank of Japan, and European Central Bank (ECB). The ECB acts as a common central bank for 17 European countries: Austria, Belgium, Cyprus, Estonia, Finland, France, Germany, Greece, Ireland, Italy, Luxembourg, Malta, the Netherlands, Portugal, Slovakia, Slovenia, and Spain.

Countries have a system designed to protect depositors and the economy as a whole against bank runs (a financial crisis where banking customers panic to withdraw funds). This system has four main features:

- *Deposit insurance*: Guarantees that a bank's depositors will be paid even if the bank can't come up with the funds, up to a maximum amount per account.

- *Capital requirements*: Regulators require that the owners of banks hold substantially more assets than the value of bank deposits.

- *Reserve requirements:* The rules set by the federal reserve that determine the minimum reserve ratio for banks.

- *Discount window:* An arrangement in which the federal reserve stands ready to lend money to banks in trouble.

The central banks are responsible for the issuance of paper currency and the minting of coins with a government decree in the fiat currency system.

Figure 5-1 shows how money is created to circulate in the economy through the interaction of banks and individuals. The figure depicts a simplified presentation assuming that initially the money supply consists of only cash in the hand of a customer and that she deposits the cash into a checkable bank deposit.

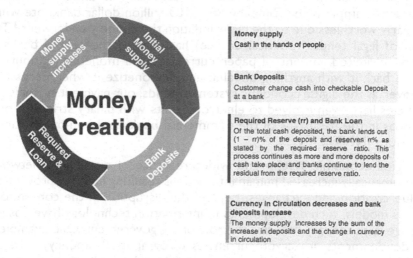

Money supply
Cash in the hands of people

Bank Deposits
Customer change cash into checkable Deposit at a bank

Required Reserve (rr) and Bank Loan
Of the total cash deposited, the bank lends out (1 − rr)% of the deposit and reserves rr% as stated by the required reserve ratio. This process continues as more and more deposits of cash take place and banks continue to lend the residual from the required reserve ratio.

Currency in Circulation decreases and bank deposits increase
The money supply increases by the sum of the increase in deposits and the change in currency in circulation

Figure 5-1. How banks create money from deposits and loans

Human developments in history have led to the creation of currency as a form of medium of exchange. It is intriguing to observe how our payment systems and monetary civilizations evolved from using shell money, stones, salt bars, precious metals, fiat currencies to electronic hashed money (Ferguson, 2008). After the end of WWII (July 1–22, 1944), the United Nations Monetary and Financial Conference (a.k.a. Bretton Woods Conference) took place to regulate international monetary and financial order through a new financial system.[1] With the participation from 44 allied nations, the conference came up with a draft for a stable currency system. This resulted in the US dollar to be the world's reserve currency backed by gold. Because the United States

---

[1]See Mikesell and Mikesell (1994).

held most of the global gold reserves following the war, countries tied their local currencies with the US dollar. Thus, with the gold standard, governments came up with the gold certificate (claim check) for a gold reserve in the treasury, thus serving as representative currencies. This resulted in the convertibility of gold for paper currencies. In 1971, this system was interrupted by the Nixon Shock following the suspension/cancellation of the unilateral convertibility of US dollars into gold or other reserve assets.[2] This was in response to increasing inflation. The shock resulted in the current freely floating fiat currency system with political decree where no currency is not backed by gold or other assets of intrinsic value.

The value in the fiat currency depends on the confidence the public has on its government. However, the government-backed fiat currency system by itself has not always proved perfection, especially in times of crisis. A prominent example is the Zimbabwean $100 trillion dollar banknote which was nearly worthless due to the hyperinflation the country underwent.[3] This notion of legal tender (political decree) has enabled the central banks to issue an unlimited amount of paper currencies and monetize without the need to back it with anything of value and demonetize it when necessary.[4] Moreover, as the digital economic system expands, our payment systems and currencies have even evolved to electronic units with binary strings of ones and zeros in the databases of the commercial banks and non-bank financial institutions (NBFIs).

The digital economic system and widespread use of distributed networks have dramatically increased human interactions resulting in the improvements of value creation and exchanges. Beyond the disruption in the conventional business models, such developments in information technology have posed a challenge by potentially reducing the role of the government. One example of such developments are cryptocurrencies (programmable money). Like any form of developments in the payment system (like a visa card), cryptocurrencies

---

[2]On August 15, 1971, President Richard Nixon closed the gold window and imposed a 10% surcharge on all dutiable imports to force other countries to revalue their currencies against the dollar. See Irwin (2013).

[3]On May 6, 2016, CNN ran a story on "The 100 trillion dollar banknote that is nearly worthless" highlighting the long-rooted hyperinflation in Zimbabwe and the failed central banknotes in the country, retrieved on April 5, 2019.

[4]The very recent example in this regard is the demonetization of all 500 and 1000 rupees banknotes by the Indian government with the goal to "curtail the shadow economy and reduce the use of illicit and counterfeit cash to fund illegal activity and terrorism." See the press release by the Reserve Bank of India "Withdrawal of Legal Tender Status for ₹ 500 and ₹ 1000 Notes: RBI Notice (Revised)," Reserve Bank of India, November 8, 2016, www.rbi.org.in/Scripts/BS_PressReleaseDisplay.aspx?prid=38520, retrieved on April 20, 2020.

are other forms of currency that revolutionize the conventional fiat currency system. One important aspect of such currencies in the private form is that they reduced the role of the government as a legal tender.

However, the innovation diffusion and survival of such a form of private currencies as a payment system have not been long rooted to date. The wild fluctuations in the prices (bubbles) and inconsistent acceptance of such forms of currencies have led to the question on whether the governments have to step up in the issuance of e-cash (or, more specifically, central bank digital currencies (CBDCs) which are deemed to be more stable). Unlike the conventional distributed network-based cryptocurrencies, the digital coins from banks have an interesting feature in that they are free of credit risk backed by the fiat currency of the issuing bank (Dyson and Hodgson, 2016). The main purpose behind this argument is to keep the payment systems secure and efficient through a government-backed currency system, unlike the private form of cryptocurrencies like bitcoin, ethereum, and so on.

Central Bank Digital Currencies

The banking sector being one of the facilitators of economic interactions is considering mirroring the digitalization of the other sectors. In today's digital society, in many countries, the use of cash as payment systems shows a declining pattern (e.g., about 2% of payment systems in Sweden;[5] Griffoli et al., 2018). As the digital society transforms into a cashless transaction behavior, there is a need for the development of a safe and efficient payment system. The sector faces some challenges from new developments in financial technologies.

The developments in the decentralized private digital currencies have made central banks question and experiment the potentials for the central bank digital currencies. Some examples of the banks involved in the exploration of CBDCs include the Bank of England,[6] Central Bank of Uruguay, Norges Bank,[7]

---

[5]www.riksbank.se/en-gb/payments--cash/the-riksbanks-task-in-relation-to-payments/what-is-money/

[6]In 2018, the Bank of England published a working paper on the design principles and balance sheet implications of the central bank digital currencies (CBDCs). The paper showed the dynamics in the initial stages of CBDC launch and the potential dramatic shift (bank run) of private sectors and users from the bank deposits to the CBDCs (Kumhof and Noone, 2018).

[7]See also a working paper series on the central bank digital currencies by the Norge Bank, Norges Bank Papers No. 1 (2018).

Riksbank, ECB,[8] Reserve Bank of Australia (on hold[9]), Federal Reserve,[10] Bank of Canada,[11] and so on. The issue has remained to be open with different levels of curiosity, vivacity, as well as fear of the need, functionality, design, feasibility, and related regulatory issues on whether these forms of government-backed cryptocurrencies are viable to develop. The idea is further circulated and discussed by various experts and international organizations.[12]

For example, in 2018, IMF Managing Director Christine Lagarde, in her speech during the Singapore FinTech Festival, highlighted the need to consider CBDCs.[13] She argued that the state has to step up in the provision of the accompanying payment systems of the digital economy for privacy, security, and consumer protection as well as financial inclusion reasons. A global survey on the central bank's cryptocurrency by the BIS shows that central banks are interested in the notion of the central bank's cryptocurrency; however, they are considering it with greater care and caution. Most are only at a conceptual stage with Sweden and Uruguay in a relatively better state of adoption.

Central bank cryptocurrency (CBCC), a.k.a. Fedcoin, refers to programmable e-money of central bank in which transfers take place on a peer-to-peer (P2P) basis without the need for intermediaries or a central server, unlike other forms of electronic means of payment systems such as mobile money and credit or debit cards (Bech and Garratt, 2017). The primary purpose behind a central bank digital currency is to provide state-guaranteed electronic means of payments.

---

[8]Bloomberg on January 7, 2019, run a story, according to which "Virtual Currencies To Go Down as 'Load of Nonsense'," says ECB's Hansson. Quoting the cryptocurrency bubble and the European Central Bank policymaker Ardo Hansson, they reported the need for investor protection from the private cryptocurrencies. Similar reports show that the European Central Bank has no plans to issue digital currencies; see story by Reuters on September 14, 2019, quoting "ECB has no plan to issue digital currency: Draghi," www.reuters.com/article/us-ecb-bitcoin/ecb-has-no-plan-to-issue-digital-currency-draghi-idUSKCN1LU1JM

[9]See the Speech by Tony Richards, Reserve Bank of Australia Head of Payments Policy Department, on "Cryptocurrencies and Distributed Ledger Technology," Australian Business Economists Briefing Sydney, June 26, 2018, www.rba.gov.au/speeches/2018/sp-so-2018-06-26.html, accessed on March 20, 2020.

[10]Up until the writing of this text, the Federal Reserve of the United States is not convinced about the idea of CBDCs.

[11]See Fintech Research by the Bank of Canada: www.bankofcanada.ca/research/digital-currencies-and-fintech/fintech-research, accessed on May 22, 2020.

[12]See, for example, Griffoli et al. (2018), IMF Staff Discussion Note No. 18/08.

[13]See the article by the IMF published on November 14, 2018, with running head: "Winds of Change: The Case for New Digital Currency," www.imf.org/en/News/Articles/2018/11/13/sp111418-winds-of-change-the-case-for-new-digital-currency, accessed on March 20, 2020.

In its form of transaction, the P2P setting of this cryptocurrency mimics a direct cash exchange that has partial anonymity. In the retail form of transaction, the P2P nature of the cryptocurrency guarantees anonymity through a decentralized setting. On the other hand, anonymity is limited, in that their central operating system facilitates such transactions. Cryptocurrencies in the wholesale transactions are thus instead preferred for efficiency and cost-effective settlement purposes.[14] For example, e-krona, one of the potential CBDCs, has two main forms of value-based and account-based. The value-based one attains anonymity where its ownership follows a prepaid business model, while the account-based one requires partnership with other central agencies in its functionality.[15]

The central bank can create one-to-one convertibility between electronic federal reserves and paper notes, implying that the CBDCs are issued (ledgers are created) in replacement to the reserves and notes or the other way round. It is common that most (if not all) of the private cryptocurrencies operate under the principle of limited supply, while the supply of CBCCs, like the conventional money supply, is meant to endogenously be determined by the market (commercial banks—credit unions and trust companies—influence the quantity of demand deposits and the money supply).

The Legacy Payment Systems vs. CBDCs

CBDCs are different from other forms of the banking digital currency system, in that the electronic currencies are issued by private entities, unlike the banknotes/coins which are issued by the central bank. Thus, CBDCs are the electronic version of the banknotes/coins issued by central banks. Central bank cryptocurrencies can give customers the option to choose over the commercial banks with risk-free central bank Fedcoin liabilities. The key feature underlying this form of currency is anonymity in the end users while the need for this is arguable (Bech and Garratt, 2017). These forms of electronic currencies have not been applied so far.

With an increase in the electronic means of payments (bank cards, mobile payment systems, and debit cards), the survey by the Riksbank on the pattern of payments shows a decline in the use of cash in Sweden (Skingsley Riksbank, 2018). One of the key factors behind this shift in the pattern of payments is related to the demographic composition of the people, where the younger generation tends to use the electronic means of payments the more.[16]

---

[14]A study by the IMF supports that CBDCs facilitate real-time and secure international settlements (He et al., 2017).
[15]See Riksbank's e-krona project report 2 (2018).
[16]See also Mancini-Griffoli et al. (2018).

Riksbank has been closely involved in conceptualizing and identifying the potentials and implications of central bank digital currencies through its e-krona project. The project works on researching on rethinking the Swedish krona in a digital form.

> *If the state, via the central bank, does not have any payment services to offer as an alternative to the strongly concentrated private payment market, it may lead to a decline in competitiveness and a less stable payment system, as well as make it difficult for certain groups to make payments. Ultimately, it may also risk eroding basic trust in the Swedish monetary system. Some of these problems could be neutralised or mitigated by an e-krona.*

—Skingsley Riksbank, 2018

Another project, Project Ubin, by the Singapore Central Bank, is also underway. The project aimed at creating a digital token version of the Singapore dollar and securities asset. The digital token is intended to facilitate the domestic inter-bank payments and international settlements that are run on the DLT platform.[17]

A similar project is the one in Uruguay. Here, a pilot program on the central bank cryptocurrencies, e-Peso, has been deemed successful for a greater governmental financial inclusion (Central Bank of Uruguay).[18] The e-Peso platform keeps the record of ownership of the digital banknotes and does not utilize distributed ledger technologies of any kind. In contrast to the private digital tokens (which are in most cases distributed by nature), central bank tokens are supposedly run under the notion of the legal tender, which passes regulatory requirements. The platform overall issued 20 million e-Pesos. About 35% of the e-Peso was distributed by a third-party PSP that held an equivalent of money with the central bank. Users own electronic wallets to hold e-Pesos, where P2P transactions take place through text messages or the mobile e-Peso application. In this digital currency system, the role of the central bank is a legal tender, which is a complementary monetary system to cash peso.

---

[17]See the report by the Monetary Authority of Singapore on "Project Ubin: Central Bank Digital Money using Distributed Ledger Technology," www.mas.gov.sg/Singapore-Financial-Centre/Smart-Financial-Centre/Project-Ubin.aspx, accessed on March 20, 2020.

[18]www.epeso.com.uy/

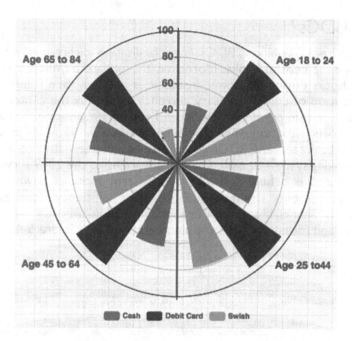

Figure 5-2. The payment behavior of the Swedish population by age group[19]

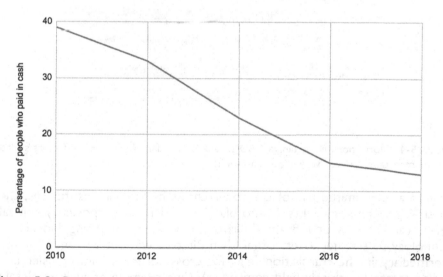

Figure 5-3. Percentage of Swedish people who responded that they paid in cash for their most recent transaction[20]

---

[19]Data Source: Sveriges Riksbank, Payment Patterns in Sweden Survey 2018, www.riks-bank.se/en-gb/statistics/payments-notes-and-coins/payment-patterns/
[20]Data Source: Sveriges Riksbank, Payment Patterns in Sweden Survey 2018, www.riks-bank.se/en-gb/statistics/payments-notes-and-coins/payment-patterns/

Why CBDCs?

The main purpose behind CBDCs is to facilitate a direct public access of money from the central banks. Moreover, the private payment systems are prone to shocks during economic instabilities and may face failure in crisis. Hence, this form of complementary currency system by the central banks is meant to create safe payment systems and secure stabilization. For instance, during a bank-run situation where the public tries to withdraw their funds due to fears of a bank failure, CBDCs can be used as an alternative to a bank run from the banking system to cash. Overall, according to the 2019 survey by the BIS,[21] the purpose behind this currency system includes payment safety, securities settlement arrangements, payment efficiency (domestic and international), financial stability, financial inclusion (mostly in emerging economies), and monetary policy implementations (see Figure 5-4).

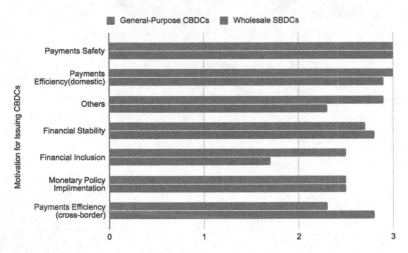

Figure 5-4. Motivations for issuing a CBDC, ranked in order of importance: factors scaled "not so important = 1" to "very important = 4")[22]

Despite a very limited use of cryptocurrencies by financial institutions, the underlying technology, DLTs, is into play for settlement purposes by central banks. Large banks and financial firms are working on using blockchain technology to transfer assets other than Bitcoins without the need for the intermediary in the transaction (e.g., for cross-border money transfer and trading shares for closely held companies). One example of such wholesale payment systems is a project run by the Bank of Canada, Jasper. Such

---

[21]www.bis.org/publ/arpdf/ar2019e3.pdf
[22]Data Source: Barontini and Holden (2019). BIS Central Banks' survey on CBDCs, 2019

settlement services (real-time settlement) are run through permissioned DLTs. DLTs allow decentralization of the notion of trust—which in the traditional system has been built by centralization either in banks or central banks and supported by the regulatory, supervisory, and legal system and by government funds—using cryptology and peer-to-peer verification to enable issuance of cryptocurrencies such as Bitcoins.

Unlike the distributed DLTs, the permissioned DLTs (Corda and Hyperledger Fabric) are perceived to be suitable for the financial markets and banks due to privacy and other administrative issues. In these forms of DLTs, the consensus is reached through trusted parties among the stakeholders (e.g., the central bank in the case of settlement services) of the transactions running on such platforms (Bech and Garratt, 2017). The transfer of central bank digital money takes place through digital depository receipt, CB's digital reserve liability for which CB tokens are issued. The technology has not proved to be better than the conventional centralized system beyond their minimized risk of a transaction through real-time settlements. Thus, the application of the DLTs in the financial market infrastructures is still in its infancy, mostly at the proof of concept and pilot stages. The technology in its current form, however, seems to be promising for cross-border transactions (He et al., 2017, and Chapman et al., 2017).

CBDC DLT Solution Concept

What should the protocol for the CBDCs look like? This depends on the roles the central banks play in the payment system and the interaction with the stakeholders of the system (including banks, NBFIs, clearing organizations, payment service providers, CBDC exchange intermediaries, businesses, and individuals). Kumhof and Noone (2018) in the Bank of England's working paper series identified three different models of CBDCs depending on the access to CBDC: *Financial Institutions Access*, *Economy-wide Access*, and *Financial Institutions Plus CBDC-Backed Narrow Bank Access*.

The access models can be summarized into two main categories (Norges Bank Papers No. 1, 2018):

- *Account-based model* (users have direct access, and CBDC account with the central bank and transfers and access take place through payment instruments—mobile devices, Web, cards, and IoT)

- *Value-based model* (an indirect access to the CBDCs, where users use non-central bank channels to buy/sell and transfer CBDCs)

Moreover, the protocol development for CBDCs, distinct from the private cryptocurrencies, should take into account for the role of the central banks as lender of the last resort, legal tender (CBDC ledger government legal decree), interest rates and monetary policy, and the adjustable unlimited supply of the CBDCs.[23] Digital wallets are developed in such a way that they preserve the cash-like anonymity of the users. The private key is composed of the information about the user, which is hashed and stored in the (distributed relational) database, and CBDC ledger stores the index of each value transfer/ transaction. Like all other cryptocurrencies, public keys hold the address of individual users. Further design concepts on the technical layer of CBDCs are beyond the coverage of this text.

Figure 5-5 shows the possible basic design of the CBDC system. It is developed based on the key classifications of CBDCs (Kumhof and Noone, 2018; Norges Bank Papers No. 1, 2018; Riksbank, 2018; and Bech and Garratt, 2017) and the general DLT technical layer network design concept.

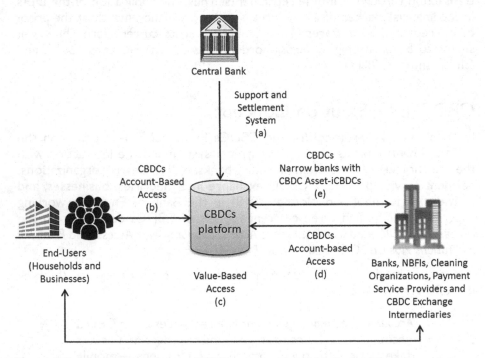

Figure 5-5. Possible basic design of CBDC system: (c) and (d) Financial Institutions Access; (b), (c), and (d) Economy-wide Access; and (a) and (e) Financial Institutions Plus CBDC-Backed Narrow Bank Access

---

[23]Here, central banks need to have the mandate and ability to increase the CBDC supply, thus the liquidity, to eligible institutions during crisis. Unlike the caped private cryptocurrency supply principle, the supply of CBDCs varies with the demand where central banks buy/sell short-term government securities in exchange for the CBDCs in the account-based CBDC system (see Bordo and Levin, 2017).

Important issues to take into account in the course of applications of the modified versions of these like digital currencies at the central bank level, beyond defining the roles and legal mandates of the central banks, include[24]

1) *Technical issues:* Mechanism design and protocol development with different denominations of the digital banknotes.

2) Privacy and security issues (anonymity of ownership).

3) *Analytical issues:* Concept design and application.

4) *Regulatory issues:* The legal standing of such currencies.

5) *The issue of interest on CBDCs:* Interest is charged on CBDCs and identifying the consequences.

6) The effects of such a currency system together with an overall feasibility analysis.

On the legal mandates and requirements side, there is a need for an amendment in the existing acts and laws defining the mandates of the banks in issuing currencies. For the Riksbank, the existing act is considered congruent for the value-based CBDCs while it requires some amendments for the account-based ones (see e-krona project's report 2[25]). Furthermore, regulation, cybersecurity, the economic cycle (during recession times, which most of the financial technologies have not encountered yet, new risk scoring and risk management models seem to have the edge over those of traditional banks), and rise in interest rates are other important factors to consider. Some of the new business models have also not been tested over the long term (through time price increase by fintech startups may result in customer attrition and lessening the effect of price erosion on the banking sector), and some broad-based structural shifts could tip a given region toward faster digitization. Denmark, for example, has adopted legislation that calls for a cashless economy within five years.

Further Considerations in the Application of the CBDCs

In this section, we will flesh out major concerns, stir direction for future work in this field, and implications of the CBDCs from different dimensions.

---

[24]See Barontini and Holden (2019), BIS Central Banks' survey on CBDCs, 2019, and Hileman and Rauchs (2017).
[25]www.riksbank.se/en-gb/payments-cash/e-krona/e-krona-reports/e-krona-project-report-2/

Implication for Monetary Policy

Interest-bearing CBDCs are considered to be alternative stable payment system in the incidence of crisis while there are some reservations on their need in some countries, for example, Norway.[26] In terms of implication to the monetary policy, there is no evidence of negative impacts of the CBDC as a payment system. The size of money (of any form) in circulation and type of payment systems do not have a direct influence on the monetary policy, but can facilitate ways to conduct a monetary policy (Bordo and Levin, 2017; Norges Bank Papers No. 1, 2018; and Rogoff, 2015). Hence, CBDCs as payment system do not create any different direct effects from banknotes than facilitating a transparent system. However, the store of value aspect of the CBDCs can create an alternative to the user; thus, central bank can impose lower-bound interest rate (negative where necessary), which will help rule out cash (resolving the zero lower bound);[27, 28] in addition, the lower interest rates on CBDCs can reduce the debt burden for CBDC-denominated ones that extend to the fiscal policy tools.[29]

Regulatory Issues

As far as the digital economy is concerned, the rule governing the digital value transfer and the need for the accompanying technology at the central bank level (financial, technical, and legal aspects) are required. Moreover, framing the ways to govern and regulate the private sectors (intermediaries facilitating the access to the CBDCs and payment systems built on top of the CBDC system) operating on the CBDC platforms is vital. With the anonymity of the CBDCs, further consideration for the ethos (ethics) such as anti-money laundering, pathos for the trade-off between privacy and digital ID management, where privacy is one of the emotional appeals for the digital society, is another issue to take into account.

Technical Layer

In spite of other complex issues that arise with the introduction and application CBDCs, the system is supposed to be viable in terms of a technological infrastructure.[30] However, the type of technology which could be deployed

---

[26]See Norges Bank Papers No. 1 (2018).

[27]See Rogoff (2015) for the details on the cost and benefits of forgoing banknotes in favor of electronic currencies.

[28]See also Friedman Rule (Friedman, 1989).

[29]See Barrdear and Kumhof (2016), Bordo and Levin (2017), and Rogoff (2015).

[30]Norges Bank Papers No. 1 (2018) states that scalability, interoperability, accessibility, security, and flexibility of the CBDCs are possible to realize assuming the associated financial costs of the system development which depends on the technology, functionality, and security and other institutional factors like outsourcing and system ownership.

for government-backed digital currencies and the design approach remain an answered. Here, to devise a system utilizing DLTs or alternative technological solutions (CBDC ledger or an XRP-style ledger) without compromising the central bank's role in controlling its currency in a secured attack-resistant way is needed. Besides, the definition of stakeholders and possible related applications running on top of the CBDC platform requires further research. Moreover, the question of whether central banks operate on a unique platform of their own or a commonly utilized global/regional platform needs to be addressed.

Disruptive Technologies in the Commercial Banking Industry and NBFIs

Banks based on their business line focus are categorized into three main types:

1. *Retail bank* (consumer banking) is the provision of services by a bank to individual consumers: services offered include savings and transactional accounts, mortgages, personal loans, debit cards, and credit cards.

2. *Commercial bank* is a type of bank/financial institution that provides services such as accepting deposits, making business loans, and offering basic investment products to individuals, corporations, or large/middle-sized business.

3. *Investment bank* is a financial institution that assists individuals, corporations, and governments in raising financial capital by underwriting or acting as the client's agent in the issuance of securities (or both) and assist companies involved in mergers and acquisitions (M&A) and provide ancillary services such as market making, trading of derivatives and equity securities, and FICC services (fixed income instruments, currencies, and commodities). Unlike commercial banks and retail banks, investment banks do not take deposits.

Overall, the key banking services provided by traditional banks are financing, investments, and transactions. Banks drive their revenue by bundling these services.

Fintech

With improved artificial intelligence, cost-effective data mining and processing, and convenient and efficient speed of operation capturing the low-end customers' preference, the financial technology wave has created noticeably significant pressure to the incumbent players in the financial markets, including banks and credit card providers (such as Visa and Mastercard). Many fintech companies operate in different business lines (including credit, deposit, settlement services, etc.). As such, fintech startups with technology-enabled financial solutions are emerging. For example, Stripe[31] is a technology company that allows both private individuals and businesses to accept payments over the Internet[32] and is valued at $5 billion and has partnered with Visa. It focuses on providing the technical, fraud prevention, and banking infrastructure required to operate online payment systems. Square,[33] a financial services, merchant services aggregator, and mobile payment company for in-person payments, is yet another example.

Already-established IT companies are also entering the traditional banking businesses. For example, in peer-to-peer money transfer market, Venmo, part of the PayPal company, allows for easy transfer of small amounts of cash. Major IT companies are joining the battle as well. Facebook has entered the money transfer market. Apple Pay, Android Pay, and Google Wallet are boosting mobile payments. IT platforms for matching such as peer-to-peer lending have provided a substitute for the brokerage function of banks, particularly crucial in transaction banking. Automation and algorithmic decision-making based on artificial intelligence have brought further competition in transaction banking. Banks could lose 60% of retail profit (in consumer finance, mortgages, small- and medium-scale enterprise lending, payments, and wealth management) to tech startups by 2025, according to a report by McKinsey.[34]

Accordingly, banks need to rethink their business models through technological solutions. Upon consideration for competitive advantage, banks can build fintech innovation labs or buy/partner with startups. Factors favoring the adoption of cloud technology by banks and NBFIs include cost efficiency, data growth, and analysis, speed, convenience, simplicity, cloud computing, automated decision-making, and so on. However, there are challenges to deal with as far as moving to the cloud is concerned. These include security and compliance, reliability (system failure and other disasters), regulation at the core of the banking industry, and the like. It should also be noted that banks are known to be risk-avert and conservative in some way. Classic examples of how banks react to fintech are the American Goldman Sachs and Spanish BBVA.[35]

---

[31]www.cnbc.com/2015/05/07/stripe-expands-into-asia-latin-america.html
[32]https://stripe.com/en-ca
[33]https://squareup.com/ca/en/payments/in-person-payments
[34]See "FinTechnicolor: The New Picture in Finance" at www.mckinsey.com/~/media/mckinsey/industries/financial%20services/our%20insights/bracing%20for%20seven%20critical%20changes%20as%20fintech%20matures/fintech-nicolor-the-new-picture-in-finance.ashx
[35]www.cbinsights.com/research/banks-record-fin-tech-investment/

De Nederlandsche Bank already uses Amazon Web Services for a host of banking services such as credit risk analysis, retail banking, mobile applications, website hosting, and high-performance computing. Bankinter, the sixth largest bank in Spain, also moved to Amazon cloud and brought down their risk simulations from 23 hours to just 20 minutes. A Dutch bank Robeco Direct N.V. (an asset management firm) managing around 8 billion euros of assets in investment funds and mortgages shifted their whole retail banking platform to the cloud.[36]

Access to CBDCs by the Households and Businesses: Implications for Banks and NBFIs

Potential effects and the disruption of the conventional banking and financial institutions systems (e.g., bank runs from bank deposits to the CBDCs with the central bank-backed deposit insurance) are some of the major concerns raised about the CBDCs. The introduction of CBDCs has an increasing effect on interest rates of extended loans and interest rate levied on customers' deposit which also depends on the lending market structure (Griffoli et al., 2018) (see Figure 5-6). With lower or no cost, people can switch between CBDCs and interest-bearing investments such as bank deposits. This has an implied effect of decreasing the quantity of real money (cash) that people plan to hold or save in checkable bank deposits. In addition to the government-backed currency security, if CBDC holdings bear interest with direct access to the CBDCs, then there are chances that households replace their deposits in the commercial banks depending on the rate of return accompanying the CBDCs. For example, consider a hypothetical money creation process between a bank and its customers. Consider that Alice has $100 in cash and that the required reserve ratio for the bank is 10%. Let's say those who borrow from the bank convert 50% of the cash into CBDCs and deposit the remaining 50% at the bank. Assume that Alice deposits all her money at the bank. Following this, the bank lends out $90 and reserves $10. Whoever borrows the $90 will convert $45 into CBDCs and deposit $45 in a bank. Given the required reserve, the bank will now lend out $40.5. Whoever borrows the $40.5 will convert $20.25 into CBDCs and deposit $20.25 in a bank. The bank will lend out $18.225 and so on. Overall, this portioning of deposits with CBDCs reduces the amount of bank deposits which would otherwise have been higher by a monetary transmission of 50% loanable funds which were switched to CBDCs. This switch also shrinks the currency in circulation.

---

[36]www.financewalk.com/2015/technology-finance-career-trends-2015/

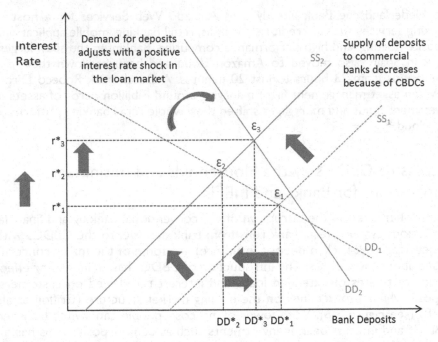

Figure 5-6. The effect of CBDCs on commercial banks' loan and deposit markets: bank deposits adjust for interest rate changes in bank loans

However, the goal of central banks, as the body of the government, is not to disrupt the banking and financial institutions' business lines than providing a secure and efficient payment system. Norges Bank identified additional factors that might lay the ground for introducing CBDCs. These include international competitiveness of a currency, where CBDCs allow a local currency to be linked to different payment systems that would otherwise be linked to other ubiquitous currencies; a payment system doesn't have a direct effect on the monetary policy tools, and thus CBDCs are taken as one of the payment systems; and that it helps in increasing seigniorage (return to central banks for issuing currency through minting coins and printing paper money).[37]

A study conducted by the Bank of England pointed out that a potential bank-run situation resulting from the access to the CBDCs is manageable as long as there is a variable rate of return on CBDC holdings and CBDCs are not convertible to either electronic federal reserves or bank deposits and if CBDCs are issued against government securities (Kumhof and Noone, 2018).

---

[37]See Norges Bank Papers No. 1 (2018). See also Bordo and Levin (2017) who have stated their concerns over the shrinking seigniorage with the diminishing use of cash in the digital society.

In the same line of reasoning, Bordo and Levin (2017) argue that CBDCs are "costless medium of exchange, secure store of value, and stable unit of account" under the condition that account-based access with adjustable interest rate through stabilization monetary policy is attained. Thus, households and businesses should not have direct access to the CBDC; rather, they can exchange CBDCs and bank deposits from the commercial banks, NBFIs, and CBDC exchange intermediaries that have direct access to the CBDCs. Therefore, in this form, the CBDCs serve as a supplement payment system to the bank deposits, banknotes, and government securities.

Outlook

In this section, we have extensively discussed the notion of central bank digital currencies. Open research questions in this regard include

1. The convertibility of CBDCs with banknotes, other electronic currencies, bank deposits, and the responsiveness of the end users to the access for the CBDCs

2. Technical layer and mechanism design behind a robust and efficient CBDCs

3. Whether central banks operate on a unique platform of their own or a commonly utilized global/regional platform

4. Bank runs and the competitive strategies of the commercial banks and NBFIs against such technological disruption

5. Financial stability, monetary policies, and the governance and regulation of the access to the CBDCs

6. Further work on the compelling evidence for identifying the value-add of CBDCs over the conventional central bank payment systems and whether central banks should indeed need to introduce CBDCs (because the idea of efficient and secure payment system doesn't affirm a decisive ground for introducing CBDCs[38]) and so on

Generally speaking, the notion of the CBDCs is too early, and it is not clear whether those involved in it in one way or another are going to consider it or if a modified notion is going to develop out of it. Various studies of different

---

[38]See Norges Bank Papers No. 1 (2018) which identified currency competitiveness, insignificant monetary policy effect, and seigniorage in support of the introduction of CBDCs, even if, according to them, the latter is not an issue for Norway's baking system.

degree echoed the need for further study and scrutiny of the system before its real-world application. Thus, there is no real-world evidence of the issuance of CBDCs so far. The main problem is that the idea of the CBDCs did not emanate from an existing problem that required such a solution concept. Instead, it comes from embracing the newly evolving private cryptocurrency notion. Thus, a whole bunch of complex issues arises in its introduction and application. Whether this remains to be an infatuation of the renowned highly conservative institution or if the institution ultimately reaches a feasible augmented version is a thing to observe in the (near) future.

Financial Technology Applications and Money

Programmable DLT-based currency system (cryptocurrencies) came into place following the 2008 financial crisis that significantly challenged the mainstream economic theories of the federal reserve system and monetary stabilization policy. This development lucid Hayek's private currency system proposed in the 1970s (see Hayek's (2009) book *Denationalization of Money: The Argument Refined* and Iwamura et al. (2014)).

Digital finance innovations of the cryptocurrencies are considered virtual game-changers, meeting the fintech business model needs for the digital value transfer and exchanges. This technology has made possible geographically unbounded frictionless, secure, and cost-effective flows of values across the globe. Cryptocurrencies like Bitcoin are peer-to-peer payment systems in which direct transaction between peers is conducted without a central party. A network of nodes confirms transactions between peers and records in the blockchain (a public mutually distributed ledger, which is a co-utile network). It uses cryptology to guarantee trust between transacting peers in a decentralized way.

Despite its promising features, these decentralized virtual currency systems also have some limitations. Some of these include

1. Difficulty in the exchange with other currencies

2. Serving as a tool for black market operation and tax evasion purposes

3. Prone to potential theft attack of private keys

4. Expensive electricity consumption in computations

5. A possible attack by selfish minors who could subvert the system for their own benefit (see Eyal and Sirer, 2014, and Johnson et al., 2014).

With the existence of selfish minors, the decentralized central bank like roles of the network of miners who keep public records can make the system inefficient. Hence, to make the ecosystem more robust and co-utile, further research work on developing incentive schemes that can hinder malicious agents from subverting the system is needed. Some traditional banks and financial institutions are working on using the technology for a cross-border money transfer and trading (e.g., CBA, Australia, utilizing the Ripple payments). A detailed discussion on further developments of this distributed currency system toward the central bank digital currency system is presented in the section that follows.

In order to see the interest rate in the cryptocurrency market, consider, for example, the arbitrage opportunity in the cryptocurrency exchange market. Let the spot price of an ETH be 1 USD; crypto investor A wants to short sell and hence borrows Ether at 10% monthly interest rate. Another crypto investor B wants to buy Ether in a forward market with a future monthly contract of $2/Ether. Crypto investor C wants to use the arbitrage opportunity in the market and hence borrows $1 at a 6% monthly interest rate to buy Ether. Then C lends her Ether to A (receiving 1.1 Ether) and sells it forward to B for $2.2, making $0.6 profit within a month.

With the speculation in the future cryptocurrency price appreciations, investors are willing to pay high interest rates. Investors in the P2P platforms for the cryptocurrencies exploit this like arbitrage opportunities in their crypto investment. It is important to note that cryptocurrencies like bitcoin are highly volatile in prices. In the conventional cryptocurrency exchange market, the competition between cryptocurrencies (Bitcoin, Ethereum, Ripple, Litcoin, Monero, Zcash, Bitcoin Gold, Namecoin, etc.) determines the price and interest rate in the market for each digital coin (Iwamura et al., 2014). Generally, an increase in the money supply, the minting of new tokens to be circulated in the network, will decrease the interest rate and increase income.

Toward a Shock-Resistant Cryptocurrency System: Stablecoins

To the other end of the currency system developments, beyond the CBDCs, is a race toward evolving the distributed cryptocurrency system via a more stable monetary system. In the sections that follow, I will take you through the major concerns of volatility and recent developments in the cryptocurrency world.

Winners and Losers of Cryptocurrency Volatility

Speculations in the cryptocurrency market fuel their price volatility. This volatility in monetary values of cryptocurrencies results in fluctuation of the purchasing power of such currencies, thus making them unstable as a medium of exchange, a unit of account, and store of value. A typical example of this can be the temporary price spike for bitcoin during the late 2017 and early 2018. Cryptocurrency price fluctuations can result in winners and losers within the blockchain community. Given economic transactions that involve long-term contracts extending over a period of time, inflating cryptocurrency can, for example, create a bias in returns.

For example, a cryptocurrency-denominated loan is normally specified in terms of the current cryptocurrency valuations. A borrower pays a specified interest rate on loan and the principal over a loan period. This return can be affected by an inflated cryptocurrency, given its prior valuation during the initiation of the loan. Consider a bitcoin denominated 5-year term loan that was initiated at the current bitcoin inflation rate of 4%. If we assume that under this loan period, the bitcoin inflation rate remains constant, then the inflation rate will be zero, which is less than the current inflation rate of 4%. The real interest rate in bitcoin is the nominal interest rate less the inflation effect; the real interest rate in bitcoin will be greater than the expected nominal interest rate. Thus, the cryptocurrency lender will gain in which case the borrower will repay a return of higher real value at maturity.

The Cryptocurrency World "Gold Standard": Stablecoins

In an appeal to keep a stable monetary environment and currency valuation, governments had been using the "gold standard" monetary system in which a country's currency was linked to the value of gold. This monetary system has its own flaws and is not functional in modern economies. Recent developments in the cryptocurrency space, however, have borrowed this notion of the monetary system. Volatility in the cryptocurrency valuations has challenged the pricing of assets through such mediums of exchange. Thus, this has been one of the main bottlenecks for the potential migration of physical assets to the blockchain space and broader adoption of this technology.

In order to avoid currency risks arising from cryptocurrency price volatilities, some traders use new breeds of cryptocurrencies, stablecoins, when transacting using cryptocurrencies as a unit of account. Stablecoins refer to the notion of price-stable cryptocurrencies pegged by other stable assets like gold or stable fiat currencies like USD or other cryptocurrency denominations. The (semi)collateralized stablecoin business model follows a hedge funding business model that creates a token for the stablecoin and pools capital from crypto investors that will collateralize the stablecoin in the form of asset, fiat currency, or another cryptocurrency through a centralized institution that serves as a custodian of reserve assets and issuer of a token, for example, Gemini Dollar,[39] Tether,[40] and TrueUSD[41] (one-to-one fiat-backed centralized stablecoins) and MakerDAO[42] and Dai[43] (crypto-backed decentralized stablecoins) and Basis[44] stablecoin, which shut down due to regulatory constraints (a non-collateralized stablecoin).

In its raw sense, the fiat-pegged stablecoins are no more than a digital representation of the fiat currencies; they are backed on a one-to-one ratio. For the crypto-collateralized stablecoins, the entire system is over the blockchain. The non-collateralized stablecoins replicate the idea of central banks controlling money supply without any collateralization. In the same fashion, business logic that defines the value of programmable money is set in the smart contract and guarantees a steady supply of the cryptocurrency through the forces of supply and demand. Note that cryptocurrency prices are unstable because the cryptocurrency supply does not respond to its demand (see Saito and Iwamura, 2019).

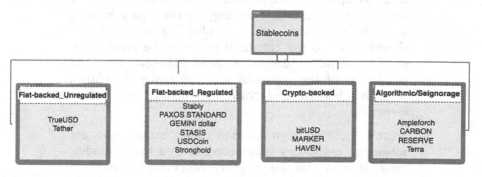

Figure 5-7. Types of stablecoins and examples

[39]Gemini Dollar, `https://gemini.com/dollar/`, accessed on April 20, 2020.
[40]Tether, `https://tether.to/`, accessed on April 20, 2020.
[41]TrueUSD, `www.trusttoken.com/`, accessed on April 20, 2020.
[42]MakerDAO, `https://makerdao.com/en/`, accessed on April 20, 2020.
[43]Dai, `https://makerdao.com/en/dai/`, accessed on April 20, 2020.
[44]Basis, `www.basis.io/`, accessed on April 20, 2020.

There are some critics on the feasibility of stablecoins (see Chohan, 2019; Eichengreen, 2018; and Fabric Ventures and TokenData report, 2018). The question of whether the stablecoins are steady, as claimed, brings us to the following key points:

1. *Fiat-pegged stablecoins*: A regulated fiat currency's valuation defines the value of the stablecoin it is backing. Stablecoin token issuers operate with accounts in the traditional banking system (like Tether's account in Cathay United Bank and Hwatai Bank in Taiwan). Thus, the trust in the central financial institution is crucial for the stability of the collateralized stablecoin (Chohan (2019) highlights the constraints in pegging cryptocurrencies with the traditional currencies).

2. *Asset-pegged stablecoins and potential risk of insolvency*: For the asset-pegged stablecoins, market risks can arise from the collateralized assets. If the price of a collateral asset drops as opposed to the price of the stablecoin, then a similar risk management strategy to the legacy banking and financial systems comes into play. That is, the curator should liquidate the collateral to close the position. A liquidity crunch situation of dried cash can limit the liquidation of the collateral asset as required. With a small number of blockchain community, this risk is inevitable.

3. Trust is built through licensed token issuers who are subject to regulatory supervision. Such a hedge funding business model of the cryptocurrency market is of no new notion than creating big tech giants that could potentially monopolize the industry. Thus, a centralized form of operation, as opposed to the inherent democratic virtue of the blockchain system, will expose the cryptocurrency ecosystem to a single point of failure, privacy, and security risks with a non-transparent off the chain verifications.

4. In addition to regulatory constraints, unlike the blockchain-based cryptocurrency, which has instant transaction validation and transfer of values, the fiat-pegged coins rely on the legacy payment channels like wire transfer which is time-consuming.

5. *Potential manipulation risk (like misrepresentation)*: With the limited transparency of how much reserves exist in the system at a given time, off-chain auditing is risky (e.g., the Enron scandal of fraudulent accounting practice[45]). Such custodians might also benefit from the exploitation of institutional features like exploitation of legislative loopholes where the industry's practice is not yet solidified. For example, money laundering and illegal practices with the anonymous features of the stablecoin (by fully or partially utilizing the innate virtue of blockchain anonymous and censorship-resistant ledger) or pricing manipulation in the case of cryptocurrency-backed fractional reserve stablecoins can be some of the underlying problems.

6. Cryptocurrency-backed stablecoins are volatile with the underlying currency they are backed with. In the case of depreciation of the values of the collateral currency, blockchain-enabled instant liquidation (bank run) can make stablecoin less stable or even worthless. The collateralization ratio used to tackle this problem is inefficient, where a fractional reserve (not the total) is recovered when exiting the system.

7. Volatility in the value of an underlying pegging asset/currency can lead to financial instability within the cryptocurrency community where uncertainty on the value of debts arises for lenders and borrowers (see the previous section for a discussion on the winners and losers of cryptocurrency price volatility for the distortion of the relationship between borrowers and lenders).

8. For asset-backed (like precious metals or derivatives) cryptocurrencies, the supply of the stablecoin depends on the rate of the asset production. When the stock of the asset increases more rapidly than the blockchain nano-economy over which the stablecoin operates, there is inflation and vice versa.

---

[45]In the early 2000s, Enron (an American energy, commodities, and services company) used a fraudulent accounting practice in collaboration with an accounting and auditing company, Arthur Andersen, through techniques of "mark-to-market accounting" and strategic transfer of problematic assets to special purpose entities (SPEs), misrepresenting its financial condition. The company consistently covered its internal problems and publicly released dubious financial statements. Enron went bankrupt and collapsed in July 2002.

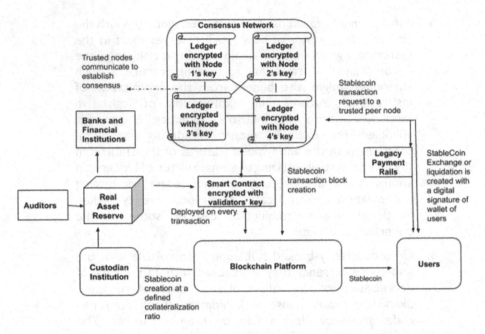

Figure 5-8. A simplified real asset-collateralized stablecoin blockchain architecture with a centralized group of institutions (trusted nodes) as a custodian institution. Note that, the consensus network, is a member of the custodian institution, and there can be a monopolistic custodian with only one member as a trusted node

Even though blockchain technology came with the notion of distributed networks, the existing trends mark the creation of centralized company ownership of cryptocurrencies and cryptocurrency exchanges. Provided that, owing to the deviation from the genesis notion of a distributed self-governing network, are we giving the monetary power to the centralized business models? As a matter of fact, to date, there is poor interconnectedness of the cryptocurrencies with the financial system. Bearing in mind the regulatory frameworks that might arise with time, further developments in the sector have to be with due consideration for approaches of financial stability in which the conventional and programmable financial systems are interconnected and co-exist. Equally important with this is the adoption of robust models of risk management for financial stability (see also the discussion under the security token offerings in Chapter 3). Summing up our discussion on the stablecoins, the following section will present a specific case of stablecoin by critically analyzing Facebook's proposed cryptocurrency initiative, Libra.

Facebook's Cryptocurrency Project Libra

With the advent of the Internet and broader digital inclusions, we are experiencing a vast range of developments in financial technologies. This has brought a number of tech giants to stare at the payment systems and decentralized global monetary systems. This brings us to several questions the conventional economic theories are not able to address. Are financial infrastructures and currency systems public goods? Is there an implied market failure of financial inclusion resulting from a poor financial infrastructural development? Are the market failures to be filled by the private tech giants as opposed to the legacy monetary system? Are the notions of distributed global scale digital currencies a substitute or complementary means of payments to the localized fiat currency systems?

Facebook is known for its business model of extracting and merging users' data for ads and other commercial purposes. The company is now entering financial services through its stablecoin. Recently, the company announced the launching of its global payment system initiative, Libra.[46] On May, 24, 2019, Forbes reported the company's plans to launch a digital payment system (cryptocurrency dubbed "GlobalCoin") in 2020 under the Libra project.[47] With the company's worldwide presence and a huge network of users, the project has a milestone contribution to the innovation diffusion of cryptocurrencies and financial inclusions. Libra is a stable cryptocurrency operating on the Libra Blockchain[48] deemed to facilitate global transactions, payments, and money transfer over the Internet, enabling further digitization of assets. It is a stablecoin planned to be pegged to a reserve of assets and basket of fiat currencies, including the US dollar, euro, and Japanese yen and short-term government securities guaranteeing the stability of the value of its digital currency.

The monetary system works in such a way that Facebook's Libra Association being the issuer of the digital currency distributes a cryptographic token, Libra, in exchange for specified fiat currency. The collateralization ratio in most of the fiat-pegged stablecoins is on a 1-to-1 exchange rate. The exchange rate, when it comes to the Libra, will depend on the real asset (currency) it is backed with, in which case it might vary depending on the type of the collateral (given the exchange rate between the fiat currencies themselves, it is not

---

[46]An Introduction to Libra, a White Paper from the Libra Association Members, https:// libra.org/en-US/white-paper/, accessed on April 20, 2020.
[47]www.theguardian.com/technology/2019/may/24/facebook-plans-to-launch-globalcoin-cryptocurrency-in-2020, accessed on April 20, 2020.
[48]See the Libra Blockchain at https://developers.libra.org/docs/the-libra-blockchain-paper, accessed on April 20, 2020.

rational to set a 1-to-1 collateralization ratio both for USD and euro, for example).

I believe it should be as easy to send money to someone as it is to send a photo.

—Mark Zuckerberg at Facebook Inc.'s annual F8 developers conference, San Jose, California, April 30, 2019

The company, like all other tech giants, was criticized for free riding consumers' digital presence in its network. Moreover, there was no compensation or reward framework to the honeypot of users over which the company's business model relies on. Its current payment system is also designed to reward users for their activities within the network, including viewing of ads, online shopping content interaction, and so on, thereupon enabling the transition from the network users' business model to that of participants. Given this, such a payment system might have the potential for compensating the free riding over the Internet.

In terms of scalability, the global network of users of Facebook is ideal to adopt the GlobalCoin as a payment system. Facebook's billions of global users promise significant network externalities and economies of scope for its new proposed payment system. Free riding over the Internet (like usage of customer data by the tech companies) is a common phenomenon of the digital economic system. As a result, the company can provide financial service at a near-zero marginal cost. Thus, the company can benefit from the low entry cost, but exit costs are questionable. This is mainly due to the implied political, economic, social, technological, environmental, and regulatory global financial environment over which the company operates.

Libra has got support from the biggest players in the industry, including Mastercard, Visa, PayPal, Uber, Lyft, eBay, Stripe, and Spotify. The project also plans to work with money transfer firms like MoneyGram and the Western Union. Facebook charges about $10 million to participate in the network with the aim to raise about $1 billion from the companies it includes in the network. Thus, Libra benefits from the huge potential where there is a requirement for liquidity and pricing of the cryptoasset since the network will be endowed with a sufficient supply of users posting collateral for the creation of the pegged asset, Libra. The company's established customer base and brand recognition are sought to benefit the functionality of this payment system. Moreover, the payment system is complementary with its core non-financial business line and to that of participating companies within the Libra network.

Libra blockchain is a permissioned blockchain with an identified network of validators under the Libra Association. A diverse network of 100 validators is planned to come from a diverse set of industries and geographic coverage, including tech companies, online marketplaces, telecom, academic institutions, payment service providers, and non-profits.[49] The association headquartered in Geneva, Switzerland, governs the system, and the underlying consensus mechanism is set based on these networks of nodes. The Libra Association, through its globally placed institutions, is to act as a central trusted custodian to store the real collateralized asset (reserve).

As it is common for the centralized stablecoin, this business model suffers from transparency and audit issues of the required reserve in the system. Combined with the privacy and security issues, this poses a significant challenge to customer protection. The company entering the financial industry will be operating in a diverse and highly regulated global financial environment. The conventional payment channels over which liquidation and transfer of payments take place also make the business distinct from the serial distributed blockchain-powered cryptocurrency system. Bridging the gap for the digitalization of assets and utilization of the existing (potentially upcoming) fully decentralized payment systems is a thing to be taken into account as far as the migration of assets to the blockchain ecosystem is in place. This requires an efficiently framed collateralization ratio and price stabilization policy that can cope with the highly volatile cryptocurrency world.

Facebook's business model, like most of the other big tech companies, is built on fetching customer data and facilitating a direct peer-to-peer interaction on its network of customers. When it comes to its new cryptocurrency initiative, the company faces a significant layer of hurdles both in terms of the exploitation of its network base and from various regulators. Even if Facebook has a big network of global users, verifiability and reliability of users' data from a virtual self of users will be in question when it comes to financial service providers. Privacy and security of users' data is another issue to take into account with the poor track record the company has in this regard.[50] The notion of stablecoins has yet to be stress-tested, and Facebook in its Libra initiative might experience a vast range of challenges from the dynamic technological environment and the financial industry as a whole.

---

[49]In its initial stage, founding members of the association are identified as Mastercard, PayPal, PayU (Naspers' fintech arm), Stripe, Visa, Booking Holdings, eBay, Facebook/Calibra, Farfetch, Lyft, MercadoPago, Spotify AB, Uber Technologies, Inc., Iliad, Vodafone Group, Anchorage, Bison Trails, Coinbase, Inc., Xapo Holdings Limited, Andreessen Horowitz, Breakthrough Initiatives, Ribbit Capital, Thrive Capital, Union Square Ventures, Creative Destruction Lab, Kiva, Mercy Corps, and Women's World Banking. See Introduction to Libra at https://libra.org/en-US/white-paper/#introducing-libra, accessed on April 20, 2020.

[50]Highlighting the data breaches of Facebook, UpGuard report on April 3, 2019, shows that over 540 million records of Facebook users detailing comments, likes, reactions, account names, FB IDs, and so on have been exposed on public Amazon cloud server, www.upguard.com/breaches/facebook-user-data-leak, accessed on April 20, 2020.

Moreover, the company so far has a limited or no footprint in the payment systems, thus posing a limit on its risk management and success of its cryptocurrency as compared to the legacy financial and banking systems which operate in a clearly defined regulatory framework. Lastly, beyond the physical world operation, the robustness of the underlying technology (DLTs in general) in its current state of development is questionable to power the stablecoins. With the major hacks and attacks we experienced, the belief that considers distributed ledger technologies as trust machines of the information society is misleading.

On the other side, if efficiently designed and implemented, the notion of a stable currency system might be promising for financial stability, mainly in developing countries. Developing countries' currencies are less stable, with governments continually printing money devaluing their local currencies (e.g., Zimbabwe's hyperinflation with a 100TN Zimbabwe dollar equivalent to 40 USD cents in 2015[51]). Thus, global stablecoins of this form could have implications for stabilization of the currencies in the developing countries, but at the cost of giving the monetary power to the tech giants instead of the central banks (Fabric Ventures and TokenData report, 2018). As far as financial technologies are concerned, regulations opening a common playfield for the tech giants entering the financial space and that of banks are vital.[52] Table 5-1 shows the major global regulatory landscape toward the tech giants. It presents four different angles of the tech regulations: limits on the use of data and restriction on entry for big techs, property rights on data to consumers, and market entry promotion for big techs.

---

[51]Could Libra solve Zimbabwe's hyperinflation whose monetary system has been on a roller coaster? BBC, on February 26, 2019, reported a running head, "Zimbabwe introduces RTGS dollar to solve currency problem," www.bbc.com/news/world-africa-47361572, accessed on April 20, 2020.

[52]See a chapter from BIS Annual Economic Report 2019 on Big tech in finance: opportunities and risks at www.bis.org/publ/arpdf/ar2019e3.htm, accessed on April 20, 2020.

Table 5-1. Regulatory landscape for big techs in finance with selected global policy interventions toward the tech giants based on BIS Annual Economic Report 2019[53]

Effect on Big Techs	Financial Regulators	Competition Authorities	Data Protection Authorities
Limited	Chinese regulations on non-bank payment firms and MMFs	–	Data privacy laws
Medium	Know your customer	Open banking (restrictions)	GDPR (customer consent)
	Grant banking licenses to big techs		
	Chinese consumer credit agency		
Large	Indian unified payment interface	German ruling on Facebook	GDPR (right to portability)
		Modernization of competition law	
		Indian ecommerce law	
		Open banking (data portability)	

Summary

As economies migrate toward the digital economic system, the wave of innovation diffusion and potential transformation has stretched out to the most rigid economic unit, money, and conservative financial institutions. In this regard, the advent of programmable money like Bitcoin (with all the arguments going around such distributed cryptocurrencies), CBDCs, and stablecoins are lending the opportunities to rethink the functionalities of centralized monetary systems. Accordingly, even if the fundamental principles and functions remain untouched, currency systems have evolved from the genesis form.

Today, the dynamically shifting digital economic environment has facilitated such developments in the currency and payment systems. Moreover, technological advancements such as the Web 2.0 developments, Blockchain and distributed ledger technology, data analytics, artificial intelligence, and cloud computing are influencing the evolution in the financial systems.

---

[53]www.bis.org/publ/arpdf/ar2019e3.pdf

> *I think that the Internet is going to be one of the major forces for reducing the role of government. The one thing that is missing, but that will soon be developed, is a reliable e-Cash. A method whereby on the internet you can transfer funds from A to B, without A knowing B or B knowing A.*

> —Milton Friedman, July 1999

To this end, CBDC systems and stablecoin (though not the ultimate developments in the field) could be the next breakthrough in the evolution of currency systems of our digital era.

Glossary of Selected Tech Terms

Artificial intelligence (AI): A machine intelligence in simulated decision-making. This intelligence is developed through a rigorous learning process from data processing for performing a task and identifying patterns.

Big data: A structured or unstructured massive volume of a systematically extracted datasets for computational and predictive analysis of patterns, trends, and relationships.

Blockchain: A technology for a distributed digital ledger system that facilitates an immutable record of data through a chain of blocks of timestamped registry.

Central bank digital currency (CBDC): A form of electronic monetary system with a legal tender virtually representing the function of money, for example, China's digital yuan, which is expected to launch in late 2020.

Cloud computing: A structured computer system that groups multiple components of on-demand network access (servers, storage, databases, networking, software, analytics, and business intelligence) into a single shared pool of optimized computing packages. Cloud computing also refers to the

© Abeba N. Turi 2020
A. N. Turi, *Technologies for Modern Digital Entrepreneurship*,
https://doi.org/10.1007/978-1-4842-6005-0

act of operating tasks on remote online platforms using computing service vendors' resources (computing power, networks, servers, data storage). Some examples of cloud computing services include Amazon Web Services (AWS), Salesforce CRM system, and Microsoft Azure.

Consensus mechanism: A common agreement over a state change of records in a distributed network, mainly in Blockchain and distributed ledger technologies.

Crowdfunding: The process of soliciting funds for a cause/project from the general public through web-based platforms.

Crowdsourcing: The practice of sourcing human capital/human resources through technology-mediated digital platforms for outsourcing a task (such as services, ideas, or content) to a large number of the online community.

Cryptocurrency: A form of electronic monetary system which is developed through cryptographic protocols and powered by blockchain technology; a.k.a programmable money.

Cryptoeconomics: A field of study that focuses on protocol development and mechanism design for a distributed digital network. It applies cryptographic science, game theory, and mechanism design to develop a self-enforcing governance mechanism (through incentive and/or penalty assignment) of distributed networks.

Cybersecurity: The act of protecting data, networks, programs, and other computerized systems from unauthorized malicious access. A cyberattack is one example of digital risk in the information society.

DApp: Is a short form for decentralized application referring to an application with back-end code running on a distributed computing system (decentralized network). It is a common term used in blockchain and distributed technologies' space.

Data: A set of values or facts characterizing qualitative or quantitative variables and which is collected for inferential or analytical purposes from which information is drawn.

Digital asset: Refers to an electronic form of resource with an intrinsic economic value of ownership. This includes digital content of any form that is formatted into a binary source (images, photos, videos, audio, text files, spreadsheets, graphics, 3D files, digital tokens, etc.). Content without a property right and a nonrivalrous one is not a digital asset.

Digital commons: A set of virtual services (Web, cloud, Internet, and ICT-powered services) that are accessible to the digital community.

Digital currency: A form of monetary system available in electronic forms serving as a unit of account, a medium of exchange, and store of value through a virtual representation of the notion of money.

Digital divide: Refers to the demographic, inter-state, and/or intra-state socioeconomic gap in access to the Internet and ICT.

Digital economy: The economic system that relies on information technology as the main catalyst. Mesh, peer, or network, knowledge, and sharing economy are the other terms that are interchangeably used to refer to the hybrid business models of this economy.

Digital financial inclusion: The inclusion of individuals to access financial services through enabling technologies such as mobile money and fintech.

Digital gender gap: A demographic gap of access to the Internet and ICT between different gender groups.

Digital ID: A system that securely builds and verifies the virtual self of a subject using the subject's personal information (and biometric information in some cases). It is a digital form of the tangible ID document system.

Digital immigrants: The information society demographic cohort used to identify the generation that was born and raised before the digital era and thus adapting to the new trends of ICTs and the Internet and transforming to a digitized lifestyle.

Digital inclusion: The inclusion of individuals to access the Internet, information technologies, and digital literacy that enables them to take part in the digital economic system.

Digital infrastructure: The fundamental hardware and software structures and facilities needed for the operation of digital services such as communication, computing, or data storage.

Digital marketing: A marketing structure that leverages online means of marketing such as search engine marketing (ads), social media marketing, email, mobile applications, and the Internet in general.

Digital natives: The information society demographic cohort used to identify the generation (Gen Z and, partly, the millennials) that is born and raised in the digital era and thus native to using ICTs and the Internet and practicing a digitized lifestyle. The age of first access to the Internet is one of the indexes used to measure demographic performance.

Digital transformation: The act of rethinking/reimagining conventional business processes using digital solutions.

Digital twin: A digital representation of a real-world entity as a virtual pair (see also, a similar concept, virtualization).

Digital waste: Underutilization or inefficient utilization of digital resources such as data, server, Web, cloud computing, network, and so on.

Distributed ledger technologies (DLTs): A digital record system in which a consensus on state changes are reached through a distributed network setting (see also Blockchain technologies, a typical DLT, that facilitates the transfer of an item of value in a distributed way).

Ebusiness: Refers to an electronic business practice using the Web, digital information, and communication technologies.

Ecommerce: The sale of goods and services online through web-based and application-enabled digital marketplaces.

E-government: Electronic government system that utilizes ICTs and web services for efficient, transparent, and more inclusive management of the public sector.

Fintech: A wide array of technological solutions used to enhance or automate financial services.

Initial coin offering (ICO): A crowdfunding model for a coin sale of tokens that run blockchain-powered applications. Investors invest in a coin sale with the expectation of future profit.

Innovation hub: A center created mainly for startups in order to pool innovative tech solutions and new ideas. Such establishments and initiatives help nurture emerging technologies and help startups to grow and, in some cases, spin back to the parent innovation hub enterprise.

Internet of Things (IoT): A system that enables the exchange of data between interconnected networks of objects with unique identifiers.

Mobile money: A mobile technology for the transfer of funds that is operated under financial regulation. Under this system, accounts linked to mobile devices serve as a bank account and are used to exchange, store, and manage money.

Network: A system for a group of interconnected computers locally (LAN) or the World Wide Web or Internet that allows communication between each evolved node.

Open data: A freely accessible systematically extracted dataset for public use and republication without restriction. Open data are nonrivalrous, thus public goods where everyone has access to use them without being depleted. The idea is to allow individuals, businesses, and governments to use underutilized data in unforeseen ways for value creation.

Open source software: A decentralized form of software development in which source code is shared to inspect, develop, refine, or change programs. Such computer programs can be used for any commercial or non-commercial purposes by the general public (see, e.g., Linux and Google Open Source).

P2P online lending: A business practice of direct and systematic loan financing through online platforms. Digital platforms facilitate the loan financing process between borrowers and lenders, cutting out financial institutions. Such marketplaces exhibit a perfectly competitive market structure with a large number of lenders and borrowers; a.k.a peer-to-peer or marketplace lending.

Protocol: A standard set of rules that regulate how computers or entities exchange information. The rules included in a computer system protocol can be related to the type of data transmitted, commands used to exchange data, and data transfer confirmation code of conduct.

Prototyping: The process of testing, simulating, or providing an early sample launch of new product development. It is commonly used for firsthand user experience in business, semantics, design, electronics, and software programming.

Secure token offering (STO): Token sale model in which tokenized digital securities built on blockchain platforms are sold. It is a prepaid funding model that mimics the initial public offering, thus also known as tokenized IPO. Investors invest in a secure token sale with the expectation of future profit.

Security by design: An approach to a system developed with security features embedded in it from the onset.

Smart cities: Urbanization powered by the Internet of Things (IoT) and sensors various other enabling technologies to extract data and draw insights for efficient utilization of physical and human capital on which the city is built (see also, a similar notion, sharing cities).

Smart contract: Refers to a commuter program for a digital agreement built on top of a given protocol. It is an automated contract execution to facilitate, verify, or enforce an agreement digitally; a.k.a chaincode of business rules

Social media: A virtual network of communities connected through web-based platforms and/or applications. Social media is one of the core developments under Web 2.0. It relies on the model of user-generated content for any form of interaction within a network.

Tokenization: A common word in blockchain tech applications, referring to the process of modeling and valuation of digital assets using native tokens in a blockchain network.

Uberification: A mobile application-enabled service provision similar to Uber's business model of app-enabled mobile services.

User-generated content (UGC): A content initiated by users of a digital platform (social media platforms and different online channels). These contents can be in the form of images, videos, text, or audio of user experience, testimonials, tweets, blog posts, virtual campaigns, and so on; a.k.a user-created content

Virtual reality (VR): A technology with a simulated artificial environment that creates a sense of real-world action.

White labeling: The protocol for a rebranding of products (e.g., a licensed software) with other established providers' brands. Some startups use this marketing strategy to access a large distribution network through the white-labeled brand.

5G: A mobile technology referring to the fifth generation of wireless telecommunications.

References

Aberer, K. and Despotovic, Z. (2004). On reputation in game theory-application to online settings. Working paper. https://www. researchgate.net/profile/Karl_Aberer/publication/247017478_ On_Reputation_in_Game_Theory_Application_on_Online_Settings/ links/0a85e534fcca53a42a000000.pdf, retrieved on May 22, 2020.

Amsden, R. and Schweizer, D. (2018). Are Blockchain Crowdsales the New 'Gold Rush'? Success Determinants of Initial Coin Offerings

Anari N., Goely G., and Nikzad A. (2014). Mechanism design for crowdsourcing: an optimal 1−1/e approximate budget-feasible mechanism for large markets. In 2014 IEEE 55th Annual Symposium on Foundations of Computer Science (FOCS 2014), Philadelphia, Pennsylvania, pp. 266–275

Anderson, S., Milam, G., Friedman, D., and Singh, N. (2008). Buy it now: A hybrid internet market institution. Journal of Electronic commerce research, 9(2), pp. 137

Arzac, E. R., Schwartz, R. A., and Whitcomb, D. K. (1981). The leverage structure of interest rates. Journal of Money. Credit and Banking, 13(1), 72–88

Atzori, M. (2015). Blockchain technology and decentralized governance: Is the state still necessary?, available at SSRN 2709713.

Baldwin, A. A., Brown, C. E., and Trinkle, B. S. (2006). Opportunities for artificial intelligence development in the accounting domain: the case for auditing. Intelligent Systems in Accounting, Finance and Management, 14(3), 77–86

Barontini, C., and Holden, H. (2019). Proceeding with Caution-A Survey on Central Bank Digital Currency. Proceeding with Caution-A Survey on Central Bank Digital Currency (January 8, 2019). BIS Paper, (101). https://papers. ssrn.com/sol3/papers.cfm?abstract_id=3331590

Barrdear, J. and M. Kumhof (2016). The macroeconomics of central bank issued digital currencies. Bank of England Staff Working Paper No. 605

Bech, M. L. and Garratt, R. (2017). Central bank cryptocurrencies. BIS Quarterly Review, September

Belleflamme, P., Lambert, T., and Schwienbacher, A. (2014). Crowdfunding: Tapping the right crowd. Journal of business venturing, 29(5), 585–609

Bianchi, D. (2018). Cryptocurrencies as an asset class? An empirical assessment. An Empirical Assessment (June 6, 2018). WBS Finance Group Research Paper

BIS Annual Economic Report 2019 on Big tech in finance: opportunities and risks at www.bis.org/publ/arpdf/ar2019e3.htm, accessed on June 23, 2019.

Bolton, G., Greiner, B., and Ockenfels, A. (2013). Engineering trust: reciprocity in the production of reputation information. Management science, 59(2), 265–285

Bordo, M. D. and Levin, A. T. (2017). Central bank digital currency and the future of monetary policy (No. w23711). National Bureau of Economic Research

Botsman (2012). The Currency of the New Economy is Trust, a speech by Rachel Botsman on the TED Talk, www.ted.com/talks/rachel_botsman_the_currency_of_the_new_economy_is_trust Retrieved on May 22, 2020.

Botsman, R. and Rogers, R. (2010). What's mine is yours: The rise of collaborative consumption. New York: HarperCollins

Brabham, D. C. (2013). Crowdsourcing. Cambridge, MA: MIT Press

Brandsen, T., Van de Donk, W., and Putters, K. (2005). Griffins or chameleons? Hybridity as a permanent and inevitable characteristic of the third sector. Intl Journal of Public Administration, 28(9–10), 749–765

Brown E. (2019) The Geopolitics of Technology Big Data, Artificial Intelligence and 5G in a Multipolar World, Global Risk Institute, available at: https://globalriskinstitute.org/publications/the-geopolitics-of-technology/

Brown, M. A. (2019). Cryptocurrency and Financial Regulation: The SEC's Rejection of Bitcoin-Based ETPs. North Carolina Banking Institute, 23(1), 139

Brozek, K. O. (2009). Exploring the continuum of social and financial returns: when does a nonprofit become a social enterprise? Community Development Investment Review, pp. 7–17. Federal Reserve Bank of San Francisco

Bruni, L. and Zamagni, S. (2007). Civil Economy: Efficiency, Equity, Public Happiness (Vol. 2). Peter Lang

Burniske, C. (2017). "Cryptoasset Valuation." Medium, September 24, 2017. https://medium.com/@cburniske/cryptoasset-valuations-ac83479ffca7, retrieved on February 19, 2019.

Cabral, L. (2012). Reputation on the Internet. The Oxford Handbook of the Digital Economy. Oxford University Press. 343–354

Cai, Y. and Zhu, D. (2016). Fraud detections for online businesses: a perspective from blockchain technology. Financial Innovation, 2(1), 20

Calviño, A., Ricci, S., and Domingo-Ferrer, J. (2015). Privacy-preserving distribution of statistical computation to a semi-honest multi-cloud. In 2015 IEEE Conference on Communications and Network Security-CNS 2015. pp. 506–514. IEEE Computer Society

Candeub, A. (2013). Behavioral economics, internet search, and antitrust. *ISJLP*, 9, 407

Caporale, G. M., Gil-Alana, L., and Plastun, A. (2018). Persistence in the cryptocurrency market. Research in International Business and Finance, 46, 141–148

Carboni, D. (2015). Feedback based reputation on top of the bitcoin blockchain. arXiv preprint arXiv:1502.01504

Carlin, W. and Soskice, D. (2014). Macroeconomics: Institutions, Instability, and the Financial System. Oxford University Press

Catalini, C. and Gans, J. S. (2016). Some simple economics of the blockchain (No. w22952). National Bureau of Economic Research

Caulkins, J. P., Bao, Y., Davenport, S., Fahli, I., Guo, Y., Kinnard, K., and Kilmer, B. (2018). Big data on a big new market: Insights from Washington State's legal cannabis market. International Journal of Drug Policy, 57, 86–94

Central bank digital currencies, Norges Bank Papers, No. 1 (2018)

Chapman, J., Garratt, R., Hendry, S., McCormack, A., and McMahon, W. (2017). Project Jasper: Are distributed wholesale payment systems feasible yet. Financial System, 59

Chohan, U. W. (2019). Are Stable Coins Stable? Notes on the 21st Century (CBRi)

Chow, R., Golle, P., Jakobsson, M., Shi, E., Staddon, J., Masuoka, R., and Molina, J. (2009). Controlling data in the cloud: outsourcing computation without outsourcing control. In Proceedings of the 2009 ACM workshop on Cloud computing security, pp. 85–90. ACM

Christensen, C. (2013). The innovator's dilemma: when new technologies cause great firms to fail. Harvard Business Review Press

Collier, B. C. and Hampshire, R. (February 2010). Sending mixed signals: Multilevel reputation effects in peer-to-peer lending markets. In Proceedings of the 2010 ACM conference on Computer supported cooperative work (pp. 197–206). ACM

Courtois, N. T. and Bahack, L. (2014). On subversive miner strategies and block withholding attack in Bitcoin digital currency. arXiv preprint arXiv:1402.1718

Crosby, M., Pattanayak, P., Verma, S., and Kalyanaraman, V. (2016). Blockchain technology: Beyond bitcoin. Applied Innovation, 2, 6–10

Cumming, D. J. and Johan, S. A. (2019). *Crowdfunding: Fundamental Cases, Facts, and Insights*. Academic Press

Cumming, D. J., Hornuf, L., Karami, M., and Schweizer, D. (2016). Disentangling crowdfunding from fraudfunding. *Max Planck Institute for Innovation & competition research paper* (16–09)

Cumming, D. J., Leboeuf, G., and Schwienbacher, A. (2014). Crowdfunding Models: Keep-it-All vs. All-or-Nothing. In Paris December 2014 Finance Meeting EUROFIDAI-AFFI Paper

Cunningham, S. (2015). Filtering P2P Loans – Part I: What is Filtering?, LendingMemo, www.lendingmemo.com/filtering-loans-part-1/

Cvitanic, J. and Zapatero, F. (2004). Introduction to the Economics and Mathematics of Financial Markets. London, England: The MIT Press Cambridge, Massachusetts

David, C. R. (1972). Regression models and life tables (with discussion). Journal of the Royal Statistical Society, 34, 187–220

Davidson, S., De Filippi, P., and Potts, J. (2016). Economics of blockchain

Dawson, R. and Bynghall, S. (2012). Getting Results from Crowds. San Francisco: Advanced Human Technologies

de Jong, A., Roosenboom, P., and van der Kolk, T. (2018). What Determines Success in Initial Coin Offerings?, available at SSRN 3250035.

Dellarocas, C. (2003). The digitization of word of mouth: Promise and challenges of online feedback mechanisms. Management science, 49(10), 1407–1424

Dellarocas, C. (2003b). Efficiency and robustness of eBay-like online feedback mechanisms in environments with moral hazard. Working paper, Sloan School of Management, MIT, Cambridge, MA

Dennis, R. and Owen, G. (December 2015). Rep on the block: A next generation reputation system based on the blockchain. In 2015 10th International Conference for Internet Technology and Secured Transactions (ICITST) (pp. 131–138). IEEE

Dietz, M., Khanna, S., Olanrewaju, T., and Rajgopal, K. (2015). Global Banking Practice, Cutting Through the FinTech Noise: Markers of Success, Imperatives For Banks, December 2015, McKinsey & Company

Domingo-Ferrer, J., Farràs, O., Martínez, S., Sánchez, D., and Soria-Comas, J. (2016b). Self-enforcing protocols via co-utile reputation management. Information Sciences, Vol. 367–368, pp. 159–175

Domingo-Ferrer, J., Martínez, S., Sánchez, D., and Soria-Comas, J. (2017). Co-utility: self-enforcing protocols for the mutual benefit of participants. Engineering Applications of Artificial Intelligence, 59:148–158

Domingo-Ferrer, J. and Megías, D. (2016). "Co-utility for digital content protection and digital forgetting," MedHocNet 2016-15th Annual Mediterranean Ad Hoc Networking Workshop, Vilanova i la Geltrú, June 2016

Domingo-Ferrer, J., Sánchez, D., and Soria-Comas, J. (2016). Co-utility: self-enforcing collaborative protocols with mutual help. Progress in Artificial Intelligence, 5(2):105–110

Domingo-Ferrer, J., Soria-Comas, J., and Ciobotaru, O. (2015). Co-utility: self-enforcing protocols without coordination mechanisms. In 2015 International Conference on Industrial Engineering and Operations Management-IEOM 2015, pp. 1–7. IEEE

Dyson, B. and Hodgson, G. (2016). Digital Cash: why central banks should start Issuing Electronic Money. Positive Money

Edelstein, R. and Urošević, B. (2003). Optimal loan interest rate contract design. The Journal of Real Estate Finance and Economics, 26(2–3), 127–156

Eichengreen, B. (2018). The Stable-Coin Myth. Project Syndicate

Emekter, R., Tu, Y., Jirasakuldech, B., and Lu, M. (2015). Evaluating credit risk and loan performance in online Peer-to-Peer (P2P) lending. Applied Economics, 47(1), 54–70

Erevelles, S., Fukawa, N., and Swayne, L. (2016). Big Data consumer analytics and the transformation of marketing. Journal of Business Research, 69(2), 897–904

Etter-Phoya, R., Lima, S., and Meinzer, M. (2019). Corporate income taxation in the digital age: Africa in the Corporate Tax Haven Index 2019, available at SSRN 3483420.

European Commission, Fair Taxation for the Digital Economy, available at https://ec.europa.eu/taxation_customs/sites/taxation/files/factsheet_digital_taxation_21032018_en.pdf

Eyal, I. and Sirer, E. G. (2014). Majority is not enough: Bitcoin mining is vulnerable. In International Conference on Financial Cryptography and Data Security (pp. 436–454). Springer Berlin Heidelberg

Fabric Ventures and TokenData report (2018). The State of the Token Market: A Year in Review and an Outlook for 2018, www.fabric.vc/report, accessed on May 22, 2020.

Falk, A. and Fischbacher, U. (2006). A theory of reciprocity. Games and Economic Behavior, 54(2), 293–315

Fan, S., Lau, R. Y., and Zhao, J. L. (2015). Demystifying big data analytics for business intelligence through the lens of marketing mix. Big Data Research, 2(1), 28–32

Ferguson, N. (2008). *The ascent of money: A financial history of the world.* Penguin

Friedman, E. and Resnick, P. (2001). The Social Cost of Cheap Pseudonyms. Journal of Economics and Management Strategy 10, (1), pp. 173–199

Friedman, M. (1989). Quantity theory of money. In Money (pp. 1–40). Palgrave Macmillan, London

Fudenberg, D. and Levine, D. K. (1992). Maintaining a reputation when strategies are imperfectly observed. The Review of Economic Studies, 59(3), 561–579

Funk, B., Bachmann, A., Becker, A., Buerckner, D., Hilker, M., Kock, F., Lehmann, M., and Tiburtius, P. (2015). Online Peer-to-Peer Lending? A Literature Review. The Journal of Internet Banking and Commerce, 2011

Galal, H. S. and Youssef, A. M. (February 2018). Verifiable sealed-bid auction on the ethereum blockchain. In International Conference on Financial Cryptography and Data Security (pp. 265–278). Springer, Berlin, Heidelberg

Gauthier, D. (2013). Achieving Pareto-optimality: invisible hand, social contracts, and rational deliberation. Rationality, Markets and Morals, 4(78)

Gerard, D. (2017). Attack of the 50 foot blockchain: Bitcoin, blockchain, Ethereum & smart contracts. David Gerard

Gerber E.M., Hui J.S., and Kuo, P.Y. (2012). Crowdfunding: why people are motivated to post and fund projects on crowdfunding platforms. In Proceedings of the International Workshop on Design, Influence, and Social Technologies: Techniques, Impacts and Ethics

Germann Molz, J. (2014). Collaborative Surveillance and Technologies of Trust: Online Reputation Systems in the "New" Sharing Economy. In Media, Surveillance and Identity: A Social Perspective. Edited by A. Jansson and M. Christensen. New York: Peter Lang, pp. 127–144

Ghosh, A. and McAfee, P. (2012). Crowdsourcing with endogenous entry. In Proceedings of the 21st International Conference on World Wide Web— WWW 2012, pp. 999–1008. New York: ACM

Gintis, H. (2009). Game Theory Evolving: A Problem-Centered Introduction to Modeling Strategic Interaction (2nd ed.). Princeton and Oxford: Princeton University Press

Greenberg, M.D., Hui, J., and Gerber, E. (2013). Crowdfunding: a resource exchange perspective. In CHI '13 Extended Abstracts on Human Factors in Computing Systems, pp. 883–888. ACM New York, NY, USA

Greiner, M. E. and Wang, H. (2009). The role of social capital in people-to-people lending marketplaces. ICIS 2009 Proceedings, 29

Guo, Y. and Liang, C. (2016). Blockchain application and outlook in the banking industry. Financial Innovation, 2(1), 24

Hamari, J., Sjöklint, M., and Ukkonen, A. (2015). The sharing economy: why people participate in collaborative consumption. Journal of the Association for Information Science and Technology

Hayek, F. A. (1978). Denationalization of Money-The Argument Refined. 2nd edn. London: The Institute of Economic Affairs

Hayes, A. S. (2019). Bitcoin price and its marginal cost of production: support for a fundamental value. Applied Economics Letters, 26(7), 554–560

He, Dong, Ross Leckow, Vikram Haksar, Tommaso Mancini, Nigel Jenkinson, Mikari Kashima, Tanai Khiaonarong, Celine Rochon, and Hervé Tourpe (2017). Fintech and Financial Services: Initial Considerations. International Monetary Fund Staff Discussion Note 17/05

Hildebrand, T., Puri, M., and Rocholl, J. (2014). Adverse incentives in crowdfunding. Working paper, http://papers.ssrn.com/sol3/papers.cfm?abstract_id=1615483, accessed on May 22, 2020.

Hileman, G. and Rauchs, M. (2017). Global blockchain benchmarking study. Cambridge Centre for Alternative Finance, University of Cambridge, 122

Hoffmann, S., Bradshaw, S., and Taylor, E. (2019). Networks and Geopolitics: How great power rivalries infected 5G. Oxford Information Labs, August, 22, 4.

www.riksbank.se/en-gb/payments-cash/e-krona/e-krona-reports/e-krona-project-report-2/

Huang, Y., Vir Singh, P., and Mukhopadhyay, T. (2012). How to design crowdsourcing contest: a structural empirical analysis. In Workshop of Information Systems and Economics—WISE 2012

International Chamber of Commerce (ICC) Commission on the Digital Economy, 2016, Regulatory Modernization in the Digital Economy: Developing an Enabling Policy Environment for Innovation, Competition and Growth, available at https://iccwbo.org/publication/icc-policy-statement-on-regulatory-modernization-in-the-digital-economy/

Intuit (2013). The Intuit 2013 – Future of Accountancy Report

Iwamura, M., Kitamura, Y., and Matsumoto, T. (2014). Is bitcoin the only cryptocurrency in the town? Economics of cryptocurrency and Friedrich A. Hayek

Iyer, R., Khwaja, A. I., Luttmer, E. F. P., and Shue, K. (2009). Screening in New Credit Markets Can Individual Lenders Infer Borrower Creditworthiness in Peer-to-Peer Lending? Management. Cambridge, MA

Jakšič, M., and Marinč, M. (2015). The future of banking: The role of information technology. Bančni vestnik, 68.

Jakšič, M. and Marinč, M. (2015). The future of banking: the role of information technology. Bančni vestnik: revija za denarništvo in bančništvo, 64(11), 68–73

Jakub, B. (2015). Does Bitcoin follow the hypothesis of efficient market? International Journal of Economic Sciences, 4(2), 10–23

Jeffries A. (2013). Indie no-go: only one in ten projects gets fully funded on Kickstarter's biggest rival, The Verge, August 7, 2013, www.theverge.com/2013/8/7/4594824/less-than-10-percent-of-projects-on-indiegogo-get-fully-funded

Johnson, J. (2019). The end of military-techno Pax Americana? Washington's strategic responses to Chinese AI-enabled military technology. The Pacific Review, 1-28.

Johnson, B., Laszka, A., Grossklags, J., Vasek, M., and Moore, T. (2014). Game-theoretic analysis of DDoS attacks against Bitcoin mining pools. In International Conference on Financial Cryptography and Data Security (pp. 72–86). Springer Berlin Heidelberg

Joshi, A. P., Han, M., and Wang, Y. (2018). A survey on security and privacy issues of blockchain technology. Mathematical Foundations of Computing, 1(2), 121–147

Kakushadze, Z. and Russo Jr, R. P. (2018). Blockchain: Data Malls, Coin Economies and Keyless Payments

Kamvar, S. D., Schlosser, M. T., and Garcia-Molina, H. (2003). The EigenTrust algorithm for reputation management in P2P networks. In Proceedings of the 12th International Conference on World Wide Web, pp. 640–651. ACM

Katz, M. L. and Shapiro, C. (1986). Technology Adoption in the Presence of Network Externalities. Journal of Political Economy, Vol. 94, pp. 822–841

Kiayias, A., Koutsoupias, E., Kyropoulou, M., and Tselekounis, Y. (2016). Blockchain mining games. In Proceedings of the 2016 ACM Conference on Economics and Computation (pp. 365–382). ACM

Krumme, K. and Herrero-Lopez, S. (2009). Do lenders make optimal decisions in a peer-to-peer network? In Proceedings of the 2009 IEEE/WIC/ACM International Joint Conference on Web Intelligence and Intelligent Agent Technology, Vol. 01 (pp. 124–127). IEEE Computer Society

Kumhof, M. and Noone, C. (2018). Central bank digital currencies – design principles and balance sheet implications. Staff Working Paper No. 725. Bank of England (2018) Working Paper

Lau, J. (2013). Dollar for dollar raised, Kickstarter dominates Indiegogo SIX times over, posted on August 28, 2013.

Leece, D. (2008). Economics of the Mortgage Market: Perspectives on Household Decision Making. John Wiley & Sons

Lehner, O.M. (2013). Crowdfunding social ventures: a model and research agenda. Venture Capital, 15(4):289–311

Lemieux, V., Hofman, D., Batista, D., and Joo, A. (2019). Blockchain technology and recordkeeping.

Lemieux, V. L., and Sporny, M. (2017). Preserving the archival bond in distributed ledgers: a data model and syntax. In Proceedings of the 26th International Conference on World Wide Web Companion (pp. 1437-1443).

LendingClub Statistics, www.lendingclub.com/info/statistics.action, retrieved on June 28, 2016.

Li, X., Jiang, P., Chen, T., Luo, X., and Wen, Q. (2017). A survey on the security of blockchain systems. Future Generation Computer Systems

Libra Association (2020). An Introduction to Libra. Whitepaper. https://libra.org/en-US/white-paper/, accessed on May 22, 2020.

Libra Blockchain at https://developers.libra.org/docs/the-libra-blockchain-paper, accessed on June 23, 2019.

Liebowitz, S. J. and Margolis, S. E. (1995). Are network externalities a new source of market failure. Research in Law and Economics, 17(0), 1–22

Lin, M. (2009). Peer-to-peer lending: An empirical study. AMCIS 2009 Doctoral Consortium, 17

Liu, Q. and Vasarhelyi, M. A. (2014). Big questions in AIS research: measurement, information processing, data analysis, and reporting. Journal of Information Systems, 28(1): 1–17, https://doi.org/10.2308/isys-10395

Mainelli, M. and Milne, A. (2016). The Impact and Potential of Blockchain on Securities Transaction Lifecycle. SWIFT Institute Working Paper

Mancini-Griffoli, T., Martinez, M. S., Peria, I. A., Ari, A., Kiff, J., Popescu, A., and Rochon, C. (2018). Casting Light on Central Bank Digital Currency. IMF, Staff Discussion Note, November

Marot, E. (2014). Predicting the Number of Payments in Peer Lending, LendingRobot, May 28, 2014, http://blog.lendingrobot.com/research/146-the-magic-number-for-lending-club-investments/2016/

Marot, E. (2016). Calculating the Expected Return of a Single Note, LendingRobot, March 3, 2016, http://blog.lendingrobot.com/research/predicting-the-number-of-payments-in-peer-lending/

Mas-Colell, A., Whinston, M., and Green, J. (1995). Microeconomic Theory, Oxford Press

McIntosh, C. (2010). Monitoring Repayment in Online Peer-To-Peer Lending. San Diego

McQuinn, A. and Castro, D. (2019). The Case for a U.S. Digital Single Market and Why Federal Preemption Is Key, available at https://itif.org/publications/2019/10/07/case-us-digital-single-market-and-why-federal-preemption-key

Mikesell, R. F. and Mikesell, R. F. (1994). The Bretton Woods debates: a memoir (Vol. 192). Princeton: International Finance Section, Department of Economics, Princeton University

Milne, A. and Parboteeah, P. (2016). The Business Models and Economics of Peer-to-Peer Lending. Chicago

Mollick, E. (2013). The dynamics of crowdfunding: an exploratory study. Journal of Business Venturing, 29(1):1–16

Momtaz, P. P. (2019). Token sales and initial coin offerings: Introduction. The Journal of Alternative Investments, 21(4), 7–12

Möser, M., Soska, K., Heilman, E., Lee, K., Heffan, H., Srivastava, S., and Christin, N. (2018). An empirical analysis of traceability in the monero blockchain. Proceedings on Privacy Enhancing Technologies, 2018(3), 143–163

Naehrig, M., Lauter, K., and Vaikuntanathan, V. (2011). Can homomorphic encryption be practical? In Proceedings of the 3rd ACM Workshop on Cloud Computing Security Workshop (pp. 113–124). ACM

Narayanan, A. (2015). Bitcoin and game theory: we're still scratching the surface, blog post on Freedom to Tinker, March 31, 2015, by Arvind Narayanan.

OECD (2014). The digital economy, new business models and key features, in Addressing the Tax Challenges of the Digital Economy, OECD Publishing, Paris, https://doi.org/10.1787/9789264218789-7-en

OECD Public consultation document Secretariat Proposal for a "Unified Approach" under Pillar One 9 October 2019–12 November 2019, available at www.oecd.org/tax/beps/public-consultation-document-secretariat-proposal-unified-approach-pillar-one.pdf

Owyang, J., Tran, C., and Silva, C. (2013). The collaborative economy. Altimeter. San Mateo, CA

Pazowski, P. and Czudec, W. (2014). Economic prospects and conditions of crowdfunding. In Human Capital without Borders. International Conference Management Knowledge and Learning, pp. 1079–1088. Portoroz, Slovenia

Petrasic, K. and Bornfreund, M. (2016). Beyond Bitcoin: the blockchain revolution in financial services, White and Case report https://www.whitecase.com/sites/whitecase/files/files/download/publications/the-blockchain-thought-leadership.pdf

Pilkington, M. (2016). 11 Blockchain technology: principles and applications. Research handbook on digital transformations, 225

Preez (2015). Sharing economy = end of capitalism? Not in its current form, a blog post by Derek du Preez, August 17, 2015, on diginomica, http://diginomica.com/2015/08/17/sharing-economy-end-of-capitalism-not-in-its-current-form/, accessed online on February 18, 2017.

Preez, D. (2015). Sharing economy = end of capitalism? Not in its current form, blog post on diginomica, August 17, 2015.

Prensky, M. (2001). Digital natives, digital immigrants part 1. On the horizon, 9(5), 1–6

PricewaterhouseCoopers (2015). The sharing economy – sizing the revenue opportunity, Consumer Intelligence Series

Prosper Ratings, www.prosper.com/plp/invest/prosper-ratings/

Resnick, P. and Zeckhauser, R. (2002). Trust among strangers in internet transactions: Empirical analysis of eBay's reputation system. The Economics of the Internet and E-commerce, 11(2), 23–25

Rhue, L. (2018). Trust is All You Need: An Empirical Exploration of Initial Coin Offerings (ICOs) and ICO Reputation Scores

Ricci, S., Domingo-Ferrer, J., and Sánchez, D. (2016). Privacy-preserving cloud-based statistical analyses on sensitive categorical data. In Modeling Decisions for Artificial Intelligence—MDAI 2016 (pp. 227-238), Springer

Rifkin, J. (2014). The Zero Marginal Cost Society: The Internet of Things, the Collaborative Commons, and the Eclipse of Capitalism. New York, USA: Macmillan

Rifkin, J. (2014). The zero marginal cost society: The internet of things, the collaborative commons, and the eclipse of capitalism. St. Martin's Press

References

Rogoff, K. (2015). Costs and benefits to phasing out paper currency. NBER Macroeconomics Annual, 29(1), 445–456

Romer, D. (2011). Advanced Macroeconomics. McGraw Hill

Sabater, J. and Sierra, C. (2002). Reputation and social network analysis in multi-agent systems. In Proceedings of the first international joint conference on Autonomous agents and multiagent systems: part 1 (pp. 475–482). ACM

Saito, K. and Iwamura, M. (2019). How to make a digital currency on a blockchain stable. Future Generation Computer Systems, 100, 58–69

Sánchez, D., Martínez, S., and Domingo-Ferrer, J. (2016). Co-utile P2P ridesharing via decentralization and reputation management, Transportation research part C: Emerging Technologies, Vol. 73, pp. 147–166

Schaub, A., Bazin, R., Hasan, O., and Brunie, L. (May 2016). A trustless privacy-preserving reputation system. In IFIP International Conference on ICT Systems Security and Privacy Protection (pp. 398–411). Springer, Cham

Schotter, A. (2008). Microeconomics: A Modern Approach, Cengage Learning, p. 524

Schwienbacher, A. and Larralde, B. (2012). Crowdfunding of entrepreneurial ventures. In D. Cumming (ed.), The Oxford Handbook of Entrepreneurial Finance, Oxford University Press, pp. 369–391

Scott, J. E. (2004). Measuring dimensions of perceived e-business risks. Information systems and e-Business management, 2(1), 31–55

Scully M. (2015). Wall Street Said to Limit Support for Online Lenders, www.bloomberg.com/news/articles/2015-08-25/wall-street-said-to-limit-support-for-online-lenders, article by Matt Scully of Bloomberg Business on August 31, 2015.

Sedlacek, Tomas (2011). Economics of good and evil: the quest for economic meaning from.

See the Speech by Tony Richards, Reserve Bank of Australia Head of Payments Policy Department, on "Cryptocurrencies and Distributed Ledger Technology," Australian Business Economists Briefing Sydney, June 26, 2018, www.rba.gov.au/speeches/2018/sp-so-2018-06-26.html, accessed on March 19, 2019.

Serrano-Cinca, C., Gutiérrez-Nieto, B., and López-Palacios, L. (2015). Determinants of Default in P2P Lending. PloS one, 10(10), e0139427

Slivkins, A. and Vaughan, J. W. (2014). Online decision making in crowdsourcing markets: theoretical challenges. ACM SIGecom Exchanges, 12(2):4–23

Sloane, P., Latreille, P., and O'Leary, N. (2013). Modern Labour Economics. New York: Routledge

Solomon, J., Ma, W., and Wash, R. (2015). Don't wait! How timing affects coordination of crowdfunding donations. In Proceedings of the 18th ACM

Conference on Computer Supported Cooperative Work & Social Computing, CSCW 2015, pp. 547–556. ACM

Soria-Comas, J. and Domingo-Ferrer, J. (2015). Co-utile collaborative anonymization of microdata, Lecture Notes in Computer Science, Vol. 9321 (Modeling Decisions for Artificial Intelligence—MDAI 2015), pp. 192–206, September 2015, ISSN: 0302-9743

Soska, K., Kwon, A., Christin, N., and Devadas, S. (2016). Beaver: A Decentralized Anonymous Marketplace with Secure Reputation. IACR Cryptology ePrint Archive. p. 464

Statista, www.statista.com/statistics/242235/number-of-ebays-total-active-users/

Strausz, Roland (2015). Crowdfunding, demand uncertainty, and moral hazard: A mechanism design approach. No. 2015-036. SFB 649 Discussion Paper

Subramanian, H. (2018). Decentralized blockchain-based electronic marketplaces. Commun. ACM, 61(1), 78–84

Swan, M. (2015). Blockchain: Blueprint for a new economy. O'Reilly Media, Inc.

Taylor, J.B., and Woodford, M., eds. (1999). Handbook of Macroeconomics, Vol. 1B. Amsterdam: Elsevier

Terwiesch, C. and Xu, Y. (2008). Innovation contests, open innovation, and multiagent problem solving. Management Science, 54(9):1529–1543

Teutsch, J., Buterin, V., and Brown, C. (2017). Interactive coin offerings. https://people.cs.uchicago.edu/~teutsch/papers/ico.pdf, accessed May 22, 2020.

The Kickstarter Blog, www.kickstarter.com/blog/by-the-numbers-when-creators-return-to-kickstarter website

The Riksbank's e-krona project Report 2, October 2018

Tolentino, J. (2016). How blockchain is transforming business models, blog post by Tolentino J. in Reinventing the World of Banking, http://thenextweb.com/worldofbanking/2016/09/16/how-blockchain-is-transforming-business-models/

Turi, A. N., Domingo-Ferrer, J., and Sánchez, D. (2016). Filtering P2P loans based on co-utile reputation. In 13th International Conference on Applied Computing—AC 2016 (pp. 139–146). IADIS Press

Turi, A. N., Domingo-Ferrer, J., Sánchez, D., and Osmani, D. (2016)b. A co-utility approach to the mesh economy: the crowd-based business model. Review of Managerial Science, 1–32

UNCTAD (2019). Digital Economy Report 2019, Value Creation and Capture: Implication for Developing Countries, https://unctad.org/en/PublicationsLibrary/der2019_en.pdf

Vickrey, W. (1961). Counter speculation and competitive sealed tenders. The Journal of Finance, 16(1), 8–37. doi:10.2307/2977633

Vigna, P. and Casey, M. J. (2019). The Truth Machine: The Blockchain and the Future of Everything. Picador

Voigt, P. and Von dem Bussche, A. (2017). The EU General Data Protection Regulation (GDPR). *A Practical Guide, 1st ed.,* Cham: Springer International Publishing

von Hayek, F. A. (2009). Denationalisation of Money: The Argument Refined. Ludwig von Mises Institute

Wang, J. L. (2005). Smoothing hazard rates. Encyclopedia of Biostatistics. Chicago

Wang, X., Montgomery, A., and Srinivasan, K. (2008). When auction meets fixed price: A theoretical and empirical examination of buy-it-now auctions. Quantitative Marketing and Economics, 6(4), 339–370

Wash, R. and Solomon, J. (2014). Coordinating donors on crowdfunding websites. In Proceedings of the 17th ACM Conference on Computer Supported Cooperative Work & Social Computing—CSCW 2014, pp. 38–48. ACM

World Bank (2013). Crowdfunding's Potential for the Developing World. infoDev. Finance and Private Sector Development Department, Washington, DC, https://openknowledge.worldbank.org/handle/10986/17626

Yang, Q. and Lee, Y. C. (August 2016). Critical factors of the lending intention of online P2P: moderating role of perceived benefit. In Proceedings of the 18th Annual International Conference on Electronic Commerce: e-Commerce in Smart connected World (p. 15). ACM

Yeoh, P. (2017). Regulatory issues in blockchain technology. Journal of Financial Regulation and Compliance, 25(2), 196–208

Zeng, R. (2013). Legal Regulations in P2P Financing in the US and Europe. US-China L. Rev., 10, 229

Zhang, Y. and Van der Schaar M. (2012). Reputation-based Incentive Protocols in Crowdsourcing Applications. Proceedings of INFOCOM 2012, pp. 2140–2148. IEEE

Zhang, X., Podorozhny, R., and Lesser, V. R. (2000). Cooperative, multistep negotiation over a multi-dimensional utility function. In Artificial Intelligence and Soft Computing, pp. 136–142. IASTED/ACTA Press

I

Index

A

ad-based business model, 27

Airbnb, 26, 27

Alibaba, 23

All-or-nothing model, 49, 50, 61, 62

Amazon, 22, 23

Amazon Web Services (AWS), 22, 171

Anti-money laundering (AML) rules, 89

Average network benefit (ANB), 97

B

Base erosion and profit
      shifting (BEPS), 36

Blockchain-based co-utile reputation
      management
   distributed identity solution, 141, 142
   eBay-like marketplaces, 137, 138
   feedback system, 137
   negative ratings, 138

Blockchain-powered nano-economies, 88

Blockchain-powered token
      nano-economies, 92–94

Blockchain technology
   applications, 91
   challenges, 125
   DApps, 136
   digitization of assets, 127
   distributed ID protocol calls, 152, 153
   features, 89

identifying participants/degrees of
      permission, 128
payment/micropayment channels, 130, 131
platforms, 90, 152
robust consensus algorithm, 129
scalability issues, 130
solutions, 90, 126
tokenization/DApps, 129
token sales, 132–134
use cases, 136
vulnerabilities, 154

Bounty model, 50

Business models, digital companies, 21
   Fintech, 28–33
   Google, 27, 28
   liquidity. PricewaterhouseCoopers, 40
   retail ecommerce, 21–24
   uberification, 25–27, 40

Business-to-consumer (B2C) model, 23

Business value analysis (BVA), 127, 128

Byzantine Generals Problem, 106

C

Central bank cryptocurrency (CBCC), 160

Central bank digital currencies
      (CBDCs), 136, 155
   business models, 167
   categories, 165
   deposits/loans, 157, 171
   design, 166
   developments, 175

© Abeba N. Turi 2020
A. N. Turi, *Technologies for Modern Digital Entrepreneurship*,
https://doi.org/10.1007/978-1-4842-6005-0

P

Payment/micropayment channels, 130

Peer-to-peer business models
  data-driven decision-making, 12
  emerging technologies, 12
  experimental phases, 13
  free digital content generation, 12
  peer-to-peer, 11
  tools, 13

Peer-to-peer (P2P)-based networks, 89, 160

Peer-to-peer (P2P) lending
  definition, 68
  investment decision, 76–78
  loans, 68, 69
  problems, 72–74
  proposed mechanisms, 79, 80
  RCA, 71
  regional volume, 69
  regulatory and policy frameworks, 70
  regulatory issues, 70, 71
  reputation protocol, 82, 84, 85
  SEC, 70
  stakeholders, 70
  value co-creation, 74, 75

Problem-solving and production model, 65

Proof-of-work (PoW) consensus
    mechanism, 97

Prosumers, 2

Q

Quadriga hack, 119

R

Return-based investment decision, 60

Reward-based crowdfunding, 45

Rotating Credit Association (RCA), 71

S

Securities and Exchange
    Commission (SEC), 70

Security token offering (STO), 132

Self-sovereign digital identity management
  Civic utility tokens, 148
  Evernym, 148, 149
  ID2020, 145–147
  non-privacy-conscious users, 145
  refugee individuals, 147, 148
  vital statistics recording, 149, 151

Shopify, 24

Smart business models, 2, 11

Stablecoins, 156, 176, 177

T, U

Tech giants, 184, 185

Token economies
  ANB curve, 97
  blockchain protocol, 102
  blockchain system development, 101
  cryptocurrencies, 99
  mining decisions, 97
  network, 96
  network effect, 102
  network externality, 98, 100
  PoW mechanism, 98
  token-based nano-economies, 96
  value, 94, 95

Tokenization, 91, 92

V

Vancouver-based blockchain platform, 99

W, X, Y, Z

Web 3.0 economies, 117–119